Second Voyage

An Atlantic-Mediterranean Circuit

1987-1991

Bruce MacDonald

Table of Contents

iv

Author's Note

If you've read my previous book, *First Voyage*, you know that it recounts the story of our three-year circumnavigation of the world in 1977-80. *Second Voyage* is the account of the four-year cruise we undertook from 1987-1991. In the first book, I attempted to give a realistic picture of what ocean voyaging is like. I made it a point to be as honest as I could about our feelings and reactions as we experienced them and to resist the temptation to sugar-coat the experience in the interest of making it more appealing. The fact is, however wonderful it can be at times, ocean voyaging is not for everyone; some passages can be grueling, even devastating, experiences, particularly if you're sailing a small, short-handed boat.

Our "second voyage" was essentially an Atlantic-Mediterranean circuit, taking us as far east as Turkey. In many ways, it was a very different experience from the first voyage. We were no longer as naïve and innocent as we'd been. We had a new boat and were better prepared in general. Our son, Jeff, was in college and only visited us sporadically. We had more money, although our resources were still relatively meager compared to those of most other people doing the sort of thing we were. And for the most part we weren't visiting out-of-the-way places or remote island villages; instead, we were in some of the most heavily trafficked areas of the world for pleasure boats: the Caribbean and the Mediterranean.

But many things remained the same. The ocean passages presented the same challenges, both physical and psychological, and I've tried again to present that aspect of it as we experienced it, with all the doubts, fears, anxieties, and questions that that entails. In addition, it was even clearer on this adventure that Liz and I often reacted quite differently to the various circumstances we found ourselves in. How that affected the voyage is part of the story.

And once again, an obvious question is: what does a voyage that took place 30 years ago have to offer the contemporary reader? I think the answer is that things haven't changed as much as you'd think. Sure, everything is more expensive now, there are more facilities for yachts just about everywhere, and in general most yachts today carry more electronics, gadgets, and conveniences than we did. But in many respects the cruising areas aren't that different—the Caribbean and the Med were pretty well inundated with yachts even 30 years ago—so many of my observations will still be relevant. And the conditions you encounter in port or on passage still have the capacity to annoy, delight, frighten, or frustrate as they always have.

Bruce MacDonald
Oriental, NC
Dec 2017

The revised edition includes many small changes, some reordering of material, clarification here and there, and a few additional insights, all with a view toward making the story more interesting and accessible. I hope you enjoy it.

Bruce MacDonald
Feb 2020

The Beaufort Scale

Throughout Europe, the Beaufort Scale is used in marine forecasts. I don't know why the US hasn't adopted it for marine forecasting, but because it's so widely used elsewhere we got used to thinking in those terms. Consequently, I often refer to wind speed in terms of the Forces on the Beaufort Scale. For reference, here's a quick summary of the wind speeds as they relate to Forces:

Force	Wind Speed in Knots	Description
1	1-3	Light Air
2	4-6	Light Breeze
3	7-10	Gentle Breeze
4	11-16	Moderate Breeze
5	17-21	Fresh Breeze
6	22-27	Strong Breeze
7	28-33	Near Gale
8	34-40	Gale
9	41-47	Strong Gale
10	48-55	Storm
11	56-63	Violent Storm
12	64+	Hurricane

1. Once Again

Every ocean passage is a step into uncertainty. However careful your preparation, however fine your vessel, however detailed your weather information, there are always things you can't control, and you're always disconcertingly alone out there.

We left Miami on a reasonable forecast: southerly winds about 15 knots with a 20% chance of showers increasing to 60% by the next day. I wasn't thrilled about the showers, but a southerly wind in the Gulf Stream is ideal for heading north, so the forecast seemed too good to waste.

It started off auspiciously enough. We had a few hours of fine sailing, and we'd started to pick up a good boost from the Gulf Stream current, but by mid-afternoon the weather had turned squally. Some of the squalls brought wind shifts and heavy rain with them, and things were starting to look a little more serious than the rather bland forecast had suggested. After a few sail changes in the downpours, we were wet and vaguely annoyed, as we'd expected to get at least one decent day out of it.

Then, as evening approached, we could see dark black clouds boiling up over the low Florida coast. I viewed them with some apprehension.

"Doesn't look good," I said.

"Maybe they're not headed this way," Liz said, ever the optimist.

But as darkness closed in, streaks of lightning began to split the clouds, and we could hear the dull rumble of thunder in the distance. It became all too apparent that the storms were getting closer.

We were fed up with getting the sails up and down in the squalls, so we decided to err on the side of caution and take all sail down to wait and see how things developed. We'd still be proceeding smartly northward at 4 knots or so, thanks to the current.

Once we had things lashed down, I checked the forecast. The news was not good. The disturbance that was moving across the Florida peninsula, the one that was supposed to cause the showers, unexpectedly intensified, and gale warnings were out now with winds to 45 knots expected. Not much we could do about it at that point, but we felt, with some justification, that we'd been suckered out there.

What followed was one of the most terrifying nights we'd ever had at sea. Liz and I retreated to the cabin, as there was little sense in standing out in the rain. It poured and blew, and as the storms descended on us there was almost continuous lightning. The interior lights weren't on, but the cabin was bright as day in a flickering sort of way, like a strobe light gone haywire. Each lightning flash was accompanied by an instantaneous ear-splitting crash of thunder that seemed to shake the whole boat, as if we were under heavy bombardment and barely escaping destruction with a series of near misses.

We sat huddled together on the settee, cringing at each crash. There was some comfort in each other's presence, but it felt like the whole world was convulsing around us in a kind of mad cataclysmic upheaval. This was not the way ocean voyaging was depicted in the magazine articles. This was grim.

At the same time, I realized there was absolutely nothing we could do. We had no control over forces this powerful. Whatever was going to happen would happen.

I'd always thought we were relatively safe from lightning in our steel boat—wouldn't the steel hull dissipate the charge if we were struck?—but I wasn't eager to test my theory. I hoped to hell the lighting would ignore our mast, even though it was the most prominent thing for miles around and hard to miss.

For six hours the onslaught continued. We sat there, eventually half-dozing at times despite the chaotic din, looking out every now and then to check for ships, although being run down seemed like the least of our worries at that point. The sea was rough, but not dangerously so, since the wind was mostly blowing with the current, not against it. But with no sail up to steady the boat, the motion was lurchy and erratic, and Liz began to feel a little sick.

The night seemed endless, but finally, toward dawn, the storms began to ease off, and with first light we ventured into the cockpit. The wind was howling now, gusting over 40, but the rain had stopped.

"Let's set the trysail," I said after some consideration. The trysail is a small storm sail that's used instead of the mainsail in heavy weather. Conditions weren't really bad enough to warrant using it just then, but I feared they might get worse, so it seemed like the right call. At least we could get moving through the water again. But to my dismay, as so often happens, no sooner did we get the trysail up than the wind started to ease off, and by noon we were flopping around in light airs, disgusted with the weather and life in general. The only bright spot was that our noon fix showed that we'd made 172 miles from Miami in the last 24 hours, even though we'd spent a good chunk of that time with no sail up.

It's hard—and probably pointless—to reconstruct the exact sequence of events, but in brief outline we were battling adverse conditions for the next four days. The short lull we'd just experienced was only a prelude to a shift to the north and increasing winds, and by evening the winds were gale force again. We hove-to—parked the boat under sail—and tried to get some sleep: there was no point in bashing into the seas with the wind that strong.

And that was the pattern. The wind was up and down, often reaching gale force for a few hours, then relenting a little. That meant a lot of sail changing for us. Sleep was difficult. Discomfort was continuous. I wrote in my journal:

> *The constant roughness is wearying. Can't sit outside. Can't do much but sit at the chart table or lie in a bunk. Another gale is forecast for our area on Thursday. Oh boy.*

The wind direction was equally distressing. We were headed for Bermuda, and with the wind in the north and the course to Bermuda now that we'd cleared the northern Bahamas about 070, we had to sail close to the wind, which only made things rougher. Gradually too, the wind shifted to the east over the next couple days, making it impossible to steer directly for Bermuda: much of the time we were 30 degrees or more off course to the south. Eventually the wind went due east, and we had to tack to the north. That was demoralizing to say the least.

We slammed on, but the fourth day, as evening encroached and with no sign of improvement in the conditions, I said to Liz: "You know, we don't have to do this."

She looked at me. "What do you mean?"

"This Atlantic crossing. We don't have anything to prove. We know we *can* do it. But do we want to bad enough to put up with this?"

"What would we do instead?"

"We could bear off and head for Beaufort. It would be a hell of a lot more comfortable. We could spend the summer on the east coast, maybe go to Maine or something."

"It does seem like we've had more than our share of this kind of weather," Liz sighed,

I was voicing doubts that lay in the background for both of us: why were we doing this? Was it worth the discomfort, the stress, the aggravation? We'd spent three years putting up with all that on our circumnavigation. It *is* an inevitable part of offshore sailing, but did we really want to do it all again?

That night Liz wrote in her journal:

We both seem to feel this kind of pain in the ass sailing may not be worth it for us. Our motivation is not strong enough, or so far the rewards or challenges have not been enough. It wouldn't take much to persuade us to abandon the Atlantic crossing. But later, thinking of giving up on the Med, I felt a sense of loss and a desire to go through with it. A positive desire—not just to avoid facing up to land life. We agreed to talk more about alternatives. We will surely need them eventually.

Neither of us really wanted to abandon our plans, but we both felt the determination to carry through with them slipping away.

So began our Atlantic crossing: with us awash in a sea of doubt.

2. New Plans and a New Boat

After you've done a circumnavigation of the world in a small sailing boat, what do you do for an encore?

That was the problem (if indeed it was a problem) that confronted us in 1987. My original, very tentative, idea was to tackle the Patagonian Channels, that circuitous route at the bottom and western edge of South America noted for terrible weather, strong winds, poor anchorages, and desolation. I'd even gone so far as to order some charts and a few guidebooks to the area. It was fun to follow along on the charts with the various accounts I had of people who'd made that trip, though I was well aware that it would probably be a hell of a lot less fun to undertake the real journey.

I didn't consciously abandon the idea; I just, quite sensibly, put it on hold while I considered other more pleasant alternatives. We could always revive that plan if enthusiasm warranted. Instead, I turned my attention to the Mediterranean. Because we'd gone around South Africa on our circumnavigation, we'd missed the Med. I'd made two long cruises to the Med when I was an officer on a Navy destroyer in the 60s, so I had some familiarity with it, though obviously not from the perspective of a small sailing vessel. I knew there was a lot of variety there, a lot of historical and cultural interest, and I suspected that the old cliché about the Med was true: that the sailing is generally lousy, with either too much wind or not enough. So we weren't likely to enjoy the kind of sailing the Caribbean offers, but other factors should compensate and it seemed worth doing.

Therefore, the Med became the immediate focus of our planning. It had been seven years since we'd returned from our last cruise. Our son, Jeff, had been 12 then. Now he was 19 and in college. Liz and I were seven years older too, in our late 40s. We'd always assumed we'd do another voyage, but real questions remained. Why did we want to do this? Would it just be a pale rerun of the previous voyage? We'd been on the steep side of the learning curve then: everything was new to us, our skills and attitudes were still developing, and we had a very clear cut goal. Things would be different now, more open ended. Would it be as challenging, as satisfying, as worth doing? It was hard to know.

If you've read my account of our circumnavigation, you know that Liz and I had very different temperaments and to a large extent we each made up for the other's weaknesses. The original idea of sailing around the world had been mine. Liz had thoroughly bought into it from the start, although the way we experienced it was probably quite different. I'm not exactly a thoroughgoing Type A personality—there are many things I'm comfortable being very lax about—but when I have a picture in my head of how things should be, I don't deal very well when reality intrudes and messes up my vision. Liz, on the other hand, takes setbacks far less personally than I do and adapts more easily to changing circumstances. I don't know that either approach is "right," but in an imperfect, muddling sort of way we made it work with minimum conflict.

At least this time we had the boat. It was sitting in our back yard in Connecticut where we'd been building it from a bare hull for the past three years.

When you're making a lot of long passages, as we were on the circumnavigation, you spend a lot of time thinking about the next boat, the one that's going to have all the virtues and none of the drawbacks of your present boat. That's a pleasant fantasy but has little to do with reality: every boat is a compromise; there are no perfect boats, though clearly some are more perfect than others for the uses you intend to put them to.

On the world cruising circuit in the 70s, many people considered steel to be the material of choice for a world-cruising boat, and I'd bought into that idea. Steel was strong, more likely to bend than puncture if you hit something, and a steel hull could we welded together to make it reassuringly watertight. There was no concern about blisters (the frequent plague of even the finest fiberglass hulls), and far less chance for water to seep through cracks or joints. If you did damage the hull in some way, a welded repair, available virtually anywhere in the world, didn't require the specialized skill that a fiberglass repair does. The big drawback to steel, of course, was the threat of corrosion, as salt water and steel don't play well together. So proper paint protection was crucial, and vigilant maintenance would be an ongoing necessity.

There were other problems. There weren't many steel boats in the US, where fiberglass had overwhelmed the market, largely because fiberglass hulls are easier to mass produce. There were many more in Europe, especially in France and Holland, but that wasn't a viable alternative for us. Of course there were yards in the US that could turn out a very nice custom steel boat for you...if you had much deeper pockets than we did. Realistically, all this meant that, if we really wanted to go with steel, we'd have a very limited number of vessels to choose from.

Then, as I mulled this all over in the early 1980s, I stumbled on an advertisement that looked promising. Sometime before our previous voyage, I'd read Arthur Beiser's 1966 book *The Proper Yacht* in which he had photographs and descriptions of vessels or designs that he considered, according to some personal criteria, noteworthy. Most of the vessels described were quite large and fancy, but the smallest was the Departure 35, a basic little 35-foot boat by the Chesapeake designer Charles Wittholz that was specifically designed to be constructed in plywood. I wasn't interested in a plywood boat, but I liked many things about the design. It had a nearly full keel, an outboard rudder, a moderate five-foot draft, and a cutter rig. So when I found that Paul Mooney in the Chesapeake was building the Departure in steel, I was immediately interested.

The upshot was that we drove to Deltaville Virgina where Paul's operation was located, went for a sail on a Departure, liked it, but considered it was probably too expensive for us, even if we bought just the hull. I'd never wanted to build a boat myself anyway, so we more or less scrapped the idea.

A few months went by, with the idea of the Departure fermenting in the back of my mind. The exact sequence of events isn't clear to me now, but I know we talked to Paul again, and he thought we could get financing if we bought the boat as a "kit," not just a bare hull. Now to me a kit implies some kind of package with all the necessary parts and detailed instructions for assembly. That wasn't exactly Paul's idea. His idea was simply to supply enough of the components necessary for a more or less functional vessel: mast and boom, rigging wire and terminals, line and blocks for running rigging, lifelines, engine sitting on its mounts, stainless steel water tanks, and various bits of teak and other small fittings. Claiming all this stuff was a kit was a means of convincing the finance company that the vessel was worth making a loan on. In a way, it was like buying a "some assembly required" piece of fantastically complicated furniture with many of the pieces missing and no instructions whatsoever and expecting to be able to come up with a product that looks exactly like the one in the advertising photo.

Actually, though, I didn't mind too much. That approach would allow us to get construction of a new steel boat underway. I'm not a natural craftsman, I'm not an accomplished woodworker or metal worker, and my goal wasn't to turn out a thing of artistic beauty. But I figured I had enough basic skills and enough practical intelligence to construct a simple and functional boat that would serve us well. I knew I was getting in a bit over my head, but I had reasonable faith in my ability to claw my way back to the surface eventually. Plus with Jeff still in school we were committed to at least another four or five years on land, and we needed a project.

So we decided to go for it.

Many years later, many thousands of miles in the boat later, I'm still not sure if it was the right decision or not. Maybe the obsession with steel was misplaced: thousands of fiberglass vessels make long voyages every year without getting into serious trouble. Maybe it would have made more sense to buy a sound used fiberglass vessel and spend three years modifying it as needed for offshore sailing: starting with a functional vessel would've left more time for getting the details right.

But by the summer of 1983, we had the Departure sitting in our backyard. We had a second-story porch at the back of the house that was just the right height to put a plank across to the deck of the boat. It could hardly be more convenient. The boat arrived as a finished hull, painted inside and out (the topsides a bright yellow, painted with Awlgrip, the very hard and glossy two-part finish). The inside was completely empty except for the engine sitting there unconnected.

One thing was obvious from the first: the boat was smaller than I thought. It was a single-chine design, which means that instead of a full and continuous curve to the hull from topsides to keel, there was just a sharp edge where the metal of the topsides meets the bottom plating. It was designed like that to avoid compound curves and to enable the boat to be constructed of plywood, or in this case steel. Working compound curves into steel plating can be done, but it requires specialized machinery and is expensive. Designing the boat so that the plates curve in only one direction is far simpler. Our previous boat, the British-built Golden Hind (also designed for plywood), had been of *double* chine construction, which meant there were two edges, allowing for a slightly more gradual curve toward the keel. I don't think either of these construction methods has much effect on sailing quality, but they do decrease the interior volume of the boat, and especially so with the single-chine design. On top of that, the grid-like steel framework that supported the hull plating also ate up a few inches of interior room; and we had an inch and a half of polyurethane foam sprayed in the hull all the way around for insulation except in the bilge area. The result of all this was that the interior was going to be quite cramped, and we spent a lot of time drawing diagrams and measuring, trying to figure out how to fit everything in, making it up as we went along.

I won't chronicle here the details of building the boat, which occupied much of my time for the next three years—I'll just mention some of the decisions we made in the process. It's said that generals always prepare to fight the last war, and that at least partially applies to some of the decisions we made about our new boat. Our previous boat had been very simple—you might even say primitive—in terms of its gear and equipment. The list of the basic stuff we *didn't* have would be substantially longer than the list of what we did. I was still in favor of simplicity, but I was willing to accept some changes. Still, I had the last cruise in mind, and that colored the choices I made. In some cases that was good; in other cases not.

For an engine, I chose the 18-horsepower Norwegian Sabb (not to be confused with the Swedish Saab, a different company). This was an older design, similar to the British Lister we'd had in the other boat. For our purposes, it was a bad choice. For one thing, it wasn't really powerful enough. If we'd been planning on doing mostly long passages, as we had on the previous voyage, it would've been fine. But in the Med shorter passages with lots of motoring prevailed, and we regretted not having a more powerful engine. Also, instead of a gearbox it came with a variable pitch propeller; by means of a separate control, you could adjust the orientation of the propeller blades, which allowed you to go into reverse or neutral. But I found it a fussy system, and because there was no fixed neutral, the boat tended to creep forward or backward when you really wanted it to stay put, as alongside a dock, for example.

I went with hanked-on sails rather than roller furling. That made a certain amount of sense. Because the boat was cutter rigged (two sails forward of the mast), it was easy to drop either the yankee (the outer sail) or the staysail to immediately reduce sail. Not quite as easy as roller furling maybe, but infinitely easier than *changing* the headsail, which is what we had to do on the other boat. Of course there'd be a lot more sail handling involved than with a furling jib; on the other hand, when you drop a hanked-on sail you can be pretty sure it's going to come down, while if a furler jams you've got problems. I'd seen enough jammed furlers to want to avoid that kind of excitement if possible.

The wind vane for self-steering—an essential device for offshore sailing—was relatively easy to engineer with an outboard rudder, and although the geometry of the layout presented certain problems, the basic design was the same as the one I'd built for our previous boat. I pulled it together for only a few hundred dollars, as opposed to the many thousands of dollars the manufactured gears were going for, and it steered us without a bit of trouble for the whole voyage.

As for electronics, satellite navigation was available in the mid-80s, but the SatNav sets were still expensive, so I passed on that. I figured celestial navigation, sextant and tables, had served us well on the previous cruise so why scrap my acquired skill for an expensive black box? I did install a radar, a little Apelco set. "It's not much more than a toy, is it?" one guy said to me. Maybe, but it worked. It had only an eight-mile range (at best), but there's seldom a need for a greater range in a small sailing vessel—in fact, most of the time we had it set on the four-mile range or less. Its low current draw was a plus. We only used it when we needed it: to confirm our distance off when sailing near a coast, especially at night, and for keeping track of other vessels at sea.

I also installed a ham radio. We'd made the previous cruise without any means of contacting anyone beyond the range of our VHF radio, about 20 miles. So at sea we were totally alone. In a sense, I liked that. Eric Hiscock, the British cruising guru, used to say that, if he were making the rules, the one piece of gear he'd *prohibit* aboard a voyaging yacht would be a radio transmitter. That idea runs counter to the accepted thinking in today's electronic world, but I can sympathize with it. If you choose to go to sea in a small sailing vessel, you're presumably doing it for your own pleasure and edification. You're not trying to make your living out there. You don't *have* to be out there. It's your choice. So to go to sea thinking that if you get into trouble you'll just turn on the radio and call for help is morally questionable. In any case, I didn't have the radio primarily for safety—it was simply a matter of convenience. With Jeff back in the States, and with our aging parents, it would be nice to have a means of contacting them (or for them to contact us) if problems arose. With the radio, we could get phone patches back home or at least pass messages if necessary. We soon found it had other uses as well. It enabled us to keep track of cruising friends and it gave us something to do when on passage.

Another major step up from the previous boat was refrigeration. Although it's probably the one thing we missed most on the first voyage, refrigeration gulps electricity. To keep even a well-insulated box cold is likely to require two-to-four engine hours a day, maybe even more in the tropics. If you're doing primarily coastal sailing, and sailing every day, that may not be a huge problem, as there's often a fair bit of motoring involved. But if you're sitting at anchor for a week or two, or making long passages, it can be a hassle. I adopted a compromise solution. I built a small, well insulated box and installed a 12-volt refrigeration unit to cool it. We didn't care about preserving big chunks of frozen meat or other frozen goodies. We just liked to be able to have cold drinks (especially beer) and to keep whatever fresh food we had from spoiling. Our strategy was to get ice whenever it was easily available and use the box primarily as an icebox. Running the fridge for a few hours a day when we had ample electricity would slow the rate of the ice melt. When ice was unobtainable, or when we were on a long passage, we'd run the fridge for a couple hours in the morning and a couple hours in the afternoon, just enough to keep the box (and the beer) cool. To help with the electrical demands, we installed a couple of solar panels. (You see how complication leads to complication.) The ideal setup would probably include a wind generator too, but in the mid-80s they tended to be noisy or bulky or both, and it was more mechanical nonsense than I wanted to deal with. Anyway, if worse came to worse, we could always drink warm beer. We'd done it before.

One other feature we installed was a plastic bubble, sort of like a gunner's turret on old World War II planes. In theory, it would allow us to look out in rough or nasty weather without actually going out. I also had some hopes that we could engineer an inside steering position that we could use while looking out of the bubble; I tried several ways of doing that but never could come up with anything very satisfactory. And I hoped that with the bubble we could do without a canvas dodger to provide shelter in the cockpit, but there were problems with that idea too, as a dodger is nice to have at anchor and in many conditions where you wouldn't want to use the bubble. After six months of cruising, I had one made in Florida.

We hadn't carried an outboard for our dinghy on our previous boat—not till we got to South Africa where we bought a little British Seagull. We rowed our inflatable everywhere, sometimes to the amusement of bystanders. We had no interest in a big outboard or a planing dinghy (more complication), but even a small outboard could be a convenience. So we bought a two-horsepower Seagull, a very basic and old-fashioned engine. That was also probably a mistake, because the newer outboards were cleaner, quieter, easier to start, and in general more pleasant to use. Still, for us, having *any* outboard was a step up.

The actual building of the boat was an adventure I can't recommend, especially if your primary motivation is to go sailing. Some people enjoy building boats more than sailing them, and for them it can make sense. Otherwise, probably not. You certainly don't save money since most things have to be bought retail without the advantage of bulk purchase. The one possible advantage is that you have the chance to get everything the way you want it. But even that is a shaky rationalization. The way you want it will probably change as you acquire experience—it did for us, and we'd already had a lot of experience. You do get a pretty good idea of where everything is in the boat and how it functions, though I had plenty of moments down the road when I scratched my head wondering, "Why did I do that?" or "Where did I put that?"

So, after three years, with everything as right with the boat as I could make it, with the name (*Horizon* once again) newly affixed to the stern, we were ready to put it in the water. That was not without its own problems. The trucking company had brought the boat into our backyard on a hydraulic trailer which could easily be maneuvered down our narrow drive and around the corner to position the boat behind the house. Unfortunately, that trailer was no longer available. We had to rent a crane to lift the boat onto a trailer. Besides the expense involved, the operation itself was more than a little shaky. The crane had to sit on rather soggy land, bringing its stability into question, and—most nerve-wracking—in order to set the boat onto the trailer, the boat had to be lifted *over* house. Liz and I watched in a state of fascinated horror, as it dawned on us that it would take only one little screw-up with that nine-ton mass of metal hanging there over the house to send it plummeting through the roof and in one stroke trash everything we owned, both boat and house. Needless to say, with the boat swinging in the slings above the house, the suspense (so to speak) was terrific. We optimistically snapped a few pictures of it as it hung there and breathed a collective sigh of relief when it finally cleared the house.

Getting ready to lift the new boat over the house

We had the boat trucked to a marina on the Connecticut River, got the mast stepped, rigged it, and launched it. Yes, it sat a little lower in the water than I'd hoped, but there wasn't anything I could do about that. A few days later, we motored down the river to Long Island Sound feeling proud and happy that we'd actually pulled the whole thing off, that we now had a brand new boat almost ready for a new adventure.

Without the time pressure we'd had last time, we were

able to spend that summer doing trial sails, getting the inevitable bugs worked out, learning the idiosyncrasies of the boat and its gear—just the way you're supposed to do it. What a contrast to the last time! We still had another year to work before we planned to leave, but that was okay because we had a lot to do to prepare. In addition to boat stuff, we had a slew of organizational things to deal with: we had to dispose of our belongings, including the house; we had to get Jeff set up; and we had financial arrangements to make.

As always, the financial end of things required careful thought. We knew we'd go without insurance on the boat. The cost was prohibitive (for us), and most, if not all, insurers required three people on board for ocean passages. That was absurd from my point of view: more voyages end due to crew problems than from any other reason; we'd heard plenty of horror stories ourselves. Our insurance was our experience, our judgment, the care we always took with the boat, and our ground tackle. Medical insurance was something else again. We were older now, and though we were both in good health, we had to acknowledge that the risk of something going seriously wrong was substantially greater than it had been 10 years before when we went without any insurance. So we opted for a Major Medical policy with a big deductible, though even that wasn't cheap. We should be able to absorb ordinary medical expenses, but we felt we needed something in case of catastrophic illness or injury.

+

As we thought all this stuff through and talked about it, there were still nagging concerns about whether this was the direction we wanted to go. It was hard to know what we expected to get out of a new voyage. Were we perhaps chasing some idyllic vision that had never really existed, except for brief moments? We were in no position to make a partial commitment. We had considerably more money than we'd had at the outset of the previous voyage, but we'd still have to sell our house and possessions for the second time, cut all our ties with friends and whatever other connections we had. Once again, we'd have nothing to come back to. That had been a huge leap out into uncertain space the first time; now, 10 years later, it seemed far bigger. One of my teaching colleagues, when he heard about our plans, said, "That's a pretty gutsy step at your age." I'd never thought of it exactly that way before. How much difference did age make? Was this perhaps just foolish, risking a secure future for a second chance to confront uncertainty? When we were in our 30s and planning a three-year voyage, we'd always felt that even if it all went balls up we'd still have plenty of time to recoup our losses, painful and difficult though it might be. Now we'd probably be in our 50s, not really old perhaps, but with far less time left to us and fewer options.

There wasn't a clear structure to the voyage this time either. Before, because we'd always planned a circumnavigation, there was a clear stopping point. We knew that after we'd circled the globe we'd be done. It was all more shapeless this time. We didn't have the money, or the intent, or even the desire to sail indefinitely. But how long would we be gone? We didn't know. All we knew was our money wouldn't last forever. Like Dickens' Micawber, I faintly hoped that something might turn up, but that was nothing more than a slightly comforting fantasy.

Anybody who's going to take off on an extended voyage, at some point, has to come to grips with *why*. What's the point? What do you expect to get out of it? Why are you doing it? Is it enough for you to simply meander from port to port? Are you satisfied to be just a sort of sea-going tourist on permanent holiday? Is the challenge of the sailing enough for you? When you're just starting out, you're on the steep side of the learning curve: everything is new, the environment demands your attention so completely that questions starting with "Why?" tend to get pushed aside. You've got other things to worry about.

But we'd done all this before. We had a pretty good idea of our strengths and weaknesses, we'd worked out ways of coping with most situations, and while there are always more things to learn and while the unforeseen can always raise its ugly head, a lot of the time we'd be dealing with situations that we'd dealt with before.

And what about me and Liz? We were different people than we'd been before the last cruise. Less naïve about the nature of ocean voyaging, certainly, but also perhaps slightly less willing to put up with the inevitable hassles of life at sea. On the one hand, we both felt a certain momentum to see our plans through. After pouring so much time and money and effort into the boat, we'd made a tacit commitment to the whole idea of a second cruise. But on some level, I knew I could walk away from it without any deep regret: it wasn't something I *had* to do. As before, we each probably looked at the cruise in slightly different ways, perhaps expected different things from it. Would that cause conflict or disagreements? Would we be able to find some sort of balance again despite our differences? We hadn't worn out that sense of it being a cooperative enterprise, had we? I wasn't sure.

Inevitably, living in the cramped space of a small sailing vessel for long periods of time, often under conditions of stress, puts a strain on any relationship. The husband-wife crew normally does best because there's a commitment to something other than the voyage to help weather the rough spots. But there's little question that such enforced intimacy can be a challenge for even the closest couples. Liz and I had done pretty well on the first voyage, but we'd grown apart somewhat in the years since. Perhaps that too was inevitable: it probably would've been more surprising if we *hadn't*. We'd both needed more space. But there's a fine line between enough space and too much, and neither of us were quite sure where that line was. We weren't naïve enough to think that sailing was going to make us into the people we were 10 years ago, but how would it affect us as we were now? Were we still close enough to make this voyage successful and satisfying, both for us as a couple and individually? Could we make it work? It was hard to know.

In any case, we were both aware that we'd need some other interests besides the sailing to make the experience more meaningful. On the previous voyage, dealing with Jeff's needs in addition to the boat problems had eaten up big quantities of time. Without Jeff, and with a new boat that, hopefully, had most things right, we anticipated a lot more "free" time. We weren't the kind of people to fill our days with cocktail parties and desultory conversation.

We took a scuba class and got certified; we bought scuba gear and read about diving sites in the Caribbean (we were planning on spending a winter in the western Caribbean before heading for the Med). We bought Spanish tapes, figuring if we were going to Central America and eventually to Spain we'd better learn some of the language. We read books about Mediterranean archeology, culture, and history. We had ideas for writing projects. We had the ham radio. I wondered if all that would be enough.

In the end, I was surprised how easy it was. Not in the details or the complexities of the arrangements that are necessary in engineering an escape like this or even in the emotional consequences: all that stuff can be difficult. The easy part was what seems at first to be the hardest: making the decision to do it. It has always amazed me that all it takes is that one let's-do-it moment to set the whole enterprise in motion. So many people say, "I'd like to do that someday..." but relatively few get to the point where they say, "Let's do it now..., and yet once you latch on to the idea in some realistic sense then all else follows. It's almost scary, having that much control over the direction of your own life.

In the larger sense, of course, I'm well aware that we were fantastically lucky to be living in a time and place and circumstances where such a decision was possible. To decide to do something that means breaking with your circumstances and all the expectations they contain, to be able to plan what you want to do and then just go ahead and do it: it's a rare kind of freedom.

So it seemed as if we *were* going to do it. In the fall of 1986, we hadn't explicitly told Jeff, who was just starting his first year at college, that our intention was to leave the following year. Obviously he knew we had the boat (he'd helped me build it!) and were planning a cruise—it wasn't like we sprung it on him out of the blue—but for him it was still in the "sometime" category. Now we had to get serious.

When at last we discussed it with him, it was hard to know what he thought about it. On the one hand, it wasn't a huge deal. He wouldn't be spending a lot of time at home anyway, now that he was in college. But on the other hand it was sort of like having your security blanket unceremoniously ripped away from you. Yes, we'd factored in provision for him to fly out to meet us during his vacations from school, wherever we happened to be, but there'd inevitably be times, before or after visiting us, when he'd have to be *somewhere*. His grandfather, Liz's dad, would help out, but we couldn't ask too much of him. It was easy enough to rationalize it all, but there was a sense in which it could seem like we were abandoning him. I didn't really look at it that way (and I don't think Jeff did either), but I did wonder if we were asking too much of him too soon.

So, once again, we had to sell our house and most of our

possessions. To our amazement and delight, the house sold quickly for about three times as much as we'd paid for it, not bad for seven years. Granted we'd made some major improvements to it (new furnace, new septic system among other things), but even so it was a nice bunch of cash, far more than we'd expected. By sheer chance, we'd bought the house at the bottom of the market (interest rates were sky high, properties weren't selling) and sold it at the height of the market. Our timing couldn't have been better, though it certainly wasn't due to our real estate acumen: it was sheer luck. And once again, we sold all our furniture, tools, and most of our other possessions in a big lawn sale. That was perhaps a little less painful than the first time, if only because we had a clearer idea of what the future would be like, a little more confidence in our own ability to deal with it. But it still wasn't easy.

"I wonder how many other people have done this," Liz said, as we picked up our few remaining possessions that hadn't sold.

"Done what? Sold their stuff?"

"No, sold everything they own for the *second* time. Made this kind of break *twice*. Are we crazy?"

"People do it once. I'm not sure about twice."

"I'm not either."

And as I thought about it, it did seem like a pretty radical move. I wondered if we'd get away with it this time.

Harder still was saying goodbye to Jeff. I hardly knew how to do it. I felt awkward and uneasy, and I'd never felt that way with Jeff. We'd given him our last car, a VW Rabbit, and he drove us to the boat. Stupidly, we shook hands in the gathering evening darkness, mumbled a few words of unnecessary advice, and a few moments later, Liz and I stood there watching the taillights of his car receding, like the end of a bad movie.

3. Back to the Tropics

It wasn't an auspicious beginning to the new voyage. We were both a little frazzled by the tension involved in arranging our departure and leaving behind everything that had become familiar in the last seven years. And we both felt more uncertain than we cared to admit about setting off without Jeff. We knew we'd see him again in a few months, and he'd already been mostly away from us during his first year in college, but there was something about depriving him of a home to come back to that was sobering, disturbing. It was a big transition, perhaps even bigger than the one we'd made 10 years before. At least then we were all in it together.

The first couple days went smoothly enough. We made the short hop from the Connecticut River to Stonington the first day, and then sailed out to Block Island on the second with a delightful wind behind us. (Goin' out to Block, as the locals say.) Despite everything, it felt good to be moving. But that pleasure was not to last. The forecast called for southwest winds, not favorable for heading for Cape May, New Jersey, our intended destination, so we planned to stay over a day. The harbor was nearly deserted—it was after Labor Day—and the island quiet, a big difference from the normal summertime crowds and confusion. It didn't much matter, for we weren't to have much of a chance to enjoy it. After a quiet day, the wind picked up in the night: it was blowing 25-30 and gusting higher in the morning, and it picked up further in the afternoon. The forecast predicted more of the same for the next few days. The big harbor was rough with white caps on the dark water and streaks of foam blown across the surface. Going ashore was out of the question—not that it would be particularly dangerous but it was obvious we'd get soaked. The water whooshed by the hull, sometimes striking it with a startling thump. We hunkered down and tried to make the best of it.

"Nice to be yachting again, isn't it?" I said.

In fact, it might not have been the worst thing in the world. A little down time after the frantic pace of the previous few months, a little time to settle in to the new environment without the pressing need to do anything much...it could be worse. We read, watched our tiny TV, worked on our Spanish tapes, determined to have at least an elementary knowledge of the language before we got to Central America. The one galling thing was that the VHF weather stoutly maintained that the wind at Block Island was 16 gusting to 22 knots. Meanwhile, our anemometer routinely recorded gusts of 50 knots or better.

"Their anemometer must be in a hole," Liz said.

"I guess they're trying to keep it out of the wind," I said.

The next day was a rerun, and by evening it was getting pretty old. But it started to calm down in the night, and we could have left and probably should have, but things still seemed unsettled, so we hung in there for a fourth night.

We had no excuse the next morning as the wind was down, so we set off in the grey day for Cape May, 200 miles away, too far to make it in one overnight unless conditions were perfect. I was leery of a night entry, which I always try to avoid if possible anyway, since I knew anchoring room was limited in Cape May Harbor. If you left at dawn, you could just about make it by sunset the next day if you could *average* 6 knots. That's not particularly easy to do in a small boat, and we certainly didn't have perfect conditions, so we resigned ourselves to two nights at sea.

On her watch that night Liz wrote in her journal:

> *It feels good to be at sea, the motion, the sounds, the watchkeeping, the routine—all good. A beautiful night. A million stars. The Milky Way right over our head. Enough starlight to see a horizon between water and sky.*

This was the first night sailing we'd done in more than seven years, and I suppose we were a little rusty. That area between Long Island and the Jersey coast has a lot of traffic—fishing boats, ocean vessels headed in and out of New York, tugs with tows and other commercial craft—so somebody has to be looking all the time. Plus the wind was fluky, finally settling down to blow from the west, making it impossible for us to steer directly for Cape May. Under those conditions, it was hard for me to relax and get any reasonable sleep. That general pattern continued the next day, with the added attraction of a few brief squalls. Where did this rotten weather come from anyway? Then, as we sailed blithely on during my watch that night I noted a large black cloud looming up ominously ahead of us. I had some idea of attempting to sail around it, but the cloud had other plans, and without warning it suddenly unleashed a huge blast of wind that it had obviously been saving for just us. We took a pretty good knockdown before I was able to drop the jib and before Liz, woken out of a sound sleep, was able to free the mainsheet and spill the wind from that sail. No harm done, but the realities of ocean sailing aren't something you can easily ignore.

Next day, after a wild sail down the Jersey coast in welcome sunshine, we entered the harbor at Cape May, squeezed in amongst the anchored boats in the very limited room available, and fell gratefully into bed.

+

So we were off at last, if not exactly as we would have wished. A few days later we entered the head of the Chesapeake, glad to be in sheltered waters in case Hurricane Emily, then stirring up the southern Bahamas, decided to head our way. We meandered south, stopping for awhile in Annapolis, then crossing to the Eastern Shore. We were still getting used to our new boat, still working out the kinks, though it was nowhere near as frustrating as our trip in the first *Horizon* when serious doubts about our mast and steering vane clouded our days, and we struggled to adapt to a new way of life. This was all familiar enough to us now, even if there was a different quality to the experience without Jeff on board.

In general, Liz and I were getting along quite well during this transition period. We both felt relief that all the pre-departure hassles were over and that we could begin to stake out a way of being in a life afloat again. In the background were memories of our previous adventures and anticipation of new ones: that helped. When there's some regret about what you've left behind, it's nice to have something to look forward to.

We'd met a couple in the Sassafras River in the upper Chesapeake, Sam and Jo, who were off on their first cruise. They were sailing a 44-footer that was absolutely crammed full of stuff, including two large dogs. They were both enthusiastic but uncertain. Sam had been a lawyer in his previous life (as of a couple weeks before), and he seemed to need all his stuff around him, as if he weren't quite ready to let that previous life go. But he told us he'd brought along a three-piece suit and smart leather shoes when they left, and then thrown them overboard off the Jersey coast. I took that as a positive sign. These transitions aren't easy, whatever your background or mental state.

We proceeded down the bay in generally fine weather, but some weird things happened.

Sailing in the shallow waters of the lower Eastern Shore one day, I thought we were going way too slow for the wind strength, and the vane seemed to be having trouble keeping us on course. I was puzzled. This had never happened before. It was as if we were plowing through the bottom muck, though the depth sounder indicated plenty of water. I tried steering with hand pressure on the trim tab arm and found that the tab wouldn't apply enough pressure on the rudder to steer the boat. Frustrated, I started mentally running through things I could do to improve the vane's efficiency and had a new vane halfway designed in my head by the time we approached our anchorage and started the engine. But when we found that the engine would barely drive the boat at 5 knots even running it flat out, it was clear the vane wasn't the problem. I couldn't understand it. What the hell was going on? We anchored, and no sooner had we'd done so, than a crab pot float popped up beside us.

"That wasn't there a minute ago," Liz said.

Suddenly all became clear: we'd hooked the pot line on the bottom of our rudder and been dragging it, the buoy and the cage assembly, for over an hour! No wonder the steering was a little difficult and the boat a little slow. We pulled the pot up and found five or six big blue-red crabs in it, enjoying their unexpected tour of the bay.

A few days later, study of the chart and the cruising guide tempted me to try something I doubt I'd want to get involved in today. A narrow two-mile canal leads from the Big Annemesex River, where we'd just spent the night, south to the Little Annemesex River. Since we were headed for Crisfield on the Little Annemesex, it would save us some roundabout miles to take the direct route offered by the canal. The only problem was, the depths were iffy...to say the least. As we approached the canal, the bottom started coming up to greet us, so I anchored and rowed out in the dinghy to take soundings. I found about five and half feet, just a couple inches more than we draw. I put the motor on the dinghy and went up to where the canal started, sounding between the entrance markers. There was five and half feet there too, but in a very narrow strip. What the hell. The day was calm, the weather nice. Give it a shot.

We started ahead with the boat, and just before the last

marker at the canal entrance we ran aground. I tried to back off but couldn't. I rowed out our little 13-pound Danforth anchor and pulled us off by taking the anchor line to a sheet winch, a more involved and time-consuming operation than the mere statement of it suggests. A crab boat came out of the canal as we working on it and we asked him how much water was in there. He said eight feet, so we plunged ahead. He was right: there was plenty of water in the canal; we didn't touch again until we came out of the canal at the other end, but luckily we bounced right off.

We motored into Somers Cove at Crisfield, a good-sized protected basin, past lots of docks fronting tumbledown seafood restaurants, a tacky commercial look to it. The cove was mostly lined with marina slips; the marina was state-run and nice enough, about an equal mix of sail and power boats, but almost nobody on them even though it was Columbus Day weekend. Obviously the season was over. We anchored—there was plenty of room and we were the only anchored boat. We went ashore and walked around, a strange grubby little town that seemed to be trying to decide if it was touristy or not. Main Street was a mixture of gift shops, restaurants, hardware and marine supply stores, a Sears catalog store. Excursions boats went out to Smith and Tangier Islands, the big local attraction.

Then, that night, we witnessed an unexpected drama. We were woken shortly after dozing off by sirens and shouting, looked out, and were shocked to see the night sky lit up in lurid shades of yellow and orange: the town was on fire! I kid you not. This was no simple house fire—it was a real conflagration encompassing a large area at one end of the town. We learned later that it had started in a lumber yard and spread from there, eventually destroying 11 buildings. Luckily we were in no danger anchored in the middle of the cove, and the boats in the marina were safe too, but a good chunk of the town was burned. Four firefighters were treated for smoke inhalation, but otherwise there were no injuries. And we had front row seats to it all—what were the chances? That initial burst of flames lasted only an hour or so, but the noise and sirens and shouting continued all night as firefighters struggled to prevent the fire from spreading further. Look it up—you can find details on the internet…and we were there!

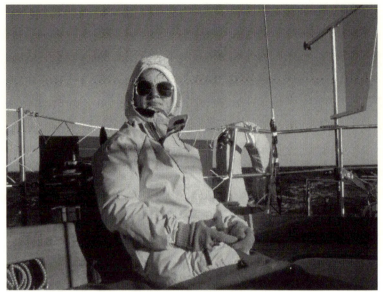

In the Chesapeake...heading for the tropics

We sailed the rest of the Chesapeake with gale warnings out, the wind 30-35 knots. Short, steep little seas just big and mean enough to fling us around, the water typical Chesapeake green, with strips of sunlight and dark cloud shadows, the air crisp. It wasn't too bad because the wind was behind us. We poled out our Yankee without the mainsail and flew. It was a windy October.

+

A couple days in Norfolk, five days in the Intracoastal Waterway (where we had gale winds again crossing Albemarle Sound and had to duck in to anchor off the chart in the Little Alligator River), and we were in Beaufort.

Beaufort was our jumping off place. From here we'd make the offshore passage to the Caribbean. No more worrying about following the markers, staying in the channel, finding an anchorage for the night. Offshore sailing has its own problems but in some ways it's easier than chugging up and down the Waterway where constant attention is required.

Things had changed in Beaufort though. The docks were no longer free of course, as they had been in 1977 when they'd just been opened. We had to anchor out in Taylor Creek in front of the town where the strong tidal current made it necessary to set two anchors, one upstream and one downstream, with all the attendant hassle involved in that. Not much of a community atmosphere any more either. The docks were filled with the sorts of vessels that could afford them: big power yachts and various gleaming sailing craft that looked like they'd recently left the boat yard. The cruising riff-raff (including us) had to anchor or take one of the few available moorings. There were some compensations. In the evening we could sit in the cockpit and watch the wild ponies grazing on Carrot Island a stone's throw away from us, but it was hard not to feel a certain twinge of nostalgia for that earlier time, which remained very special in our minds.

We did have a bit of a connection to that time though. Frank and Judy from *Moonmist* had been part of that community, and they were now living here, just a few miles out of town. They'd sailed their Nicholson 32 to the Caribbean at the same time we had (that awful passage); we'd last seen them in Grenada before they left to cross the Atlantic to Europe and we'd headed the other way toward Panama and the Pacific. Frank was a voluble and gregarious Irishmen with lots of stories to tell, and we spent several pleasant evenings with them, listening to his stories and reminiscing about people we knew in common while we waited for the weather to turn in our favor.

Just like last time, the weather was annoyingly contrary— we waited a couple weeks—though weather information now was a little easier to get. We had our eye on a tropical depression in the Caribbean that was supposed to slide into the Gulf of Mexico. It did, but then it decided to slice across Florida into the Atlantic, right where we would've been if we'd left on the otherwise promising forecast. But it sped away quickly, and once it cleared the area we seized the opportunity and left.

Our plan was to head for the *western* Caribbean and spend the winter in Honduras, Guatemala, and Belize before crossing the Atlantic next year. To get there, we were going to sail outside the Bahamas directly to the Turks and Caicos. That should make for a substantially easier course than heading for the Virgins because we shouldn't have to struggle to get east against the prevailing winds: our course was close to due south which should put the trade winds on the beam when we reached them.

We left about 1100 on November 5th after a quick trip ashore for ice. With a nice moderate breeze from the southwest, we made good time, crossing the western wall of the Gulf Stream in the late afternoon. The forecast promised a front passing with an accompanying windshift, and that happened in the early evening. The wind went into the northwest and quickly veered to the north. That wasn't ideal for the Gulf Stream, as it created a wind-against-the-current situation, but by the time it got serious we were out of the worst of the current. By morning we were down to the double-reefed main and storm jib, zinging along with the wind on the beam. The sea was slate-grey with dull-white crests and streaks of foam under an overcast but non-threatening sky. It was rough as hell but our good progress made it easier to bear. Wind was about 30 knots with higher gusts, seas about 10-15 feet. Not dangerous conditions by any means but uncomfortable and we were taking quite a bit of water: I got my boots filled while trying to get the noon sight.

Things stayed pretty much like that for the next three days, with the wind increasing a bit, so that we went down to the trysail for one night. But we were knocking off 150 miles a day or so, noon sight to noon sight, even with a northerly set. And unlike the last time we headed south from Beaufort, the wind was consistent, none of that up and down nonsense that can drive you crazy and quickly exhaust a small crew.

"This isn't so bad," I said to Liz.

"No," she said without enthusiasm. The motion was making her a little queasy.

But I was glad to see that after seven years we still worked together instinctively. There's a big difference between taking a "crew," somebody who may be an experienced sailor but doesn't know the boat well, probably doesn't know you well either, and sailing with someone you've already spent hundreds of nights at sea with. There's a level of trust and competence there that's almost impossible to duplicate in a casual crew.

I was pleased with the way the boat handled the boisterous conditions too. The one thing that gave me pause was the way the end of our long boom threatened to dip into the tops of the bigger seas. The boom was positioned pretty low on the mast, nice for furling the mainsail but not so nice if it happened to dig in and break. That didn't happen, but in later bouts of heavy weather I sometimes felt compelled to pull the end of the boom up a little with the topping lift and let the sail bag out: sail shape usually didn't matter so much off the wind in a blow, and I felt better about it. Much later, when I had a new mainsail made, I had it cut so that the clew was several feet higher.

On the third day out, Liz wrote in her journal:

Fastest 24 hours we've ever had on a passage. We've carried only the double-reefed main and either the staysail, no jib, or at present the small Yankee. At all times speed between 6 and 8 knots. Big seas, more or less confused. Very blue now with lots of Sargasso weed. Good-sized flying fish on deck this morning. He didn't have to fly on. We just scooped him up along with some Sargasso. Saw 2 ships last night, One passed close in front of us before Bruce saw it. A good scare. We're looking out every 10 minutes now.

A little rough but good progress

So on we went, eating up the miles and trying to get some sleep. It was almost as if the seven years on land hadn't happened, this all felt so familiar. On the evening of our fourth day, the wind started to ease off, and the next day was sunny and warm, the wind moderate. The wind gradually went down even more, straight to calm for awhile, but the night of Day 6 found us in the Caicos Passage, sailing slowly downwind with the sails banging since a big swell from the northeast was rolling the wind out of them. By daylight we could see the island of

Providenciales ("Provo"), and we proceeded slowly in toward the pass through the reef. I marveled at the clarity of the water—it had been so long since we'd been in tropical waters that it amazed us to be able to see the bottom in more than 60 feet, and I loved the colors. I found myself choking up. This was why we'd come. This was why we did this. This was so beautiful. It was one of those moments.

Once through the pass, we still had 10 miles to go over shallow water to the anchorage at Sapodilla Bay. It seemed to take forever, but I didn't care. We were back in the tropics.

We anchored near the little Aquatic Center that was in operation there at the time which also seemed to function as an informal yacht club. There were a few other boats in the anchorage, including *Ta-Tl*, a 36-foot steel boat with Canadians Don and Ann, and their two kids Kyle (4 ½) and Eric (1 ½) aboard: they had their hands full. One day we looked out and saw Don up at his masthead—he had steps on his mast to make climbing it easier; we looked closer and saw that Kyle had followed his father: he was halfway up, as far as the spreaders, a good 20 feet or more above the deck! A little adventurous for a not-quite 5-year old, but Kyle moved around the boat with the ease of an orangutan in the forest. Don and Ann were good with the kids though, watchful but not overprotective, and we enjoyed their company. The boat was built in England and they'd sailed it across, but they'd been in Provo for 11 months. Don had been managing the new boatyard there, something that ultimately "didn't work out." *Ta-Tl* was just a foot longer than *Horizon*, but it could comfortably have contained two or three of our interiors; I was envious of all that room. But my envy stopped there because they had massive paint problems, with rust breaking out all over. They were trying to get some satisfaction from the builder for the mess.

They gave us information about the island. Nothing, apparently, was real convenient. We didn't need much from town, but a couple days later we went in to check it out, easily hitching rides both ways. The "town" (sort of a misnomer) proved to be nothing more than a collection of buildings squatting under the tropical sun in the middle of nowhere with no discernible order to them: a few stores, a few government offices, everything looking sort of half-built or in various states of disrepair. There were a couple of fairly well-stocked grocery stores, and a "department" store consisting of one room with little bits of this and that. All the earth was white coral sand and rock, hot and windblown. We had no reason to linger.

The real attraction of the Turks and Caicos was in the water. We had yet to do a scuba dive on our own, so we signed up to do one with the Aquatic Center. We were the only customers. We went out in their boat, driven by Carl, a big jovial Caicos Islander. Our Dive Master, Jody, was a 40-ish divorcee living the good life here. She let little bits about herself drop out: she had kids in Idaho, 13 and 16; her ex-husband used to run a dive operation in Cozumel. She said the only time she felt truly alive was under water. There was a story there, but our acquaintance was too brief to allow it to unfold. So be it. The tropics tend to attract people whose lives have taken a disappointing turn in one way or another, as they hope to find fulfillment in the easy living, warm breezes, and tropical sunshine. Perhaps some of them do.

The first dive was spectacular. We went down to 35-40 feet, to the top of a wall. It only dropped another 50 feet or so, but it was a tremendous aspect: a deep blue sense of space, fish patrolling the wall almost totally oblivious to us, the water so clear that you felt like you were hanging in air. We descended to 70 feet and hovered along the face of the wall: huge elephant ear sponges, brilliant colors, black coral, a big overhang. Jody moved slowly, taking pictures, pointing out stuff to us. I was a little too overwhelmed to *look* at stuff very carefully. I had to keep checking my gauges for the amount of air I was using and the depth. I finally started to relax a little. I used more air than anybody though, probably because my nervousness increased my demand for it. I did better on the second dive when we went down to only 35 feet or so. We were in a sort of coral garden, clumps and heads of coral with white sand in between, and lots of life: triggerfish, big barracuda, angelfish, parrotfish, blue chromis, and a bewildering variety of other species, all quite lovely. We'd seen all this stuff while snorkeling, of course, but the ability to take our time, to get up close without needing to surface, to become a part of the environment was quite fantastic. We couldn't have had a better first dive experience.

We were in Provo for almost two weeks. We would've done more diving, but the weather was a little too boisterous, blowing 20-30 knots most of the time and gusting higher. So we reluctantly said goodbye to Don and Ann, not expecting to see them again (though in fact we did encounter them again in the Virgins three years later), and left, headed for Central America.

4. The First Winter

Look at a map of the Caribbean. For some people, the geography of the area is a little hazy. Some seem to think the Bahamas are in the Caribbean; I've even heard references to Bermuda, hundreds of miles to the north, as a Caribbean island. But the Caribbean Sea is actually a pretty defined area, bounded by the coast of South America to the south, Central America to the west, and the long arc of islands extending from Cuba to Trinidad, on the north and east. When sailors talk about cruising the Caribbean, they're usually talking about the *eastern* Caribbean, the string of islands just a day sail apart that sit in the heart of trade wind country, where the breeze is consistent, the weather usually fine (except in hurricane season), and where all the clichés about the tropics are true. We'd been through those islands twice before, which is why we were heading for the western Caribbean now, a less-visited area. To get there from the Turks and Caicos, we'd enter the Caribbean through the Windward Passage between Cuba and Haiti, make a right turn and pass between the south coast of Cuba and the north coast of Jamaica, and stop at the Cayman Islands before proceeding on to the Bay Islands of Honduras.

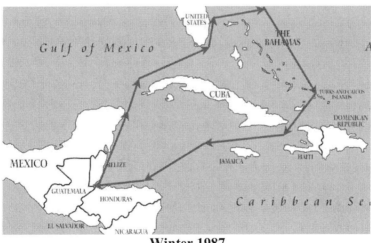

Winter 1987

As we headed south from Provo into the Windward Passage, we had Haiti, on the western part of the big island of Hispaniola, to port, and Cuba to starboard. Castro's Cuba was known for detaining yachts who wandered too close to their coast. In Haiti, as we heard on the news, sporadic violence was occurring ahead of elections scheduled for the end of November; in fact, people were being machine-gunned in the streets. We'd originally planned to spend some time visiting ports in Haiti—and even had the charts—but we decided that wasn't the smartest plan in the current climate.

So as we proceeded between these less-than-welcoming two islands on Thanksgiving Day, 1987, we kept to the center of the passage, well clear of both coasts, though we could see mountains in the distance on both sides. We'd had a very squally night after leaving Provo, courtesy of a front stalled over the Virgins to the east, but by the next afternoon things were settling down, and at dusk we were doing about 6 knots with the wind behind us, the jib poled out, feeling quite content.

That didn't last long. As darkness closed in, a bright searchlight was suddenly trained on us. My first thought was a fishing boat. But when the light persisted, I started to think pirates, or perhaps some government vessel from one of the two countries. Neither alternative was particularly attractive.

I got on the VHF and said, "Vessel with the searchlight, this is the US sailing yacht *Horizon*. Please identify yourself."

Nothing. No reply.

My stomach tightened. It's times like that that it suddenly hits you how vulnerable you are at sea. I tried a couple more times and was greeted only by silence. Meanwhile, the searchlight stayed on us, so bright in the otherwise black night that there was no hope of identifying its source. Finally, after a very long ten minutes, a voice came over the VHF: "This is the United States Coast Guard…"

I didn't know whether to be relieved or annoyed. I wondered exactly what coast they were guarding here in Windward Passage. I wondered why they'd chosen to let us sweat for so long before replying. The voice on the radio proceeded to ask a long list of questions about me, about the boat, about our last port and destination, the number of people on board, and so on. And after we got through with that, the voice said: "Please continue on your present course and speed. We're going to lower a boat and board you."

Great. Just what we needed.

It took them half an hour to get their boat in the water, and meanwhile the searchlight stayed trained on us, making it impossible for us to see anything else. Liz, who was very tired, and had just gone to bed before this all started, finally staggered out into the cockpit. We waited, feeling like sitting ducks. The seas were only about three or four feet, but with our rolly downwind motion, it wasn't easy for them to bring their big inflatable alongside. They finally managed it and deposited four guys on board, all of them armed. An additional four people on our little boat made for very cozy quarters. They had us stay out in the cockpit while three of them went below to "check the spaces" as they termed it, poking into all the various compartments and raking through our stuff. Obviously they were looking for drugs, though they never explicitly stated that. When they got done with the initial sweep, they had me open the fuel and water fills, peered in them with a flashlight and sniffed around. They were polite and businesslike, but it still felt like a hell of a violation. In the middle of all this, just to add to the interest, a squall came through with pouring rain and shifting wind. Some of the guys, especially those who had been below, started to look a little queasy. They were on board for an hour and a half and found no violations of anything for all their bother.

Do they have the right to do this? Apparently they do, even in international waters, even if it's sort of like having the police bust into your home unexpectedly and go through all your drawers and closets: just checking the spaces.

"The thing is," I said to Liz when they'd finally left, "I guess they suspected us of running drugs *from* the States *to* the Caribbean. Does that make any sense?"

"They said they just had a big Thanksgiving meal. I'll bet their Captain just wanted to exercise the crew."

Maybe, but they'd certainly managed to wreck our routine, and because I hadn't been able to pay attention during the squall, they'd messed up our DR too. I asked them for a position, but all they'd give me was a position at our first encounter. Anyway, it wasn't my choice of a way to spend Thanksgiving night.

+

Next morning as we turned west on the underside of Cuba, the wind went light and shifted into the west. That's right. Here where the easterlies reign, where westerlies are almost unknown, where we could legitimately expect fair winds and easy sailing, the wind came ahead of us. I noted that sardonically in my journal: "Course to Grand Cayman 275. Wind 275." The forecast predicted easterlies 15-25 knots, perhaps an exercise in wishful thinking, We spent the day sailing slowly against light wind, tacking every few hours to stay close to the direct course. But at least we weren't having the weather the Virgins were having, where it had been raining for a week or more. By the next morning the wind had frittered out. The sea went glassy calm. We took down the sails and sat comfortably. The sun was hot, the day brilliantly clear, the water an incredible blue. I was in no mood to shatter the tranquility by turning on the engine.

We could see the mountains of Jamaica in the distance. It was tempting to head over there, but stories we'd heard of hassles and the thriving drug trade discouraged us. We'd just wait for wind.

And we did get wind, sort of, a real variety over the next few days. First it went into the north and blew 15-20. Then it swung around to the east and then the southeast. Unfortunately, that proved too light to sail, and we had to take the sails down again. All this in an area where we should've been creaming along with the wind behind us, eating up the miles, watching the flying fishes flash in the sunlight. No such luck. I was annoyed but not surprised. We were dealing with weather, after all, and anything can happen.

Finally, with about 60 miles to go, I gave up and started the engine. We motored into the night until about 0130 when a south breeze came up and we were able to sail slowly along the south coast of Grand Cayman, using the radar to check our distance off. With daylight, we rounded the southwest point of the island, and proceeded to an anchorage off the town near the main cruise ship pier.

Grand Cayman isn't really on the way to anywhere for cruising yachts. Those headed from the States to Central America are more likely to go from Florida through the Gulf of Mexico, and it's a slog against the trade winds (normally) for boats headed east *from* Central America. Consequently, it doesn't get much yacht traffic. For most of our two-week stay, we were the only yacht there. We cleared customs painlessly, went for a snorkel on a little reef in the harbor (water deliciously warm and clear, clouds of fish) and watched a continuous stream of water traffic: boats from the cruise ships (Song Of Norway and

Scandinavian Holiday were in port), dive boats, glass-bottom boats, all rushing here and there. The scene was a little too frantic for us, so we moved up the coast along Seven-Mile Beach to an anchorage off the Holiday Inn. That was fine: we could land on the beach among the vacationers and walk into town or catch a ride. But the anchorage was really sheltered only from northeast to south; it was fine in normal trade wind weather, but we weren't having normal trade wind weather. A persistent swell made it uncomfortably rolly and the landing and exit from the beach tended to be a wet experience. We took to wearing bathing suits under our shore clothes so we could wade out and get the dinghy past the breakers before jumping in. During the day, jet skis buzzed around us like annoying mosquitoes; as the only landmark in the water "that yellow boat" became a convenient turning pylon.

Despite all that, we enjoyed our stay—with one exception which I'll get to in a moment. There was a modern shopping center only a longish walk (or a short ride) away, boasting a huge supermarket chock full of American goodies; we'd only been away from the States for a month or so, but a convenient, well-stocked supermarket is always a welcome sight. Usually we were able to hitch a ride, either to the supermarket or into George Town. The town had an air of prosperity, signaled by the many banks, havens for people from other countries looking to hide their money, or perhaps to launder it. Once we got a ride with a couple of young accountants out from England on their first overseas assignment; they didn't look or sound like shady dealers, but you never know.

But scuba diving is the big thing in the Caymans, and that was well worth it. We asked at one of the dive operations, and they said it was fine to pick up the moorings that marked the dive sites. Despite the often unsettled weather, the dives were great. We'd always enjoyed snorkeling, but as we'd found in the Turks and Caicos, the scuba gear added a different dimension to the underwater experience: to be able to linger, to hang off the face of a wall, to feel like part of the environment, was magical. We mostly dived on our own, but we did go out for a couple of dives one morning with a group on one of the commercial boats. We were getting more comfortable with the gear and with being under water; even a school of three or four barracuda tagging along with us on one dive hardly disturbed us.

Then, one day, trouble with the weather. It had rained all night and most of the morning. When it let up, we'd just started considering a trip to shore, when a northwest swell started coming into the anchorage. We had no shelter at all from the northwest.

"We better wait and see what this is about," I said.

Good thing we did. A few minutes later the wind came in strong from the northwest with heavy rain. I started the engine. The wind and seas increased. I figured we'd better get out of there, so I started to crank in the anchor with our manual windless. It was heavy work because it was blowing so hard and we were bouncing up and down in the swell. I decided to wait and see if it would calm down a bit. We sat there with the engine running for half an hour and saw gusts to 60 on our anemometer. The rain continued. There was nothing on the weather forecast predicting this kind of chaos. The anchor was holding, but it was an uneasy situation. The wind and rain showed no sign of letting up, the seas were getting bigger, so I went back to work with the windless, cranking frantically because I knew as soon as the anchor let go we'd be at the mercy of the wind and sea with limited maneuverability until we got all the gear onboard. Nothing like a little raw panic for motivation: we were soon free and set off motoring down the coast in the driving rain and high wind.

We couldn't see much, but we could see that all the dive boats had bailed out too. We watched the radar, but the rain clutter and sea clutter made it tough to see much on it. The dive boats, mostly large flat-bottom vessels, were headed around the south end of the island. We followed them, hesitated as they ducked in behind the reef there, but finally followed them in cautiously, well aware that they were much shallower than we were. We worked our way in behind Sand Cay and the reef, where there seemed to be just about enough water for us and got the anchor down. The dive boats had moorings in closer to shore, obviously for just this eventuality. We were well sheltered here but were rudely awakened in the middle of the night when we bumped on the coral beneath us. I pulled in some chain to get us away from the offending head, and we were okay till about 7, when we bumped again. Enough was enough. At that point we re-anchored, trying to position ourselves clear of the coral and in water deep enough in the limited room available. A tight spot, but we finally seemed well situated.

Apparently these sudden bursts from the northwest aren't uncommon here, and they often set in with little warning. This one lasted for three days, so we had to stay put till things straightened out. We could still get ashore here, but it was a two-mile walk into town, not nearly as convenient. Eventually, though, the wind went back to the northeast where it belonged, and we were able to return to our beach anchorage.

+

But soon after that it was time to leave. Jeff would be joining us in the Bay Islands of Honduras over his Christmas break, and we wanted to get there in time to check things out and be ready to meet his flight. Luckily the weather had more or less settled into normal trade wind conditions. We had a nice easterly breeze for the first couple days out from Grand Cayman, doing 153 miles one day, with just a few squalls tossed in to keep us from getting too complacent. On the third day the high island of Guanaja appeared just where it should be (always reassuring), and we spent the afternoon and evening sailing past it, enjoying the scenery. It looked green and lush with jagged valleys on the mountainside, reminding us of the Marquesas. But we were headed for Roatán, so we passed between the two islands and sailed along the south coast of Roatán during the night, arriving at Coxen Hole, the port of entry, at dawn.

We anchored first but a guy came out in a *cayuco* (the generic word for canoe in this area) and said the Port Captain wanted us to come in to the dock for clearance. It had taken us three tries to get ourselves positioned in the tiny anchorage, but, okay, we picked up the anchor and did as asked. Officials came and poked around the boat. Don, the guy from the cayuco, spoke English and accompanied us to the Immigration office and to the Port Captain, where he helped with translation. Later, he got ice for us and exchanged money, charging us $15 for his efforts. A little steep, I thought, but he did perform some useful services, and it was better than paying some uniformed goon to fill out papers in an office. As for the exchange rate, we found out from Don that the "official" rate, the one given at the banks, was something of a joke. The rate on the street, dollars for lemps (or more formally, *lempiras*, the Honduran currency) was at least a third better, though technically those exchanges were illegal.

Coxen Hole was a quintessential little third-world

settlement: partly paved main street, bustle of people, mixture of Spanish and English, trash everywhere, ramshackle houses sitting on piles over the water, a hotel of sorts hosting a group of servicemen from mainland Honduras on a dive vacation, chickens in the street, a blacksmith shop, a few bars, a semi-modern grocery store.

Liz and Jeff on the main street of Coxen Hole

The inhabitants of the Bay Islands were a real cultural and ethnic mix, some of them descended from 18th century English buccaneers who used to hide out here and raid passing ships; as a consequence of this heritage, English remained the first language in the islands, still widely spoken, though the islanders learned Spanish in schools. The Honduran government, however, had been encouraging migration of mainland Hondurans to the islands, apparently in an effort to make the islands less culturally different from the mainland, and the use of Spanish had increased. One consequence for us was that when we'd meet someone on the road or walking in the hills, it was hard to know whether to say "good morning" or "buenos dias." It amused us to find that, almost invariably, if we started in one language, the reply would come back in the other.

Later that afternoon, after we'd moved back out to the anchorage, we talked with three guys on another boat who had just cleared in. The owner of the boat, Trevor, was a filmmaker who lived in the old Spanish capital of Antigua in the Guatemalan highlands. He told us that we shouldn't miss a trip up the Rio Dulce in Guatemala, something we hadn't been considering, but we put on it our mental list as a result of his enthusiasm.

Roatán is a long thin island, more than 30 miles long and only a mile or two wide. It has an embarrassment of good harbors on the south coast, while the north coast is less well-endowed: the anchorages there are more exposed to the prevailing ocean swells and more reef-encumbered. In some respects, the island was quite civilized. There were two major dive resorts, one on the south coast and one on the north, and a few smaller dive operations. And there was a substantial shrimping fleet based in Oak Ridge which had made some people wealthy. But in the rolling hills and valleys of the interior, third world conditions prevailed.

In the 70s a charter boat operation had been started based in Brick Bay between Coxen Hole and French Harbor. The company went to a lot of trouble to do it right with a fleet of CSY vessels, a marina, and a detailed cruising guide (which we had—it was useful but overly optimistic). Unfortunately, the operation failed, at least in part because the sailing was a bit too boisterous much of the time: to go east along the south coast is a windward bash in the open ocean, a little more than most charterers were up for. We found out ourselves just how uncomfortable that could be as we tried to go to French Harbor the next day, only about 6 miles away, but we had 30 knots on the nose, thought better of it, and ducked into Dixon Harbor about halfway between.

We were only gradually to discover how much of a factor the weather patterns played in this part of the Caribbean. The area is much more affected by weather systems moving off the continental US than is the eastern Caribbean. Fronts slide across the Gulf of Mexico and often stall out over the Yucatán Channel, between Mexico and Cuba. From there, they pump strong winds and squally weather over the whole region. It didn't take long for us to start missing the fine trade-wind weather of the eastern Caribbean.

For the moment. though, all we knew was that hard squalls were likely to trouble us at just about any time, day or night. But we pressed on to French Harbor the next day and spent a few days there before heading back to Coxen Hole where the airport was located so we could pick up Jeff. At least that was the plan.

We trekked out to the airport on December 22, the day he was scheduled to arrive. The only planes of any size they were flying into Roatán at that time were World War II era DC3s, antiques even then. The plane came in, we waited expectantly but...no Jeff! We were anxious but not too surprised. Night landings weren't permitted here, so if Jeff's plane from Miami to mainland Honduras was just a little delayed, he'd be a day late. We knew that. We heard via ham radio—we had several contacts back in Connecticut—that Jeff had gotten on his plane in Connecticut on time; he'd apparently got on the flight to Honduras in Miami too. So we figured he was in San Pedro Sula on the Honduran coast and would arrive the next day.

Next day, out to the airport again. Waited for the plane. It arrived but once again...no Jeff. Back on the ham radio. Jeff *didn't* get out of Miami after all—some problem with the plane—but he should be on the 1100 flight from Miami today. Out to the airport again to meet the 1730 connecting flight from the mainland, the one he should be on. At 1725, we learned that the flight to Roatán had been *cancelled!* What a comedy of errors.

The next day, December 24, he finally showed up on the 0700 plane.

So here's this kid who's never flown before, forced to spend a night in Miami, then another night in La Ceiba in Honduras, without benefit of Spanish. What should've taken about 12 hours took more than 48 with two nights in hotels. He seemed remarkably unfazed by the experience, probably less so than his parents. He only commented that it was "a little difficult" to understand the airport announcements in the mainland Honduras airport. I was just glad we'd had the ham radio and had been able to get at least some idea of what was going on. Few things are more disconcerting than waiting at an airport for someone who doesn't arrive, and we'd had that dubious pleasure three times.

+

We were glad to see Jeff. It wasn't just an empty-nest reaction, though I expect that was part of it. It was also that we missed him as a participant in our adventures, something he'd always been before. With just the two of us on board, things were easier in some ways, but we were aware of something missing as well; it was as if the experience was somehow less meaningful without him along. Liz and I still worked together pretty well at sea and in handling the boat, but we also tended to snap at each other a lot, to get on each other's nerves at times, probably inevitable living at such close quarters for an extended time. We were still adjusting to this new way of cruising (for us). I'm not sure that either of us was entirely sure what we wanted or expected from the experience: we were still finding our way.

Jeff was with us in Roatán for nearly a month. It was probably a little too much time for what the area had to offer, especially given the weather we had. We'd planned it that way because we hoped to do a lot of diving and snorkeling. Thanks to all the weather fronts though, it rained and blew much of the time, which was not only annoying in itself, but all the run-off from the island didn't do much for water clarity either. Still, we managed to keep reasonably busy. A smattering of other boats were in the area, a slightly more oddball assortment than usual because Roatán wasn't exactly on everyone's list of must-visit places. They tended to be Californians who'd come through Panama from the West Coast or people from Gulf Coast states who'd wandered down here. Most were primarily coastal cruisers, though Bob and Betty on *Kalona* were planning to cross to Europe in the spring at roughly the same time we were. In any case, the anchorages were never crowded—we often had them to ourselves—but we could keep track of where others were through ham radio.

Unfortunately, in addition to the disappointing weather, I developed an ear problem which put a further crimp in my underwater activities and made me cranky and irritable a lot of the time, not the best qualities to have on a small boat. I struggled with it for several weeks: it was only mildly painful but I couldn't hear out of the affected ear. Our medical books suggested it was probably "serous otitis media;" in plain language: fluid in the middle ear. I took decongestants, and it improved slightly. To be able to snorkel, I used a flotation cushion to keep my ears out of the water...mostly. When it persisted, I finally went to a "doctor" in the clinic in French Harbor, a fellow who had "some" US training. What that meant, I don't know. We had to wait nearly three hours, but he was nice enough when I got see him. He said the ear looked a little inflamed, recommended an antibiotic, and wanted to give me some expensive Vitamin B shots. I passed on the shots. Eventually the ear got better, as did my attitude, but I learned that I had to be very careful of my ears when I was doing a lot of diving.

We moved up to Port Royal at the east end of the island, a large, well-sheltered harbor with another defunct marina tucked in one corner. It was a lovely spot though, with fine snorkeling on the protecting reef, and we stayed about a week. I had no trouble imagining a fleet of pirate ships anchored here, their crews whooping it up on shore far into the night.

One day, as we were exploring around the port with the dinghy, we spoke to some people standing on a dock who turned out to be Americans. The invited us to come over to their house that evening for drinks. We did and had a most enjoyable time. Marvin and Romaine were about our age, and their kids were with them: Alexandra, with boyfriend David, and Andrew, about Jeff's age. They had just a little dock house, but they owned five acres of land. They'd lived in Honduras for over 30 years, outside of the capital, Tegucigalpa, on the mainland, though Marvin now had a job in Haiti working with USAID. We talked about life in Honduras, about the situation in Haiti (Marvin acknowledged the risk but downplayed the danger), about kids going back to America for schooling. Alexandra, now in her mid-20s, talked of entering a US school for the first time at age 13 and being totally at a loss. Jeff, who'd entered junior high at close to the same age after three years out of the country, could well relate to that. An interesting evening with interesting people.

The island of Barbareta sits off the east end of Roatán, like a little extension of that island, and on a day with squalls and water spouts around, we moved over there. We had some anxious moments approaching the anchorage through the reefs because the poor light made the coral difficult to see. We dithered around outside the reef for more than an hour, trying to decide what to do, which put me in a foul mood, but we finally made it through and got the anchor down in a reasonably secure spot near Pigeon Point, the southern tip in the middle of the island.

Barbareta is a small island, only a little more than three

miles long, but we stayed their comfortably for five days, the only boat. The day after we arrived, we walked along the southern shore to the Barbareta Beach Club where we met Mike, the manager. He was a short, sharp-faced guy, slightly too obsequious for my taste ("Yessir" and "No ma'am" flowed freely from him) but a fund of information. The Beach Club, he said, was owned by a guy from Mobile. They'd been doing package tours for the military, but they were no longer advertising for business. The idea now was to divide the island up into lots, some of which were already presold, and the club would then function solely as a facility for the owners. Like so many similar places in the tropics, plans changed frequently; some worked out and some didn't. Mike was going a little stir-crazy; he said he'd seen only five "white people" (his expression, not mine) in the last three months. He would've been glad to take us diving, but neither the weather nor my ear was up to it.

Later in our stay we walked into the steamy jungle, an eerie hothouse landscape filled with vines and the kind of palms that are all fronds. Colorful parrots fluttered around in the trees; Mike said there were at least 900 pairs of parrots on the island. Who'd counted them, I didn't know.

We climbed a hillside, bushwhacking through the undergrowth, looking for pottery fragments. Mike had told us about the ancient native inhabitants of the island who, it was said, every seven years, smashed up all their pots as a way of letting go of material things. (We could relate to that idea, having twice divested ourselves of almost all our possessions.) Supposedly, fragments of that orgy of destruction could be found in the jungle here. I was beginning to think it was just a story when Jeff's sharp eyes spotted a small shard lying in amongst the leaves and twigs and decaying vegetation. And suddenly, bits and pieces were everywhere, once we knew what we were looking for. Some even had designs still evident on them. I wondered how many years, or hundreds of years, those things had been sitting there.

When we left Barbareta, we sailed down to Cayos Cochinos (literally, Hog Islands, not nearly as euphonious in English as in Spanish), a group of little islands just off the Honduran coast, about 25 miles from Roatán. We had a nice reach across the trade winds, doing seven and a half knots at times. Anchoring off Cochino Grande, we found *Double Decker* there with Bob and Fran on board, the only other boat in the group. They were about our age, had been knocking around the Caribbean for several years, taking it slow: eight months in the Grenadines then to Venezuela, working their leisurely way west. I could never be satisfied with a pace like that, but some people can, and they seemed happy.

It was another beautiful spot: steep green hills sloped right down to the water, lots of palms along the shore, houses nestled in the trees. A more or less defunct dive resort occupied the southern end of the island. We chatted with Fran and Bob for awhile, and later met Jim and Gae, residents of the island who were, essentially, homesteading there. Jim was a short, stocky Irish guy, a former Navy man, down to earth, practical; Gae was talkative, rather dour-looking but pleasant. Jim's mother was living with them too in a little house next to theirs. I couldn't imagine living in such an isolated spot, but they seemed happy and self-sufficient. The only complaint they voiced was the difficulty in getting anything shipped to them, which often took weeks or months. We took freshwater showers at their outdoor shower facility—hard to imagine a more lovely tropical setting for a shower with a splendid view through the palms and out over the anchorage while soaping up. Jim needed some caulk, so I took a couple of tubes of 5200 marine caulk in for him; I wanted to give it to him, but he insisted on paying.

We spent a few days exploring the islets and reefs in the group, then sailed back to Roatán so that we'd be sure to be there in plenty of time for Jeff to catch his flight out. Luckily, everything functioned as it should for his trip back, and he made it to Connecticut right on schedule. It had been good, though different, having him with us, and the boat felt empty without him. Liz complained that she was feeling too isolated. It was true that, although we'd met many people and had some interesting conversations, we hadn't found much in the way of continuing relationships. Chats on ham radio weren't the best way to develop meaningful friendships. The other factor was that on our circumnavigation we were all making the same passages, so we had something in common with most people. Here, people were on various schedules and various routes—or just stuck—so that instant bond didn't really exist.

We stayed in Roatán for another 10 days or so after Jeff left. My ear felt better, so we did manage some dives, but the weather remained unsettled, squally, with lots of rain, which limited our activities. We left Roatán with few regrets. It had had its moments, but we'd been there over six weeks and were glad to move on.

An overnight sail in good weather brought us to the mouth of the Rio Dulce in Guatemala. The bar over the river mouth has only a nominal six feet, and then only if you're in the right place, but the "right place" is a little difficult to determine without navigational markers of any kind. All we could see as we approached was an expanse of water in front of a wall of tropical jungle; it was even difficult to tell exactly where the river was. We'd heard stories of boats not much deeper than ours having to be towed over the bar, so there were a few white-knuckle moments as the water started to shallow. But the bottom was soft muck, so we just went for it. The depth sounder went down to five feet but somehow our five and a half feet made it across.

Once we got anchored off the town of Livingston, the officials came out and rifled through our stuff, opening lockers and cupboards, poking into everything. This was getting to be a habit. When they'd exhausted that amusement, they told us to come ashore where the stack of forms awaited us. We'd heard that some yachts had been unable to enter at Livingston and had to go to Puerto Barrios some 10 miles down the coast (and back over the river bar), but they cleared us in and gave us a 30-day visa along with some tourist information for roughly $35. You just never know with officials.

Livingston was an attractive little town, cleaner and more orderly than Coxen Hole. It had several paved streets; colorful little stores—*tiendas*—selling all manner of stuff: pots, straw hats, clothing, line, outboard motors, a real miscellany; several hotels and a fair number of tourists; people of all hues from white European types, to Mayas, to black Caribs; the usual pigs and chickens in the streets; and almost no cars, for there weren't any roads *to* Livingston.

We went up the river the next day, motoring of course. The gorge was scenic: high green cliffs mixed in with a few bare rock cliffs, white heron-type birds in the branches of the trees, the occasional cayuco going by. The river turned and twisted, and the sunlight on the cliff faces was spectacular: one side in the light, the other in the shadows. Once out of the gorge we started to see Mayan settlements and houses tucked into the trees, thatched-roof houses with cayucos out front. In front of one, a man was building a large cayuco. There were lots of Mayans on the river, fishing from cayucos, mostly with hand lines. They'd paddle up river and then drift back down with the current, fishing. We anchored near a hot sulfur spring we'd heard about, just a rock basin by the side of the river. The water bubbled out of the rocks and mixed with the river water, creating pockets of hot and cold water. We slid into the pool, and the water felt lovely, but we had to be careful to avoid the hottest spots—they were too hot to touch.

Starting up the Rio Dulce

Just beyond the spring, the river widened out to a narrow lake, El Golfete, and we anchored for the night near a little nature center. We dinghied ashore, listened to the caretaker's explanation in Spanish, and took the dinghy up a narrow jungle stream. This wasn't the Amazon, but it wasn't hard to imagine jaguars and snakes and various other tropical beasts slinking around in the dense undergrowth, just waiting for some clueless yachties to stumble through. We spotted a trail leading off from the stream but decided we were out of our element here and passed on it.

When we got to the Catamaran Hotel the next day, after a less interesting motor through El Golfete, it was as if we'd returned to the modern world. There were 25-30 yachts anchored or at the slips. Many of their owners were off traveling inland, for the hotel was known as a safe place to leave the boat. It was convenient enough, the management was friendly, and the town of Fronteras, about a mile away by dinghy, had basic supplies. But the weather was less accommodating: it rained incessantly, sometimes hard, sometimes just a drizzle, and we were hard put to find a break in it for any outside activities. *Kalona* and *Double Decker*, friends from Roatán, were there. Bob and Betty were just back from a trip inland, but Bob and Fran were interested in a day trip to see the Mayan ruins at Quiriguá, so we decided to do it together. It proved to be quite an adventure.

It rained hard during the night before we planned to go; it wasn't raining in the morning but it looked like it might. Liz and I were ready to cancel, but about 10 Bob decided he wanted to go. Okay. We dinghied over to Fronteras and caught a bus. It wasn't crowded, but it did stop in Morales, the next good-sized town, where it circled the market, trying to pick up business, the conductor calling "Guate, Guate, Guate," for Guatemala City, the final destination. After many stops to load stuff on top and help people on and off, we arrived at the access road to Quiriguá, but it was still six kilometers to the park. A young fellow on a red Suzuki motorcycle was eager to take us but dismayed that there were four of us. A bus arrived headed down the road to a huge banana plantation, but it was mobbed and there were a bunch of locals waiting to get on. Bob and Fran managed to squeeze on, but Liz and I gave up, remembering the motorcycle as an option, so they got off. We ended up letting the guy with the motorcycle and his friend ferry us down there in two trips for one Q (a *quetzal*, the Guatemalan currency) each.

The park was low-key and interesting. It drizzled most of the time we were there, and there were few tourists. The carved stellae were the big attraction here, tall columns carved from hard red sandstone, protected under little thatched roofs, about 10 of them with glyphs on two sides of them, pictures of heads and arms on the other sides, all dating from the 700s. We climbed around on terraces surrounding the amphitheater where grass-covered mounds were still evident, waiting to be excavated. I would've enjoyed spending more time there if the weather had been better and if it hadn't been getting late.

We had to wait in the rain for our motorcycle guy when we got back to the park entrance, taking shelter under a cantina roof. He finally showed up, but instead of a second motorcycle he was accompanied by a decrepit-looking car. The car could take only three people, we were told, probably because the motorcycle guy didn't want to lose his fare. I volunteered to ride on the motorcycle while the others climbed into the car.

Back at the road junction, we waited for a bus in the rain, and gratefully grabbed the first one to come along. That might've been a mistake. Many of the buses in Guatemala were old US Bluebird school buses, usually painted blue. This one was possibly the most miserable excuse for a vehicle it's ever been my misfortune to ride in. Whenever it hit a bump or pothole in the road—and there were plenty of both—it felt like the bus would break in two, drop the transmission, snap an axle, something. We were sitting in the back of the bus, in a prime spot to get the full effect from the rear axle—I felt like I was being physically abused—and at every bang or crash, some of which nearly threw us out of our seats, the locals would turn and look at us, grinning, curious to see how the gringos were holding up. To add a little spice to the drive, the windshield wipers didn't work; the driver sat hunched over straining to see though the rain-smeared windshield, though I didn't notice that he slowed down at all. We feared for our lives.

We got off the bus—to our great relief—at the road to Morales and walked about a kilometer to a gas station at the road junction at Ruidosa. We optimistically waited for a bus as darkness descended. A few mini-buses passed through but they were so jammed full we had no chance of getting on. Our optimism began to wane. We were told that the buses stopped running after dark. Luckily the rain had stopped, for I was beginning to think we might have to spend the night by the side of the road, not a pleasant prospect. A young couple of indeterminate nationality were trying to get a ride to Tikal; there were no private vehicles, but there were a number of trucks, all of which had to stop here to be fumigated, a precaution against the Mediterranean fruit fly. The girl approached each truck to ask for a ride without any luck. It wasn't encouraging, but we began to realize we'd have to do the same if we had any hope of making it back. Liz approached the drivers, asking in her best Spanish for a ride. After a number of refusals, we finally got lucky with a couple of fuel trucks. Liz and I got in one, Fran and Bob in the other. It was about 15 miles to the bridge over the Rio

Dulce near where we'd left the dinghy. In the dark tropical night, the truck struggled to make it up the hills, the speedometer didn't work (I noted that the needle was resting comfortably on zero), and the driver's replies to our questions in Spanish were incomprehensible. Nevertheless, we made it. Our driver didn't ask for money, but we gave him five Q; it seemed like the thing to do. It started to rain heavily again as we motored back to the boat in the dark. We didn't care: it was infinitely better than a night by the roadside.

+

We left Guatemala for Belize shortly after that. The trip down the river on a grey day was decidedly less interesting than it had been going up. Were we just getting jaded?

Belize remains mostly a blur in my mind, with just a few images standing out. That may be because so many of the anchorages were unmemorable: mangrove lagoons or low sand islands. Belize is protected by a long barrier reef, the longest in the western hemisphere, if that has relevance to anything. For the most part, you're sailing *inside* the reef, where most of the islands are. That's nice in a way because it's fairly flat-water sailing, no ocean swells to toss you around, and there's plenty of room because the reef is roughly 10 miles from the mainland for much of its length. But the water there is often murky (though it's beautifully clear *outside* the reef). The charts were notoriously unreliable at the time too, many of them based on surveys done in the mid-19th century: that doesn't inspire confidence in coral waters. There was no real cruising guide to the area to help us along either, though we had bits and pieces from various sources that were helpful but short on specifics. I can remember sailing along happily in water 30-40 feet deep and suddenly passing over uncharted eight-foot spots. Since the water was too opaque to see the bottom, that sort of sailing tends to get your attention.

Other than Belize City, there were only a few small settlements on the mainland: Punta Gorda, the southernmost, where we checked in, Placentia, a pleasant little town with a decent anchorage, Dangriga, and a few others. Belize City had a reputation as a pretty rough place. One guy we met in Roatán described it graphically: "You'll be talking to somebody on one side of your boat, and his buddy will be unscrewing your winches on the other side." Well, maybe. The anchorage off the town was rolly enough all right, and the town wasn't particularly attractive, but we had no trouble there.

Mostly we spent time among the islands. Many of them were islands in name only, without much land, if any: just clusters of mangroves enclosing a body of water. They provided good protection, but not much else. While we could appreciate the positive qualities of mangroves—they provide a breeding ground for many varieties of sea life—we got awfully sick of looking at them. The sand islands were a little more interesting; some of them allowed us the opportunity to get ashore, and some even had small diving or fishing resorts on them. We spent several days at South Water Cay and took advantage of the little resort's dive compressor to fill our scuba tanks for several dives. We were able to dinghy out through the pass in the main reef and dive on the walls out there in beautifully clear water.

At South Water Cay we met John and Sandy, guests at the lodge, and Jackie, a grey-haired Belizean friend of theirs. If John was to be believed, he was a physicist who'd worked for NASA in Houston. Now he was a rancher in Belize while Sandy was a travel agent. John was something of an amateur philosopher, with opinions about everything, teetering on the edge of coherence as he freely imbibed at the resort's bar. We listened. Ranching was tough in Belize because of the difficulty of getting supplies. If you got a tractor stuck, John said, the only way you could get it out was with a bulldozer; he had a bulldozer, but he never used it because if the bulldozer got stuck, he'd be out of options. You always had to hold the bulldozer in reserve. I suppose that makes some kind of sense.

According to John, Jackie was a bush expert, jaguar hunter, orchid exporter, tour operator, and deep sea fisherman. Jackie didn't deny any of that. He said jaguars were plentiful in the Belize jungle, and he had a wild tale about grabbing a jaguar by the tail and swinging him over his head. He was a neat old fellow, but how much either of these guys said was to be believed was questionable at best. But it made for an interesting evening.

Because the cays were so small, shelter was often minimal, and sudden wind shifts could create problems. We got blown out of Laughing Bird Cay one night. The cay is only a thin sand spit, though it does have some palms on it, and there were some Belize fisherman camped there. It was calm when we arrived, but I woke about midnight to find a north wind had come up. It was only about 10 knots, but it was making the anchorage bouncy. I tried to go back to sleep, but an hour later the wind had increased to 25-30 knots and the seas had started pouring into the anchorage, getting really nasty. I decided we had to get out of there. Maybe we didn't need to: the anchor was in sand and well dug in, but we had a drying reef behind us that posed a legitimate worry. Could we do it though? There were shoals and reefs and islets all around and the night was inky black.

We got the anchor up with some difficulty and motored out downwind, our hearts pounding. It's no fun in reef-strewn waters when you can't see anything. The radar proved its worth that night. We plotted an intricate course out through all the hazards by using the radar returns on the various little islets— Laughing Bird, Colson, Scipio, and eventually Harvest, where we intended to anchor. As we approached Harvest Cay, which we'd picked up on radar at about six miles, we couldn't actually see it visually at a half a mile: it was a black night. Luckily, the British chart for the area that we had was quite accurate. We got anchored by 0500, red-eyed and still tense, with the first signs of dawn already appearing in the east. By then the wind was down to five knots or so (wouldn't you know), but I still think we made the right decision in the conditions we had. Some nights are like that.

We'd been in Belize for nearly a month before Jeff came during his spring break. This time the plane made it more or less on time. We'd arranged for a trip the next day to the Mayan ruins at Altun Ha, so we took the boat to the little marina at Moho Cay where it would be safe. (Safe enough, but the channel in to the marina lagoon was very shallow—we made it in all right but had to be pulled out the next day.) The driver the tour company provided—his radio name was "Fireball"—was competent but hardly a ball of fire and not very talkative: we peppered him with questions but got only short answers in reply, so the drive was more tedious than anything. The ruins were moderately interesting: no carved inscriptions as at Quiriguá but big stone pyramids to climb over and a Mayan-built reservoir. I liked picturing the Mayans working away in the hot steamy jungle building these things some 1300 years ago.

Jeff looked good. He'd taken a scuba course so that he

could dive with us. Once again, the weather limited what we could do, but we did manage a couple of dives. We talked about plans for next summer when, hopefully, we'd be in Europe and he would join us. He only stayed a week this time and the weather was far from the best (which was starting to seem normal), but we all enjoyed it anyway.

+

When Jeff left, we were ready to go too. We sailed up to northern Belize inside the reef, over some very shallow spots in gusty winds, stopping at Cay Caulker and San Pedro. Both were a little more upscale and touristy than what passed for resorts in southern Belize, with plenty of vacationers from the States working on their tans and testing the limits of their alcohol consumption. Not really our thing,

We turned our attention to the problem of getting out through the reef so we could sail north to Mexico. Not quite as easy as it might've been because the pass at San Pedro was unmarked and not readily apparent, the occasion for some confusion as we approached the reef. We scanned the line of breakers, looking for the gap we knew was there somewhere. Of course today GPS would've removed all that uncertainty and possibly some of the adventure. But after due consideration and discussion, and a fair bit of waffling around, we finally agreed on a likely looking spot and went for it. There's something a little unnerving about simply *hoping* you're in the right place, and I confess to some apprehension as I watched scattered lumps of coral pass beneath our keel as we headed out. It was a little rough too with substantial seas rushing in—I was glad we had the reefed main up to help steady us—but it must've been the pass all right because we made it through. I relaxed my grip on the tiller and breathed a little easier once we were in the open ocean.

The next 24 hours were pretty miserable though. The wind blew from somewhere north of east, which meant it was hard to steer our northerly course: we kept getting shoved over toward the Mexican coast. Friends on the boat *Our Natasha* that we talked to on the radio had tried to go north the previous day and come back. We stuck it out, but we certainly weren't comfortable. The current flows north through the Yucatan Channel (it's the beginning of the Gulf Stream) which creates a wind-against-the-current situation when the wind's in the north.

We crashed and banged and lurched our way along, but at least we were picking up miles with the current.

The night was squally and dark. We spent a lot of time dealing with the sails in the changeable conditions, so at least one of us was almost always on deck. In those circumstances, we usually didn't show any lights, figuring we'd see any vessel who happened along and could turn on the lights to make ourselves visible if necessary. At one point, I was involved in reefing the main, Liz was in the cockpit, when I caught a glimpse of lights to starboard, only about 50 yards away. I felt a stab of panic and then quickly realized that the lights were receding: they were *already past us.* I gulped as the implications of that became clear. It was another sailboat heading south and I'd seen their *cabin* lights: neither one of us was showing navigational lights! Scary and stupid. I have no idea whether they saw us or not, but that little incident cured us of sailing without lights.

The radar showed us how far off the Mexican coast we were, but the coast was so featureless, it didn't tell us how far *along* we were. By the time daylight came, we had no radar return, we could see no land, and we had no idea where we were. I took an early shot of the sun with the sextant, and the resulting line put us 10-12 miles off the coast, headed up the slot between Cozumel and the mainland. That was comforting. By 0900, we had Cozumel in sight, and we proceeded in to the anchorage. The current had booted us along far more than we'd realized.

We didn't bother to go ashore, and after some much-needed sleep that night, we sailed the 45 miles over to Isla Mujeres, a little island a couple miles off the coast from Cancún (whose high-rise hotels were visually unmistakable and provided good radar returns as well). We went ashore to try to check in, but it was Friday afternoon and all offices were closed till Monday. We changed some money at a restaurant, and a guy told us to enjoy the weekend and check in on Monday. Okay. With any luck, I figured, we'd be gone by then. The island was attractive, quite a few tourists around, a nice place to walk around or go for a run. There were lots of cruising boats in the anchorage too, most of them from the US, but the bay was large enough to accommodate them comfortably. The chief activity for many of them seemed to be yakking incessantly on the VHF radio, a pleasure that never did much for me.

One bizarre thing happened while we were there. For

some reason I stepped out into the cockpit around 0230 at night for a look around—a calm, starlit, lovely tropical night—and saw, in a moment of disbelief and rising panic, that our dinghy was gone! Not trailing off the stern where I usually tied it. Not alongside. Just not there. That's almost equivalent to discovering your car missing from its usual parking spot. Had I not secured it properly? Had somebody taken it? That was hard to believe, as there were much more attractive dinghies at other boats. There was nothing I could do in the dark. I retreated to the cabin and lay awake stewing about it, thinking about our options: we were nearly helpless without a dinghy, our lifeline to the shore. We'd have to buy one in Florida.

At first light I went out in the cockpit again, scanning the shoreline behind us with the binoculars. And there, barely visible, were a couple of inflatable dinghies washed up on the shore. I was pretty sure one was ours. While I was trying to decide what to do, a guy came floating by in the water, wearing a life jacket. "Going after my dinghy," he said, as if that were something he did regularly. I grabbed my snorkeling fins and jumped in. It was about a quarter of a mile to the dinghies, but I realized if the wind direction had been just slightly different, the dinghies could easily be in Cancún by now. When I reached it, I was glad to see there was no damage. We learned later that several other dinghies had also gone mysteriously adrift in the night. Somebody's idea of a practical joke? We never knew. But thinking about how severely handicapped we'd be without a dinghy I realized we'd needed some kind of a backup plan. So when we got to Florida, I bought a cheap plastic dinghy at a discount store for less than a hundred dollars. It probably wouldn't last long if we ever had to use it, but at least we'd have an option. We've carried it around, still in its box, ever since.

+

Now the problem was to get to Florida. It's not that far, only about 350 miles to Key West, but I'd been worrying about that trip ever since we decided to go to the western Caribbean. The problem is, it's against the prevailing easterly winds. Of course "prevailing" doesn't mean "inevitable," and we'd had plenty of evidence of winds from other directions over the last few months. And even light easterlies shouldn't be too bad, for the current would be with us. That current we'd experienced in the Yucatan Channel makes a right turn, flowing north of Cuba into the Straits of Florida (between Florida and the Bahamas) where it gathers momentum and becomes the Gulf Stream. All well and good—a favorable current is always welcome—but if the easterlies piped up, the wind *against* the current could create some very nasty seas. So we listened carefully to the weather forecasts, looking for mention of wind from any direction but east, or, failing that, light airs.

On Monday morning, we had to decide whether to go ashore and check in to Mexico or just leave. The wind was in the east about 15 knots, but the forecast was for southeast winds, and in a phrase we were to grow to loathe, they claimed that "a moderate southerly flow" existed over the eastern Gulf of Mexico. I wasn't crazy about the conditions, but I latched onto that idea of a southerly flow and decided to leave. As it turned out, that was a mistake.

Once we got clear of Isla Mujeres, we found the wind a little *north* of east, which meant we couldn't steer a direct course for Key West; we'd have to tack. That complicated things. We didn't want to get too close to Cuba, so we'd have to tack whenever that seemed likely to happen. But tacking made it more difficult to keep an accurate DR, especially with the unknown effect of the current to factor in. Obviously, once again GPS would've made things easier, but GPS was still in the future, so we just dealt with the situation we had.

Beating to Key West

Conditions weren't too bad that first afternoon, but with the wind in the northeast at about 20 knots, the seas got short, steep, and nasty. We were uncomfortable as we lurched and crashed and banged our way along, well heeled over, and it only got worse that night. Despite all the talk of a "southerly flow," the wind obstinately refused to go at all south of east, and it frequently went well into the northeast, the direction we wanted to go. Navigation was difficult because of the crazy motion and the constant flying spray: it was tough to control the sextant and keep it out of the splashing water. Sleep was nearly impossible. Life below in the cabin got very primitive. Off watch, I was reduced to lying down on the cabin sole, still with foul weather gear and life harness on as the motion was a little easier there and it was too much trouble to remove anything. It was doubly discouraging when the best course we could get on the starboard tack (away from Cuba) was about 010, nearly due north. The seas weren't particularly big, but they were steep and close together, so that it just wasn't possible to sail very close to the wind or we'd get almost stopped after slamming into two or three in a row.

"We're making progress," I said to Liz. "We just have to tough it out." Easier to say than do. Where was this "southerly flow" they were still talking about?

And just to add further interest to the trip, I broke my little toe when I stubbed it hard on a deck fitting (I often go barefoot at sea in the tropics, which may not be very smart). There's not much you can do for a broken toe other than tape it to the toe next to it and wait for it to heal. I did that, and then I put my deck shoes on. That was such a painful exercise that I dreaded repeating it, so I didn't take my shoes off for the rest of the passage. Of course they got soaked and squishy over the next four days, but among the many unpleasant things on this trip, that was only a minor bother.

On the third night, the wind increased. Our anemometer showed the apparent wind at 35 knots, which meant a true wind of about 30 knots. We were using the double-reefed main and staysail, but I wondered how long we could stand the punishment. I wasn't worried about the boat, but we were getting ground down. I raised the possibility of going back, though I really didn't want to.

"We can't give up all those miles," Liz said, and I knew

she was right. But when you can't even steer in the direction you want to go and you're getting beat up by the sea conditions, it's tough to steel yourself to keep at it. Finally, with about 90 miles to go, and the wind still 30-35 on the anemometer, I decided to heave-to and wait for the wind to ease a bit. We needed a break. That was in the late afternoon on the third day. I got a good star fix at twilight, and then we both went to bed. The hell with the shipping—we needed some rest. We stayed hove-to till about 0300. The wind was down to 20-25 then, so we got moving again, just slightly refreshed after eight hours or so but it made a difference.

My noon sight the next day showed us just south of the Dry Tortugas and on the edge of soundings. I turned on the depth sounder, and sure enough we had a reading. We decided to tack out, but when we did so we immediately encountered tons of big-ship traffic. There was a constant parade of them, all following the same route. I didn't like the idea of tacking around out there at night: it would be like stepping out onto a bowling alley blindfolded with the balls rolling down toward you one after another. I checked the chart again and saw that if we went in east of Rebecca Shoal light and west of the Marquesas Keys we could proceed to Key West north of the islets extending to the west from the tip of Florida and be out of the traffic. We spotted the light tower in the late afternoon, and spent the night tacking our way to Key West with no worries about big ships, though we did have to dodge a lot of fishing boats. Luckily, the wind was quite moderate by recent standards, and the night was beautifully settled, clear, and even cool.

But we weren't quite done yet: in the morning we had to slog our way down the Northwest Channel against a strong current: it took us nearly three hours to go six or seven miles. When we finally came to anchor off the town, a little dazed and very exhausted, we'd taken almost five days to cover 350 miles in very difficult conditions. That "moderate southerly flow" had never shown up; it apparently had existed only in the imagination of the forecasters. But it didn't matter now. We'd arrived.

+

So ended our first winter. We'd been out for five months, and it had been a mixed bag. The biggest disappointment had been the weather. It had been continuously unsettled, and while there'd been nice days mixed in, there'd never been the sort of consistency the eastern Caribbean offers. And we'd had an unbelievable amount of rain. Whether that was "normal" for that area or not, I don't know, though in my experience normal is never what it's cracked up to be.

On the plus side, the diving, when we were able to do it, was fantastic; we both enjoyed it, and so did Jeff when he was with us. We'd had some interesting experiences too, and met some interesting people. But the cruising people we'd met had their own itineraries, which were usually different that ours, so there wasn't much chance for continuing friendships: with only a few exceptions, we'd see people for a few days, after which we'd go our separate ways and never encounter each other again.

Lingering in the background too, the question of why we were doing this still remained. Were we on a permanent vacation? Were we early retirees? Were we just looking for fun-in-the- sun, something that inevitably palls after a while? Maybe we'd just stayed too long in one area. I still had high hopes for the Med, and the challenge of the Atlantic crossing still appealed to me. But I knew if we were to keep at this, we'd have to find some *reason* for it beyond simply meandering from port to port.

I knew too that Liz and I needed to find a better way to be. We were still close in many respects, but there was too much friction in the air when we were confined to the boat by ourselves. In some sense, I think, though we both wanted to do this, we each had our own reasons for wanting it, mostly unarticulated. Maybe we were both hesitant to open that Pandora's box for fear of what might emerge, and so we carried on.

5. Atlantic Crossing

"Oh, the water's cold," Liz exclaimed after she jumped in. It was 76 degrees, not exactly frigid, but we'd been swimming in water of 80 degrees or more all winter. The air felt cooler too. We were out of the tropics—just barely.

We were subject to instant culture shock too. We dinghied ashore and were immediately floored by rampant American tourism: dozens of bars and restaurants; shops selling T-shirts, jewelry, and other junk; overfed, red-faced Americans lapping it all up. We joined the tourists for the sunset ritual at Mallory Square, a sort of pointless celebration (after all, there are sunsets everywhere) featuring an endless supply of street performers: jugglers, escape artists, musicians, contortionists, acrobats, scam artists, and just about anything else you can name. For us, fresh from the backwaters of Central America, it was a little much to take. But we did manage to locate a grocery store and load up with some US goodies we hadn't seen in a awhile.

We had several projects we wanted to get done before our Atlantic crossing. We had paint bubbling along the waterline of the boat. We needed to get the boat hauled and try to deal with that. And we wanted to have a dodger made.

Our topsides had been painted by the builder with Awl-Grip, a hard two-part paint that looked very nice, but it had to be applied over a special sanding sealer. It turned out that the company specified that the sanding sealer was not for use below the waterline. That was fine; strictly speaking we weren't using it below the waterline...except that when sailing heeled over our topsides were often submerged for long periods, which one would suppose qualified as below the waterline. The result was the sanding sealer absorbed water, held it against the other layers of primer, and ultimately got to the steel. For that reason, I wasn't impressed with Awl-Grip. This was hardly as serious as the paint problems *Ta-Tl* had been dealing with, but I wanted to resolve it if I could. In any event, we hauled out at a nearby yard, spent a depressing week living aboard in the dust and grime and confusion of the yard ("dirt yachting" the guy in the boat next to us called it) while I sanded and applied layers of primer along the waterline.

And we arranged to have a dodger made. We hadn't had one on our previous boat and thought we could go without it on this one, especially because we had the bubble. The bubble was a nice feature at sea, but for ordinary coastal sailing or island hopping, or for just sitting at anchor, a canvas dodger can keep a lot of wind and spray off you and make life in the cockpit much more pleasant. So we relented and called the canvas maker.

Through all this I was still dealing with my broken toe which seemed more painful now than at sea, probably because I was abusing it more.

Back in the water in mid-April, we left Key West and headed toward Miami. Unfortunately, there aren't a lot of good anchorages in the Florida Keys for a boat of our draft—five and a half feet when fully loaded—so we stopped only three times. We needed to go to Marathon where the canvas shop was located for the final fitting of our dodger. The harbor was crowded, and most boats, we noted, were on two anchors. Somehow I managed find a spot with enough swinging room to sit on one anchor, and the next day we took the boat in to the dock near the canvas shop.

Our dodger was a pretty complex affair because of all the things it had to wrap around. "We'll see," the guy said. "Sometimes these things fit on the first try and sometimes they don't." But incredibly he had the thing fitted in an hour, and it looked great.

So we left Marathon feeling quite happy and pleased with ourselves, content with the way both the paint job and the dodger had turned out…and promptly ran aground. We were rounding Boot Key just outside of Marathon, and apparently I got in too close to the Key, crunched to a halt, and we had to kedge off. I'm sure it didn't do our new bottom paint any good…or my ego either.

A few days later, we were in the Dinner Key anchorage in Miami, along with a few other cruising boats and a slew of questionable vessels who'd apparently been taking up harbor space for quite some time with no intention of going anywhere anytime soon. Some places seem to collect craft like that.

We now had a decision to make. We knew that Jimmy Cornell was organizing what he was calling the "Trans-Arc," a cruising event for boats crossing the Atlantic to Europe. We knew Jimmy because we'd been in the Pacific at the same time during our circumnavigation, and our kids had played together. Jimmy was an energetic hustler, and in the ten years since we'd last seen him he'd become something of a sailing guru, having written numerous articles for sailing magazines and several cruising manuals. He'd also established the successful "Arc" event for transatlantic boats. It wasn't a race but rather a "cruising rally." Jimmy knew that many boats from Europe crossed to the Caribbean in November and December when the hurricane threat eased and the trade winds started to re-establish themselves. He hit on the idea of injecting some organization into that annual migration. He could charge an entry fee and in return the participants would get pre-departure seminars and advice (and a T-shirt), they could set up radio schedules, they'd could have some form of competition (though it clearly wasn't a race in the traditional sense), and they could partake of various social events before and after the crossing. It appealed particularly to first-timers who couldn't quite deal with the idea of being alone out there. The Arc was amazingly successful, and it spawned a bunch of similar events. As Jimmy told us at one point, "I really stumbled onto a good thing."

The Trans-Arc was a similar event for boats headed the other way across the Atlantic in the spring. One group was to leave from Miami and another from Antigua. Liz and I kicked around the idea of joining the group from Miami. Liz was more attracted to the idea than I was.

"I think it would be a great way to meet people," she said. "It would be nice to know some people who are cruising the Med when we get there."

That part of it was fine with me, but there were things about the whole cruising rally concept that didn't appeal to me. I didn't like being part of a group at sea—one of the big attractions of ocean sailing for me was precisely the opposite idea: I liked the independence of it, the whole idea of being dependent only on your own resources and abilities, not counting on someone else to bail you out if you got into trouble. Further, if you go as a group, in daily radio contact, if somebody else has trouble, it's pretty much your trouble too. If somebody else has been careless about boat preparation or maintenance or has health problems you could easily be drawn into a situation that compromises your own safety or, if not that, at least messes up your passage. Of course there's a certain obligation to come to someone's aid if he's in your vicinity and in trouble, but it seemed to me that going in a group, even one that gets quickly spread out, far from making you safer, just multiplies the possibilities for trouble. I didn't like being tied into a particular day to leave either. I'd always made my own decisions about that: sometimes I'd been right and occasionally wrong, but at least I stood or fell by my own decisions.

So maybe I had a sort of curmudgeonly attitude toward the whole thing, or at least I had misgivings, but I was willing to check it out. We'd met some people in Marathon on a boat called *Second Wind* who had signed up for it, two couples (and a baby!) in a boat about our size. We told them we knew Jimmy.

"Are you going to come?" they asked. "It's going to be a blast."

They were so full of naïve enthusiasm that Liz and I didn't have the heart to disillusion them. None of them had made an offshore passage before, and we suspected it'd be an eye-opening experience for them.

We contacted Jimmy who was in Miami organizing things. He was glad to hear from us and wanted to recruit us too. "I won't charge you anything," he said. "Come on over to the yacht club and we'll talk about it." The participants were gathering at the Miami Yacht Club, but we learned from Jimmy that there were only nine boats signed up for the event, although twenty were leaving from Antigua. I was frank with Jimmy and told him I doubted that we'd be joining the group. "Come to the party anyway," he said.

We took the boat over to the yacht club, went to the pre-rally party and met most of the participants. The party was bizarre. Jimmy was dressed in a suit to impress the local officials in attendance. He seemed embarrassed that there weren't more boats entered, and he included us in his introduction: "…and circumnavigators Bruce and Liz MacDonald…." Our position was a little awkward since we really weren't intending to participate, but for Jimmy's sake we sort of let on that we were. Strangest of all was the assortment of participants. Virtually none of them were cruising people; most seemed to have entered just to have the experience of an ocean crossing and were not intending to do any extensive cruising once they arrived in Europe. One guy on a 30-footer was sailing his boat over in the Trans-Arc intending to come back in the Arc in the fall. So that pretty much sealed it for us: there was little reason to get involved. However, we did get T-shirts out of it!

+

We left on our Atlantic crossing the next day, a day ahead of the Trans-Arc boats, and plunged directly into that hell of thunderstorms and four days of strong, adverse winds that had us talking about giving up on the whole enterprise. Maybe we were no longer cut out for this kind of punishment. After all, we'd just had five days of it on that bash from Isla Mujeres to Key West. How much could we take? Maybe we'd be happier putting up and down the waterway, where at least we could count on getting a decent sleep most nights. Maybe this ocean sailing business was no longer for us. Maybe we just didn't care that much.

But inexplicably, the wind shifted into the southwest the next day, directly behind us, we poled out the jib, and enjoyed fine downwind sailing for the 450 miles still to go to Bermuda.

Finally--good sailing to Bermuda

I can't say what we would've done if that hadn't happened, if the atrocious conditions had continued for another day or two. I don't know if we would've had the fortitude to stick it out. I do know that that whole experience points up an important difference between our attitudes now and on the previous voyage. We weren't paranoid to the extent we'd been before, but we just weren't sure if what we were going through was worth it. As I'd said, this wasn't something we *had* to do.

And yet, once things improved, once the sun came out and the wind settled in behind us, once we started lapping up the miles in the right direction, the misery of the last few days all but disappeared. Sitting in a dry cockpit in sunshine, with the relatively easy downwind motion, we almost began to enjoy the passage.

A few days later, much refreshed, we motored in through Town Cut to the harbor at St. George, Bermuda, tied up to the customs dock and were quickly cleared. The 977 miles had taken us

64

just under nine days. The Trans-Arc boats had left Miami a day after we did and therefore missed the thunderstorms, but only two of the larger ones had arrived so far. It was several days later when we encountered the people from *Second Wind*, the ones who were so full of enthusiasm in Florida.

"How was your trip?" we asked them.

They looked at us for a long moment before one of the guys said, without a trace of a smile: "A hellish nightmare."

We didn't press them for details. We'd been out there too. Offshore sailing can quickly shatter any illusions you have. We tried to reassure them that it wasn't always like that. That was a lesson I was still struggling to learn.

+

It was the first time we'd been to Bermuda. St. George was neat, clean, touristy in a low-key way, and very expensive. Next day we took the bus into Hamilton through the thickly settled countryside: little concrete houses, pastel colors, tiled roofs for water-catching, narrow winding roads with drive-on-the-left traffic. Hamilton was much more big city-ish than St. George. Two cruise ships formed a wall in front of the harbor. There were almost no yachts there except for a few at the yacht club, for it's a long circuitous route through shoals to get there. For us, it didn't seem to offer anything that St. George didn't.

Walking around back in St. George the next day, an old guy pulled up in his car asked us if we wanted a ride. Why not? He looked harmless enough. His name was Simon Oakley, 81 years old, and he'd lived in Bermuda since the 1920s. He took us for a tour of St. George, pointing out all the places he'd lived over the years, singing snatches of old songs to us, telling us stories of old Bermuda. He didn't strike me as loony: he just enjoyed sharing his knowledge and experiences with us. For us, it was delightful.

My broken toe had finally healed, and I was able to go jogging through the back streets of St. George. It felt good to be able to get some exercise ahead of the long passage to the Azores. Liz had invited a friend of hers to come to Bermuda to visit. Our cramped little interior was not really set up for guests, but Judy was adaptable and we made out fine. She even went for a run with me one day. We rented motor bikes and—possibly taking our lives in our hands—explored the island from the Dockyard Museum to the pink sand beaches on the ocean side where rocks and ledges isolated neat little pockets of sand caressed by beautiful green water, all quite lovely. Considerable interest was added to the day by the challenge of driving on the left in the persistent traffic; nevertheless, we all escaped unscathed. Clearly, everything in Bermuda revolves around tourism, but it's all so tastefully done it's hard to quarrel with it, and we enjoyed our time there.

+

After Judy left—she'd been with us for five days—we started thinking about the upcoming passage to the Azores. Bermuda, at roughly 32 degrees latitude, sits in the middle of the "horse latitudes," that area of variable winds between the easterly trade winds further south and the prevailing westerlies further north. Conventional wisdom suggests that the best strategy is to steer a more northerly course leaving Bermuda than the "direct" great circle course to the Azores. In other words, so the wisdom goes, you should try to get north quickly so you can pick up the westerlies to blow you on your way. If only things were that simple. You can usually count on the trade winds, but the westerlies are far less reliable, and while winds with a westerly component *prevail* in those latitudes, the hard truth is you're very likely to encounter winds from any direction there as various weather systems move through.

I decided that we'd head directly for the Azores and only turn more northerly if we encountered headwinds or calms; as long as the wind remained fair, there seemed little point to heading north. So, after nearly two weeks in Bermuda, we cleared out on May 21 for the 1800 mile passage. I wasn't particularly worried about the passage itself, but I was aware that we were getting away from what could be considered home waters. To some extent, we were shutting the door behind us. In the Caribbean or even in Bermuda we were only one long passage away from the east coast of the US. Now, getting back would be a lot more complicated and time consuming. It wasn't quite like striking out into the Pacific, but there was still a considerable commitment involved. Of course we could always hop a plane to get back in an emergency, but that would be a stopgap measure at best.

Questions of why we were doing this still lay in the background too. There was a certain challenge involved—there always is in any ocean passage. But the challenge didn't loom as large and important as it had in the first year or so of our previous voyage. For many people, this passage, as the main component of an Atlantic crossing, would be the adventure of a lifetime; for us, it was just another couple weeks at sea. I don't mean that we were jaded exactly, and I don't mean to minimize the thought and preparation and psychological adaptation necessary to have a successful passage, but we'd made many such passages so that it didn't quite have edge of excitement it did for many. We knew we could tough out just about anything and had the skills to weather most crises. So we weren't really doing it for the thrill it. And if in heading for Europe our main objective was tourism, well, there certainly were easier ways to do it. But we had the boat, we'd done the organization and planning, all our efforts had pointed in this direction. It only remained now to go.

The passage started out a little ragged. We had moderate winds the first day and night, but the wind increased the second day until it was blowing a steady 35-40 knots with higher gusts and building seas, and for a while we couldn't steer the course. All I could think was, "Uh-oh, here we go again!"

But it wasn't to be. The wind gods must've talked it over and decided they'd punished us enough. The wind eased off toward evening, we had a settled night with moderate winds, we could actually steer the course, and thereafter the passage was, all things considered, quite bland.

Basically, my strategy worked. Looking back on it, it's pretty easy to see what the weather situation was. In simplified terms, a big area of high pressure was centered southeast of us and a low pressure system was centered to the northwest of us. If you sketch it out on the chart, you can see that with the high spinning clockwise and the low spinning counter-clockwise, with us in between them, the result is southerly winds. For us, a southerly meant a beam wind, and that's what we had for virtually the whole passage. It wasn't quite as consistent as that sounds. Winds were mostly moderate, but some days they'd pipe up a bit, other days they'd ease off; some days were cloudy and vaguely threatening. But we had no real gales and no real calms, seas were often big but not nasty. Mostly we were quite comfortable and progress was gratifyingly good. All this was very welcome after our previous two passages.

On Day 3, Liz wrote in her journal:

1520 miles to Horta. Thank goodness a settled night last night. Cloudy all night but no rain. No sail handling! This morning the sky cleared and was sunny or partly cloudy till mid-afternoon. I feel much better. Washed myself and my hair. In the afternoon I wrote Spanish exercises and did leg exercises. A semblance of normal routine.

And on Day 7:

1153 miles to Horta. Today I actually found myself enjoying the journey rather than just wanting to get there. A combination of good sailing, no threats around, having been out here long enough to get adjusted, and being pretty well rested. And it's too soon to be really focusing on the destination.

And on Day 10:

715 miles to Horta. Continued all night and day with strong SW wind. About 11 last night I dropped the Yankee and put up the staysail. Very exhilarating and a little scary on the foredeck in moonlight. Big seas. Cloudy skies. Scurried back inside to my little nest.

Life at sea. Sometimes it can be almost pleasant in mid-ocean.

Just about the best it gets at sea

The ham radio proved to be a worthwhile diversion. I'd never considered it anything like an "essential" piece of equipment, but it did have its uses. Quite a few other boats were making this passage at about the same time, some with ham radio, and it was fun to be able to keep track of them and know where they were in relation to us. To do that, I'd check into the Transatlantic Maritime Mobile Net each morning. A "net," in radio parlance, denotes a time and radio frequency for interested people to get together and exchange information. There's usually a designated "net control" station to ensure that a certain order prevails and everyone isn't squawking at once. The net control for this net was Trudi, who was land-based in Barbados, and had the call sign 8P6QM (or as it invariably came out on the radio, Eight Papa Six Quebec Mike).

I have to admit there was something reassuring about hearing her voice every morning as the various vessels checked in and she chatted with each of us, asked about the weather we were having, and gave us the chance to talk about any concerns we had. It wasn't a busy net: only a maximum of about 10 boats would check in on any given morning and often fewer, so there was plenty of time to talk or complain or ask questions of one another. As it turned out, there was one boat just about a day behind us and another one just about a day ahead of us, and we kept that same relative position for the whole passage. That was ideal for us, because it gave us a good idea of what the weather was like a day behind us and a day ahead, and it gave us a better idea of what to expect. In a sense, I missed the total isolation we'd had at sea on the previous voyage, but there was something to be said for keeping at least a tenuous connection to the rest of the world.

Perhaps the most notable thing about the passage was the prevalence of Portuguese Men-of-War. We'd seen them before, but never in such profusion. At times the sea was absolutely littered with them, their little purple jelly-bubbles bobbling along on the surface, their tentacles dangling down 30 feet or more. In a way, they were quite beautiful creatures (if "creature" is the right word), but it occurred to me that anybody who went overboard would be in danger of being stung to death before he had a chance to drown. Not a pleasant thought.

Progress got even better the second week, as we reeled off a succession of daily runs of around 150 miles. One day we did

166 miles, our best ever, and without much help from the current. "Some of the best sailing we've done in a long time," I wrote in my journal. I'd also written some days before: "I know this wind can't last, but it sure has been fun." But last it did till almost the end. On Day 13 I noted that we'd made 1043 miles in the previous seven days. And then, on Day 14, we sailed into the big Azores high that normally dominates this part of the ocean at this time of year, and we ran out of wind.

Reluctantly, I turned on the engine. It would've been nice to hold the wind right up to the harbor entrance at Horta, but that was not to be. Neither was I about to sit there a daysail away waiting for wind. However you looked at it, we'd had a great trip, and the fact that we had to motor a good chunk of the last 24 hours didn't bother me.

At dawn, we motored along the south coast of Faial for about 12 miles, watching the island as the sun hit it: green fields separated into rectangles by hedgerows, little red-roofed houses scattered on the hillsides, steep cliffs dropping to the sea, the top of the island shrouded in cloud. The conical peak of Pico, the neighboring island, was an amazing sight, nearly 8000 feet high. By early morning we were tied up at the customs dock in Horta, Faial, just a little over 14 days out of Bermuda.

+

The Azores were a delight. As a natural mid-ocean stopping point for yachts headed for Europe, they went to some trouble to make everyone feel welcome. They'd built a 150-slip marina well-protected by breakwaters; the charge was very reasonable, only about $4 a day for us that year, and that included water and electricity. The town of Horta was wonderfully clean, neat, picturesque: little parks in European-type squares; old-fashioned buildings; streets with hand-laid stone patterns. An air of prosperity, civility, friendliness—everything positive. Beautiful scenery too, with the dramatic cone of Pico, just a few miles away, appearing around just about every street corner, like an improbable backdrop for a movie set.

A lot of our time in Horta was spent catching up with friends, meeting new ones, enjoying the convivial atmosphere among the yachties. Everyone here had had to make a substantial passage to get here, so we all had that experience in common. Jimmy was there wrapping things up as the Trans-

Arc boats had just left—they were on a faster schedule than we were. Other boats we'd known in Bermuda came in, passage times varying widely. *Blue Mermaid* left two days before us and got in the day before. Steve and Dave on *Lindy Lady*, a boat about our size, had one day's run of 183 miles. *Xanth*, a 32-foot Canadian boat, left the day after we did, followed conventional wisdom and took a northerly course from Bermuda; we started worrying about them when we'd been there a week and heard nothing. They finally turned up after a 26-day passage (!) during which they'd struggled with headwinds, gales, and gear failures. So much for conventional wisdom. Later, *Wassail*, a funky little British 36-footer, came in dismasted after slogging into northeast winds for five days. I felt smug with the way my strategy had worked, though, if I were being honest, I'd have to admit that however carefully you plan, the weather you get on any given passage is at least 75% luck.

A little French Canadian boat, *Elegie*, came in and tied up in the slip next to us. The guy, Paul, was singlehanded and crossing the Atlantic in the other direction, *from* Europe, which in these latitudes is essentially against the wind, a tough way to go. His boat didn't inspire confidence either. One morning I happened to look up at his masthead and noticed a strand of wire sticking out. I got out the binoculars and took a closer look. At least three strands of the 19-strand wire were broken! I told him about it. He said he'd just had a new roller furling gear put on, so I strongly suspected that an incorrect installation must have been responsible. Later, I spent most of one day helping him replace the forestay and get his end fittings installed correctly. I hated to think what might've happened to him if he'd set out for a windward bash with his forestay barely hanging on.

With Rob and Ray, a British couple on *SkyDiver*, we rented a car and explored the island of Faial, driving out to the cliffs on the north side and the caldera from a 1957 eruption which left a real lunar landscape and impressive sand dunes. Flowers were everywhere—it was spring after all: roses, daisies, pinks, hydrangeas, nasturtiums, growing in gardens, on stone walls, out of crevices in the walls. Ray knew all the flowers and identified many as the same as those in her garden in Falmouth. We had lunch at a little restaurant run by an American woman and her Azorean husband, maybe the only restaurant outside of Horta. Then we drove by a meandering route through walled villages where we had to ask directions to the main caldera. When we reached it finally, it proved to be a huge thing, 500 meters deep, 2000 meters across. We climbed up the wall to the highest point, but it was discouragingly cold up there with a stiff wind blowing, so we passed on climbing down into the crater bottom. That sort of touristy excursion wasn't really our thing, but for the most part we enjoyed it.

After looking at Pico—you could hardly help it— sticking up there just a few miles away, I decided I'd like to climb it. It was a little more than Liz wanted to get into, but Steve and Dave, the two young Brits on *Lindy Lady* were up for it, so we chose a day. Unfortunately, the day we chose was exceptionally windy. We almost cancelled, but Dave wanted to do it, so we caught an early ferry. Liz came along, and so did Peter and Ada from *Cougar*. Peter was 61 years old, a former British army officer in India and later a banking executive; he was on the last leg of a circumnavigation. He told us he considered the circumnavigation "easy," but then he had a 44-foot boat and always had two or three people as crew. Ada was crewing on this stretch. She was an attractive 57-year-old whose husband had left her for another woman in December; by March she had divorced him, sold her house, and headed for the Caribbean. There she signed on to *Cougar* and here she was in June: big life changes in a very short period of time that she seemed to be handling exceptionally well.

Liz and Ada were going to tour the island while we climbed the mountain. I was a little skeptical about Peter, particularly when he showed up in regular street shoes, but there he was. It was cloudy in Madalena, the little town where the ferry landed. We got a taxi to take us to the starting point for the climb, and it was almost raining on the way up. But the taxi got us up above the clouds into brilliant sunshine, though a chilling wind was blowing. We were all afraid the climb would be too short because we were already pretty high up and the summit looked close. We needn't have worried. We figured later the ascent was more than 4000 vertical feet.

**Dave, Steve, and Peter, getting directions for the Pico climb
from the taxi driver**

We started off through barren-looking fields with only low, heather-type vegetation mixed in with volcanic rock. Dave and I went ahead while Steve stayed back with Peter, who was much slower. The trail was moderately but consistently steep, a good workout as it threaded its way over loose rock and vegetation and passed conical peaks of old eruptions. Near the top we got to a ridge that appeared to be the rim of the crater, while the center peak jutted up on one edge of the ridge, a conical monolith that looked like a huge pile of lava. The wind gusts were so fierce on the ridge that we could barely hold on, and we almost considered not going on. But we persevered, crawling along on all fours at times, and reached the summit about 1230. We climbed the peak in the lee so we were out of the worst of the wind until the very summit. The cloud layer was 4000 feet below us, a huge white field. Faial, to the west, was only partially visible through the clouds. Just below the summit in a dip in the rock we found a hot steam vent: standing near it quickly soaked us, as the hot steam condensed in the frigid air.

Steve came up about a half hour later. Peter didn't do the final ascent. Going down wasn't as bad as I'd feared, though Peter was painfully slow. At one point we rested for 20 minutes or so, and Peter got a cramp. We thought for a while we might have to carry him, but he walked it out, and we were down by 1630 to meet our taxi friend who showed up an hour later. Whatever we might think about Peter's judgment in attempting the climb and in his choice of footwear, he certainly had that unflappable British quality of carrying on in adversity.

One evening we went to a "fish soup" event at the local yacht club. All the visiting yachts were invited, but maybe the name didn't appeal because only a few showed up. We enjoyed it though. We talked for a while with a couple of Portuguese people and got to see some traditional dancing: colorful and interesting. I was impressed by the way the local people tried to involve the visiting yachts.

Liz on the marina wall with Pico in the background

One of the long-standing traditions in Horta is painting the boat's name on the surrounding breakwater wall. In some places this would be considered graffiti and humorless officials would take pains to have the paintings eradicated. Here, it was encouraged—there was even a rumor that failure to do a painting was bad luck—and it made a colorful background to the marina. Some boats must have been carrying resident artists, because some of the paintings were quite elaborate, verging on the professional. Others were more basic. My artistic skills were rudimentary, but I found an empty spot on the wall and made a stab at it. It took me a while, but the end product wasn't too bad. A couple years later when friends of ours passed through Horta, they wrote to tell us our painting was still there; even better, they sent us a tourist poster for the Azores that featured a photograph of the marina with our yellow boat—photogenic as always—prominent in the center. Our limited claim to fame.

My artwork

We'd been in Horta for 17 days and were sorry to leave.

"We've met the nicest people here," Liz said. It was true. A good percentage of the people were real voyagers, either homeward bound to Europe at the end of a circumnavigation, or, like Steve and Dave, at the end of a year's Atlantic circuit. We had a lot to talk about because of the experiences we had in common—the joys, anxieties, and rigors of life at sea—but perhaps even more important, we shared similar attitudes with many of them, a perspective on life, a sense of valuing things other than high paying jobs and expensive cars. That's a generalization of course, for in a time of general prosperity people with many different motives will buy a boat and sail off in it, just because they can afford to. But the fact remains that it had been a long time since we'd been in such a congenial atmosphere and enjoyed it so thoroughly, or that we'd experienced such a welcoming attitude that the Azoreans provided. Maybe this voyaging business wasn't all gales and headwinds after all. Maybe it had its redeeming aspects after all.

+

We said goodbye to friends we'd never see again, and left

for Spain. We were going to the Med, but rather than heading directly for the Strait of Gibraltar, which has several difficulties associated with it for small sailing craft (current, traffic, funneling winds), we'd decided to stop first at Cádiz on the Atlantic coast of Spain. That way, we'd be able to pick our time for going through the Strait a little better.

The distance was a little over a thousand miles, and we had a reasonable passage although conditions were never as consistent as they were on the passage to the Azores. Boats headed for the UK or northern Europe had a tougher time of it because of the prevalence of northeast winds. We struggled with that the first couple days too, and while we were still threading our way through the islands of the Azores, the wind was maddeningly inconsistent. But things eventually settled down. and we had some decent days' runs.

The most memorable night occurred as we were approaching Cádiz. The night was clear with an almost-full moon, slight seas, and mostly good wind: ideal conditions, in other words. But ships! It was like they were lying in wait for us. The onslaught began just at dusk as lights seemed to pop up in every direction. At times we had nine or ten in sight at once, and even with the radar going it was a challenge to keep track of them all and to ensure we knew which ones were going to be close. I had one close call when both the red and green sidelights appeared suddenly, seemingly out of nowhere, indicating that a very large vessel was headed directly for us, and I had to drop the sails in a panic and start the engine so I could maneuver to get out of his way. Never had we'd seen so many ships in such a short period of time, probably 30-40 altogether in the· hours of darkness. We figured this was the traffic heading in and out of the Med from the Straits. It was sort of like trying to walk across the Interstate at rush hour.

Somehow we survived the frantic night, though neither of us slept. The next morning we entered the harbor at Cádiz, with some confusion as to *which* harbor for there were several indicated on the chart. The cruising guide assured us we should head for the fishing harbor, and once we'd located that, things became a lot clearer. There were only a couple other yachts in there—most of the harbor was understandably filled with fishing craft—so we tied up to a Norwegian yacht. The guy onboard wanted to talk, but he seemed a little drifty and we were far too spacey from our long night to have much appetite for casual conversation. He looked scornfully at our fenders and declared they were "too small." He may have been right, but it wasn't what I most wanted to hear just then.

Two officials showed up almost immediately with a bunch of forms in hand. We filled them out dutifully, and the officials left. We were a little unclear whether or not that was all there was to the entry procedure. They didn't stamp our passports. They didn't say anything about how long we could stay in Spain. They didn't indicate that we had to seek out any other officials. So in the absence of any evidence to the contrary we figured we'd arrived.

Things are much different with the European Union these days. Theoretically, at least, things are a lot more formalized, and the rules and regulations apply to *all* the EU countries, so if you enter one country you're considered to have entered all the countries, and the time limits for both crew and vessel apply. You can't go from Spain to France, for example, and expect to be restart the clock of your permits: all the EU is considered one country. Of course, exactly how stringently the rules are enforced is, as is the case almost everywhere in the world, up to the discretion of the officials you encounter. For us, though, we apparently never formally entered Spain. We encountered officials many times in various Spanish ports, we spent the winter in a marina in Spain, and no-one ever stamped our passports, nobody told us we had to leave Spain at any particular time, nobody gave us any trouble at all. They seemed happy to have their individual forms filled out, and as long as they were happy, so was I.

So, we'd made it. We'd covered 3856 nautical miles from Miami in 32 days—almost exactly an average of 120 miles a day. We'd motored 37 hours, the biggest chunk of that the last day and a half approaching Horta, which amounted to less than 8% of our time underway. We were tired, but we were in Europe. It felt good.

Liz doing a sail change on the foredeck on passage to Spain

6. Summer in Spain

Cádiz is an ancient city—founded in 1104 BC by the Phoenicians it says in our guidebook—one of the oldest in Europe, and it's hard to imagine a better introduction to Europe: narrow winding streets shaded by the facades of buildings; balconied windows with wrought iron railings overlooking the street below; dozens of little shops, cafes, tapa bars; beautiful plazas with splashes of greenery. Through open doorways we could glimpse lovely patios and courtyards. Not many tourists, at least not many non-Spanish tourists. It was delightful just to walk around.

Preparations were underway for a folklore festival, with costumed groups from various cities of southern Spain in attendance. Beautiful black-haired Andalusian girls abounded. Flamenco guitarists sat on streetcorners. Music was in the air.

Our third night there we attended the festival, a parade through the streets and performances at an outdoor theater. Things happen late in Spain though, and by 11:45 they'd only reached intermission with half the groups still to appear. Much as we were enjoying it, we were still somewhat sleep deprived and definitely not functioning fully on Spanish time yet, so we left them to it. We had a long walk back to the boat through midnight streets that were well-lit with plenty of people enjoying the night, including very young kids.

Things were always in flux in the fishing harbor. The crazy Norwegian we'd tied up to at first claimed—on Friday—that he was leaving with the boat the next day. He didn't; he disappeared for a few days, leaving his boat in place. He also claimed he'd sailed from Falmouth to the Azores, 1200 miles, in six days; I didn't believe him. A French couple on another boat had asked us over for drinks the evening of the day we arrived; we had a good time trying to converse in French, English, and Spanish. At least I think we did—I was too spacey to be sure. They were leaving their boat and going to Paris to work for a month; meanwhile, they planned to move their boat over next to the other yacht in the harbor, a Belgian boat, so the Belgians could watch it for them. I figured we'd be in a more settled situation if we could tie up next to them outside of the Belgians. We asked, but the Belgians said there wasn't room. I thought there was, but they didn't seem real friendly so I didn't press the point.

We wanted to go up to Sevilla and needed to make sure the boat was safe while we were gone. The Norwegian we were tied to was actually tied up to *Chellah*, a large Moroccan fishing vessel. Two guys from that ship, Magid and Abrahim, asked us over and showed us around. They had radar, SatNav, all very sophisticated, although the hull looked pretty basic. We had a beer with them and a long talk in Spanish and French. They showed us pictures of their families. The boat had a crew of 16 or so—these guys were the engineers. They assured us that they wouldn't be leaving until at least Thursday—it was then Monday—so we figured we'd be safe to go.

It was about a two-hour train ride to Sevilla, through fields of sunflowers, grapes, and olive trees. After Cádiz, Sevilla was much more a big city, busy with traffic and tourists, and overall less attractive to us. We walked around, guidebook in hand, looking for a suitable hotel. We settled on one recommended in the guide even though that worthy volume cautioned that the maid "sang shamelessly." She did, her voice ringing out as she went about her tasks, but that didn't bother us half as much as the church bells which seemed to ring every ten minutes through the night. We managed to see some of the major sights: the cathedral (where we climbed the Girlada, or belltower, originally built by the Moors as a minaret and got a great view of the city); the Alcazar (a Moorish palace); the Archives of the Indies (where photocopies of letters of Columbus, Magellan, and Vespucci were on display, the originals apparently buried somewhere in the bowels of that institution). We had an early dinner (early for Spain, about 9:30) at a café and walked around the city till after midnight.

All that was well and good, and it was nice in a way to see some of the highlights of the city. But on the way back on the train, as we half-listened to a group of kids across from us talking in rapid-fire Spanish and only catching a word or two, I thought that that kind of tourism—checking off the must-see sites in any given city— doesn't really appeal to me. Hotels, whether they're cheap or expensive, are always a gamble too. Traveling by yacht has its own drawbacks, but at least you're staying in your own space, your own bed, with your own stuff around you, and you can take your time exploring whatever city or location you happen to be in.

Back in Cádiz we found that the Norwegian had indeed left, and we were now tied directly to *Chellah*. Nobody had bothered to rig spring lines, but luckily the weather had been calm. A strong levanter—east wind—was predicted, which would mean a headwind in the Strait, so we figured we were stuck for a few more days. A good place to be stuck though.

An American boat came in, *Swan*, a 42-foot ketch, with Kellogg and Diana aboard. They'd been in the Med for a while and gave us information, singing the praises of Italy in particular. Kellogg had built the boat—out of *wood*—and it had taken him 13 years! It was a beautiful job and very luxurious inside, but I couldn't imagine working that long on a project like that. I was about at the end of my patience after a couple of years. Somehow, you'd have to be able to keep a firm vision of the ultimate outcome in mind, along with the confidence that you could pull it off. It takes some special quality that I know I lack.

+

When the levanter finally eased off, it was time for us to go. We proceeded down the coast, threading our way through big tunny nets, a common hazard in this area. The wind picked up as we rounded Cape Trafalgar until it was blowing 25 knots or so, and we blew by our intended anchorage, thinking we might just go through the Strait at night with the good wind. But the wind soon died, and we ended up anchoring in a large open bay, Ensenada de Bolonia, realizing we'd have to leave if the wind came into the west. Ashore were big sweeping dunes in front of craggy mountains with people riding horses on the beach, a wild and weirdly beautiful spot.

The next day we entered the Med. The wind was fluky at first, but it increased as we got into the Strait and remained behind us, so we raced in toward Gibraltar with our jib poled out. We were supposed to have the current against us, according to the tables, but in fact we had little current. The day was clear with outstanding scenery: rugged rocks, bare mountains, the little port town of Tarifa looking like an isolated outpost at the tip of Europe, the forbidding mountains of Morocco to the south, the bulk of the rock of Gibraltar ahead of us.

Approaching Gibraltar

Gibraltar was set up to deal efficiently with yachts. We cleared customs in about five minutes, and got a berth at Marina Bay, one of the two marinas. Anchoring was possible in Gibraltar, but only in an inconvenient and out-of-the-way spot, so most yachts opted for a marina; luckily, prices were quite reasonable.

After our circumnavigation, during which we'd been in many different kinds of anchoring and mooring situations, we figured we had things pretty well together and were unlikely to be surprised. The Med, however, is different, and surprises awaited. As we approached our assigned slip, which was perpendicular to the pier, an attendant was there, I presumed to handle our bow lines. I handed him a bow line and in return he handed me the end of a rather heavy line the other end of which disappeared into the water. I had no idea what to do with it, but the guy on the next boat said, "Take it and walk it aft—that's your stern line." It turned out that line was shackled to a very heavy chain laid underwater astern of the boats, and all the boats attached to it. Once we snugged up bow and stern lines, we were securely moored.

The guy who'd spoken to us was Les on *Solitaire*, a funky little boat. He was a white-haired old guy, very British, very friendly, living very simply. He said he'd circumnavigated twice, once nonstop around Cape Horn, although he also confessed to some weird mistakes in navigation. I was never quite sure how to take these British types who, like Peter in the Azores, set off on adventures that were possibly a bit more than they'd bargained for, figuring they'd tough it out somehow. But he was helpful to us, even scrounging up a cruising guide to the Balearic Islands that we were looking for and that was unavailable in any shops in town.

Gibraltar itself proved to be overwhelmingly British (though also racially varied), a jumble of "duty-free" shops and tourist honky-tonks, with the Rock presiding over everything, a huge lumbering presence. We walked around it in the afternoon heat, then retreated to the boat.

Jeff was due to arrive two days after we did. Naively, in light of our previous experience, we didn't anticipate any problems. The marina was very close to the airport runway, which extended out over the water on built-up land—there's not a lot of flat land in Gibraltar. In fact, you had to walk across the runway to get to the air terminal. We were there to meet the plane: it landed, we watched *all* the people coming out of customs—hundreds of them—and when they stopped coming we had to face the fact that, once again, Jeff wasn't there. The nice man at the Air Europe counter ascertained that Jeff's reservation had been cancelled.

Cancelled? Liz and I were dumfounded.

We called Liz's dad, with some difficulty. What happened?

Jeff had *lost his passport*! He therefore didn't get on his flight to London.

We were both upset, particularly because we weren't sure at that point whether he'd even be able to make it at all, although he had made a reservation for the next day's flight.

Next day, with no more information, we went out to the airport when the flight from London was due to arrive. It was listed as two hours late, but to our great relief a J. MacDonald was on the passenger list. We didn't totally relax, however, until we saw him emerge from the customs area.

We soon got the whole story. He'd been on a shuttle bus from Hartford to New York to get his flight when he realized he didn't have his passport. When he got to JFK (after the bus driver's "slowest trip ever"), he changed his flight, caught the return bus, and went to check the storage unit where he'd moved his stuff a couple days before. Sure enough, there was his passport in an envelope with some other papers.

We didn't ask why he hadn't checked for his passport the day before: there was nothing to be gained by exploring that aspect of it. We were just glad to see him. Not quite as wrenching as his flight to Roatán, but still a fair bit of anxiousness on both sides.

+

So with Jeff finally with us, we were set for a summer in Spain. We spent a day exploring the Rock. There was a cable car, but we passed on that and walked up along the switchbacked road, saw the Barbary Apes (whose presence assures that Gibraltar will remain British, or so the story goes), St. Michael's cave (impressive, with incredible stalactites and stalagmites), the Mediterranean Steps leading down the back side of the Rock, the Upper Galleries (long tunnels chipped out of the rock with openings for gun ports), and were suitably impressed by the near vertical North Face. But with all that taken care of, we were ready to leave.

Summer 1988

Our departure was delayed a bit when I managed to wrap that stern line, the one attached to the marina's heavy chain,

around our propeller shaft as I attempted to back out of the slip: not the smoothest of moves. Jeff had to go in the water to free it. But once we put Gibraltar astern, we had our first introduction to Mediterranean sailing. Our plan was to sail overnight to a marina about a hundred miles down the coast where we could safely leave the boat while we went up to Granada. The wind was light at first and behind us, but it gradually increased during the day until shortly after dark we were getting gusts over 50 knots. As an experiment, I dropped all sail and let the vane steer us downwind with no sail up. We careened along at five to six knots with the vane steering and doing a good job of it.

"Who needs sail?" I said.

Jeff and I stayed out in the cockpit and watched it. It was only Jeff's second day on the boat and he was feeling a little queasy. But things soon moderated, and by the early morning hours we were losing the wind: we ended up motoring the last five miles or so. Talk about changeable conditions. In compensation, with first light, we got to see sunrise over the Sierra Nevadas, quite lovely, long purple shadows creeping over the brown earth.

Marina del Este was nice enough, expensive enough too, I thought, at about $15 a day, considering it was essentially in the middle of nowhere. But it served our purposes. The manager at the marina managed to find us a car, which we rented for three days. This was not our normal method of cruising—marinas, car rentals—but we thought we ought to at least make an attempt to see what there was to see. As I've noted, tourism for the sake of tourism was never high on my list of must-have experiences in life, but I was willing to give it a limited shot here. I had only a hazy idea of Spanish history, though we'd all read Michener's *Iberia* and a couple of trusty guidebooks which at least gave us a bit of context.

So the next day we took off for Granada, and I have to admit that the two-hour drive was spectacular. The road wound through rocky gorges and bare brown hills studded with olive trees and terraced fields, little white villages clinging to the hillsides, the sky bright blue above, ascending around wicked switchbacks, each turn revealing incredible vistas. It required all my attention to keep the car on the road while sneaking quick glimpses at the scenery. From the high point we could see the snow-capped Sierra Nevadas. When we descended to Granada though, we found it situated on a barren, arid plain. The Alhambra, the big attraction, had all the aspects of a big theme park, without much in the way of maps or guides. We wandered around in confusion for a while but eventually managed to see the major sights: the Alcazaba, the Court of the Lions, the Generalife (summer palace). In true theme park fashion, there were tons of tourists though judging by the babble of languages few Americans. It was interesting enough, the gardens were attractive, but I could've used a little more background.

On the second day with the car we drove up into the Sierra Nevadas. through the towns of Pampaneira, Bubión, and Capiliera, little white-washed buildings standing out starkly against the brown hills and overlooking a breathtaking gorge. We continued on the road past Capiliera, through wicked switchbacks again, to an altitude of about 2500 meters. We left the car there although the road continued and plodded up to the summit of Mulhacén, the highest mountain in Spain at 3478 meters, well over 11,000 feet.

Jeff near the summit of Mulhacén

It was an easy climb made more difficult by the altitude, which had us sea-level folks all breathing hard. The route led through fields of alpine flowers, loose rock, clumps of grass, and the occasional snow field. From the summit we looked over the incredible drop on the north side to the valley below. An ascent from that side would be serious business, and in fact people have died in the attempt. On the descent, Jeff and I tried to "ski" down some of the snowfields without a lot of success, though we had fun trying.

That probably would've been enough for us with the car, but we managed to fill the third day by driving through the Alpujarras, visiting the towns of Albóndon, Bérchules, and Trevélez, all incredibly picturesque and set in fantastic scenery. From Trevélez, Jeff and I climbed a 2000 meter peak that looked closer than it was and proved to be a long hot slog, though the views were still impressive.

So much for our land-based tourism. We were all a little worn out at that point and ready to move on.

+

Southern coastal Spain had some interest for us because it was our introduction to Med cruising, but it had its downside too. Rampant development had blighted it—this was not new: it had been going on for many years. The hot sunny summers attracted the package tours and hordes of people from more northern Europe out for a good time. Multi-story hotels and apartment blocks lined much of the coast. Still, there were some good harbors here and there, and somehow approaching the various ports from the sea made the less agreeable aspects a little easier to take.

The sailing was frustrating though. Occasionally the wind would pipe up to 30 knots or more, only to die away to nothing in a few hours. Even in calms or light airs there always seemed to be a short little chop which our low-powered engine had trouble coping with when it was ahead of us. It was hard not to envy the big motor-sailers that could power through those conditions with little trouble.

There's a certain vision of the Med as the domain of luxury yachts and European playboys, of jet-setters and movie stars with bottomless pockets. When we were initially planning the cruise, various sources assured us that there were few anchorages, that we'd be sailing (or more likely motoring) from marina to marina, that it was no place for a small boat with a crew on a limited budget. We found that to be a collection of half-truths. Certainly the gold-plated cruising scene does exist there, as it does almost anywhere there's a high concentration of pleasure vessels. But it's far from the whole story. There were plenty of boats of all descriptions, from the most opulent to the most basic, and their crews were equally diverse. Anchorages abounded too. In our nearly two years in the Med, we went to marinas only about a half dozen times, and that was usually because the marina happened to provide the best access to something we wanted to see. By careful study of the cruising guide and in consultation with other yachties, we were able to choose suitable anchorages in most areas. Sometimes there were nominal port charges; more often there weren't, especially if you were only staying a night or two. If you chose to tie to the city wall, there would normally be a charge, but that too was quite nominal. In the same way, sometimes the officials boarded us; more often they didn't bother. We learned not to seek them out, since that was time-consuming and unnecessary. No one ever questioned our right to be there despite the fact that our passports were unstamped.

We day-sailed all along the southern coast: to La Rábita, an open anchorage where a fearsome roll in the middle of the night destroyed our sleep; to Almerimar, the last marina we went to in Spain that summer, a strangely quiet place in a desolate, arid landscape, not far from where Sergio Leone's spaghetti westerns were filmed; to an anchorage under the lighthouse at Cabo da Gata, the southeastern tip of Spain; to the fishing harbor at Garrucha; to the tight little harbor at Cala Cerrada, where the photograph in the normally accurate cruising guide clearly showed the entrance to the *wrong* harbor; to Torrevieja, a good anchorage behind breakwaters and a pleasant, low-key little beach resort and town; to Alicante, with typical eyesore beach front development fronting a very attractive city, the nicest we'd seen since Cádiz; to Calpe with its distinctive rock formation.

Although we managed to get ashore in most places, look around, buy a few grocery items, this was probably the least interesting stretch of time we had in the Med. We all started to get a little bored, although the frustrating sailing kept our attention.

In Calpe we anchored outside the port area. It was a little rolly but we hoped it would be okay for the night. Unfortunately, at 0100 we woke up to find the wind blowing 20-25 knots from the southwest, to which the anchorage was open. We got the anchor up and cleared out, and once we were out of there we figured we might as well sail out to Ibiza, as the wind was ideal for that direction. With the annoying inevitability that often accompanies decisions like that, the wind died after about an hour. We spent some time changing sails, decided it was hopeless—the wind was all but gone—and started the engine. We motored the rest of the way to Ibiza.

+

The Balearics are a group of islands about 60 miles off the coast of mainland Spain. There are three major islands—Ibiza, Majorca, and Menorca—and a smattering of smaller ones. This is resort country with a vengeance, lots of package tour people, maybe a shade more upscale and perhaps a little weirder than those of mainland Spain. But the islands are quite beautiful, spectacular in places, despite the throngs that descend on them in the summer.

We anchored on the west side of Ibiza, at San Antoni, a crowded harbor with mostly local boats. The town was only moderately interesting from our point of view, the usual jumble of souvenir shops, beach gear, big-breasted girls and muscular guys strutting their stuff in bathing suits, vying for the darkest tan. At night, I supposed, the discos would be full of them, but we'd never know for sure—disco wasn't exactly our thing. We took a bus over to Ibiza city (Eivissa, in Catalan, for the Balearics are part of Catalonia) which was more urban, a little less focused on fun-in-the-sun, though there was still plenty of that. We walked around the old walls, through a dark, twisting tunnel to the cliffs on the outside, and through the streets inside the walls where the cobbled stones were worn smooth by people walking on them over the years. Hot and thirsty in the Spanish sun, we had a Sprite at a little bar on top of the walls.

Leaving Ibiza to the disco crowds, we sailed down to Espalmador, a strip of sand north of the island of Formentera, south of Ibiza. There were plenty of yachts in the anchorage and, when the tour boats pulled in from Ibiza and disgorged their tourists, plenty of people, in various stages of undress, enjoying the beach and the green mud pools, said to be good for the skin. I was dubious. We stuck our hands in but had no desire to proceed further. When the tour boats left, the people remaining seemed inclined to disrobe more fully, some of them fully immersing themselves in the green mud, giving them the appearance when they emerged of weird extraterrestrials in a campy sci-fi movie.

Women routinely go topless on Spanish beaches and throughout the Med. Full nudity is less acceptable in some places, though certainly not on Espalmador. When I suggested going ashore the next morning, Jeff said, "Let's wait awhile. The scenery's better later." I had no quarrel with that. Liz smiled.

The whole nudity thing is strange, as is people's reaction to it. Some people feel compelled to remove their clothes as soon as they hit a beach. Why? One wonders. There's a certain feeling of freedom, I suppose, and a certain element of egotism too: see how uninhibited I am. In general, it's not particularly sexual. The sight of lots of naked or semi-naked bodies isn't very arousing for most people. The only problem I have with it is when it's done with no regard for the feelings of the local people, in which case it becomes almost an affront. It requires a healthy dose of insensitivity to parade around naked in front of black-clad Spanish or Greek peasant women, as we witnessed in some places. Strangely, when we returned to the Caribbean after two years in the Med, the beaches there seemed full of over-dressed people, as nudity is less generally acceptable there. It all depends on what you're used to.

After taking in the "scenery," we left Espalmador and sailed up to Ibiza city where we anchored in the fishing harbor with several other boats. That was fine, but about seven in the evening, as we were preparing to go ashore, a couple of uniformed guys in an inflatable came by and told us we couldn't anchor there, we'd have to move. They were clearing all the anchored boats out. It seemed like a pretty poor time to be asking people to leave, but we had no recourse. We picked up our anchor and at the same time picked up *another* anchor, a huge barnacle-coated grapnel of some kind, and it took us nearly an hour—working with line, gloves, and dinghy—to set it free.

So where to go at eight at night? We took a look at the mouth of the bay, but it was awfully rolly, so we went around the corner to Cala Talamanca. The cala, or cove, was wide open and didn't look encouraging at first, but we found a spot on the west side just inside the bay. We had some trouble anchoring because most of the bottom was impenetrable grass. I had to go in the water with a mask and direct the anchor to a patch of sand; luckily the water was beautifully clear. In the end, though it squelched any thoughts of going ashore, we had a reasonably comfortable night, only rolling a little when the wind died. As with so much else in traveling by sailing vessel, flexibility is an often-required attribute.

Leaving Ibiza to the disco crowds, we motored out to Majorca, the biggest island in the group...motored the whole 55 miles because there was no wind at all. We entered the harbor at Palma, at the head of the large Bay Palma, and anchored in front of the "paseo," the waterfront promenade, with a few other boats. We managed an excursion ashore and found Palma to be an attractive city, a real city, not just an excuse for a resort. At first sight it looked like a place we might want to consider for the winter. We spent a comfortable night, went back into the city the next morning, but when we returned to the boat we found that the officials had moved the other anchored boats out and left a note for us saying that we had to move too. Anchoring, apparently, was not allowed. This was starting to seem like a habit.

We could have moved to the wall, where boats were moored stern-to, but rather than go to the trouble of doing that for a short stay, we decided to leave. We could explore Palma more thoroughly when we came back, which we had to do because Jeff's flight left from there. Instead, we tried to beat out of the bay. That proved to be difficult. The wind was blowing directly into the bay, but beating out should've been a simple matter of making a few tacks. Not quite. In tack after tack, the wind followed us around so that, to put it bluntly, we got progressively screwed.

Jeff couldn't believe it. "The wind is against us whatever we do," he declared.

"Don't worry," I said. "As soon as we get to the head of the bay we can turn to sail along the coast, and we'll have the wind on the beam."

That was the plan, but when at long last we reached a point where we could make the turn to a more easterly course, we found the wind had made a turn too and was now blowing *parallel* to the coast...directly ahead of us!

I threw up my hands in disgust.

By then it was getting late and it was clear we weren't going to make our intended anchorage till well after dark. So at about seven o'clock, to our intense frustration, we gave up, turned the boat downwind and headed in the opposite direction across the mouth of the bay. It would still be awhile before we could get to an anchorage since the bay is roughly 10 miles wide at the mouth. This time the wind didn't follow us around; instead, it died soon after we made that turn, and we had to turn on the engine if we had thoughts of getting to *any* anchorage that evening. As it was, darkness descended, and we ended up entering a strange harbor—Andratx, if you can believe that name—after dark anyway. It was an easy entrance, but the harbor was crowded and it was nearly midnight before we were anchored and secured. Not the most satisfying of days.

All that is pretty typical of the Med. The problem is, there's often no real wind generated by large weather systems in this part of the Med in the summer. The breeze you get is usually some form of a seabreeze, generated by the difference in the way the sea and the land heat up during the day. In a big island like Mallorca, with an irregular mountainous interior, the wind, if there is any, is likely to be doing just about anything. Because of that, the next couple of weeks that we spent on the northwest coast of the island were supremely frustrating (to me, anyway) in terms of the sailing. I still had the odd idea that we were supposed to be a sailing vessel, but the wind had other ideas and seemed determined to prevent us from making much use of the sails. If we started off sailing with a favorable wind, it would invariably come ahead of us or die way to nothing within half an hour. Obviously, I should have simply declared us a power vessel and left the sails in their bags, but I couldn't bring myself to do that.

Still, the anchorages on this stretch of the island were spectacular. Steep cliffs lined most of the coast, and in most places you could sail close enough to them to touch them with a boat hook and still be in 60 feet of water. We explored the island of Dragonera off the southwest tip of Mallorca. We visited the town Deià where the writer Robert Graves had lived: terraced olive trees, a huge mountain wall looming over everything, and the village all brownish-grey stone as if an architect had planned it. We spent a couple days at Puerto Soller from which a nice little tram ran back to the town of Soller about five kilometers inland. From there, we hiked up into the hills on the Pilgrim's Way, an ancient cobbled pathway leading ultimately to the monastery at Lluc by means of carefully engineered and constructed switchbacks—all built back in the 12th and 13th centuries. At Cala de la Calobra we found another beautiful anchorage at the mouth of a torrent where the surrounding cliffs were graced with fantastic shapes, caves, and stalactite formations; but when we came back to the boat after exploring ashore we saw that a large power boat had dumped a mess of oil in the harbor, coating the beautifully clear water with a large slick of oil, rendering it unswimmable, reeking and unappealing. I said something to the guy on deck. He said it was "an accident." Some accident. Vessel was British registry but the crew seemed mostly Spanish.

Horizon **in one of the spectacular anchorages on northwest coast of Majorca**

It was getting near time for Jeff to leave, and frankly I think we were all ready for it. Not that we didn't enjoy having him, not that he didn't enjoy being with us, but in a small boat like ours it's hard to avoid rubbing up against each other: we all needed a little more personal space. And Liz and I had to remember that this, this sailing business, was *our* thing, not necessarily Jeff's. From an outside perspective, it might seem like a great deal for him: a month or two in Europe or the Caribbean on a sailing yacht every so often. And to some extent it was. But it also meant he was with his parents all the time doing *their* thing without much chance to strike off on some direction on his own. It was another form of the same sort of thing we faced during our circumnavigation when he was much younger.

The other aspect of it was that Liz and I were still trying to work things out in our minds. It would be easy to say that we were both uniformly positive and delighted with the cruise—that's the way many accounts of similar cruises read—but it's seldom the case. It was too easy for us to snap at each other when things weren't going smoothly. I was probably the worst offender. I knew that and disliked myself for it. I think part of the problem was that our cruising at this point was rather aimless. With the Atlantic crossing, we had something to focus on. After that, we were determined to show Jeff a good time. With his time with us winding down, we felt ourselves in some kind of unfocused state, not sure what we were supposed to do next, and that brought up all the questions of why-are-we-doing-this-anyway.

So, we returned to Palma and tied stern-to the paseo. That was something of an adventure in itself. Some boats back as easily as cars; ours doesn't: we have to get up to about 3 knots before we have any real control in reverse. The strategy for stern-to mooring involves dropping an anchor at your best estimate of the distance off the wall that will allow you to let out enough chain for security but not enough to empty the chain locker—that requires some judgment. Then, you back down toward the wall, pulling against the anchor to keep yourself straight while the person on the anchor windless lets chain out gradually, snubbing it as necessary to straighten the boat out. When you get close enough to the wall, the person on the stern finds a way to throw a stern line to someone on the wall or to otherwise get it across somehow. This can all be very dicey when there's limited room and a beam wind is blowing…which seems to be most of the time. Looking the situation over in Palma, I decided the maneuver was too complex in the prevailing conditions, so Liz got in the dinghy to row a line ashore. Somehow, and I don't know exactly how—maybe she was standing on one of the inflatable's tubes in an effort to reach the line up to the wall—she managed to fall in in the attempt, surprising both of us. Only a little rattled, she clambered back into the dinghy sopping wet, got the line ashore, and we pulled ourselves into position. Not exactly a study in grace, but it got the job done.

A few minutes later, we watched another boat come in. The expertise he exhibited put us to shame. He backed down easily into a tiny slot between two other boats, friends magically appeared on the dock to take his stern line (you can't script that), and two minutes later the whole crew was enjoying drinks in the cockpit as if they'd been there a week. Oh well—we can't all be master seamen.

A few days later we said goodbye to Jeff. We'd see him next during his Christmas vacation. And we wondered what to do with ourselves. The question of where to spend the winter was becoming more prominent in our minds, so we canvassed the marinas in Palma. They were asking about $250 a month, a little rich for our blood. The charge for the paseo was about half that and it had the virtue of being in the center of an attractive city, but it was noisy, not particularly well-protected, and there were scant amenities. I couldn't see spending four or five months there. We decided to look elsewhere.

We spent a few days at the island of Cabrera south of Majorca where I filled most of my time varnishing our teak bulwarks. Somehow a whole week slipped by there before we mustered the enthusiasm to sail up to the well-sheltered Puerto Colom on the east side of Majorca. There were a lot of cruising yachts there, and the harbor had some appeal as a place to winter, but the marina charge was about the same as in Palma, and it was obvious we'd be a lot more isolated. Another week slipped by. We did little maintenance jobs and visited with other yachts. Finally we motored (in the usual no-wind conditions) out to Menorca, the third big island in the group, where we found *Sunflower*—another yellow boat!— with Al and Beth aboard, last seen 10 years before in Indonesia. The cruising world is sometimes surprisingly small.

Al and Beth were long-time voyagers. They'd done a circumnavigation back in the 1960s, then built their present 42-footer, a Robert Perry design, from a bare hull in Guam, of all places. Now here they were again, a little older like us, but still doing it. They'd worked out a system of cruising for part of the year, leaving the boat for a few months (in Tunisia for this winter), flying back to Florida where they'd rent an apartment and work for a while to build up a little capital. It seemed to work well for them, but I knew I'd have a tough time with that sort of schedule.

Menorca was different than either Ibiza or Majorca, less overrun with package tours, a far less dramatic landscape, flat and dry, at least at that time of year. It was dotted with prehistoric ruins though, the Bronze Age megaliths called *talayots* and the Stonehenge-like *taulas*, which usually consisted of a huge stone 12-15 feet high with another stone placed across the top to form a T. These things dated from 3000 years ago or more. We visited several. I liked looking at them, trying to imagine what had motivated those long-ago people to erect these huge stone monuments. We took a bus to Ciutadella on the other side of the island. Ciutadella had a long narrow harbor, which, we were told, was occasionally subject to a tsunami-like surge of water. The surge could arrive and depart in a few minutes, often causing serious havoc among the boats and shoreside facilities. We had no desire to visit the town by boat.

In nearly three months in the Med, we'd barely seen a cloud: the skies had been postcard blue the whole time. But suddenly in Ciutadella things unexpectedly changed. It clouded over, and the heavens opened up, giving graphic meaning to the term "cloudburst." We huddled in a doorway for half an hour while the stone streets turned into fast-flowing rivers six or eight inches deep—the drains couldn't handle it. It didn't last long, but it was a potent reminder that the Mediterranean summer was almost over.

Back in our anchorage, *Sunflower* was having trouble recovering their anchor. It had snagged something on the bottom. Al had tried everything, but he couldn't free it. I volunteered to go down with scuba gear and have a look. The water was murky, visibility less than foot, but I found that his chain was wrapped—several times—around a huge old fisherman-type anchor, the kind you might expect to find on an 18th century sailing vessel. It's surprising that kind of thing doesn't happen more often in the Med, where thousands of years of shipping have undoubtedly littered the bottom with all kinds of nautical junk. I worked at trying to unwrap it for nearly an hour without success. I surfaced and told Al what I'd found. I suggested cutting the chain and using a chain-joining shackle to put it back together, but that idea didn't appeal to him. I could understand that. So later that afternoon I went back down again, tied a line to Al's anchor which lay some distance beyond the wrap, and we were able to pull that up and unshackle it from the chain; then it was a fairly easy matter to unwrap the chain from the other anchor. Such are the joys of yachting.

+

It was late September, time to leave. People talk about the "equinoctial gales," storms that occur during the time of the equinox. Apparently there's little scientific foundation for that, but the weather does deteriorate as summer wanes and high pressure loosens its grip on the Western Med, allowing more active weather systems to pass through. At any rate, it was time for us to get serious about finding a place for the winter.

We sailed back to Majorca and spent more than a week at Pollensa which sits in a bay near the northern tip of the island. It was clearly post-season, though there were still a few holiday-makers straggling about. We weren't sure what to do. We realized we'd have to go back to mainland Spain since we'd failed to find a spot in the islands that grabbed us. We went hiking in the hills, visited with other yachties, biding our time.

Meanwhile, the elephant in the room raised its head.

Liz woke me up in the middle of one night and said, "I don't think I want to continue sailing,"

I took a deep breath. "A great time to decide that," I said, meaning it in several senses.

"I don't mean I want to quit this minute. I just feel like I need something else in my life."

"It's been a weird summer," I said, not eager to probe further.

The truth is, I'd been feeling much the same thing, though probably for different reasons. The last few months had been sporadically interesting, but too much of it had just been trying to get from one point to another without much consistent wind. It frustrated me, and it was too easy for me to take it out on Liz, one way or another. But beyond that, I think neither of us had found the experience particularly meaningful. Being a tourist, on permanent holiday, just wasn't enough for us. For some people, maybe it was. I'm not making a judgment. I think it's more a matter of temperament than anything. Without a clear cut goal, I had the sense of wasting time, just letting the days slip by. For the most part, we both enjoyed seeing the sights, meeting people with varied backgrounds and motivations, having the freedom to go when and where we wanted to. But was that how we wanted to spend the rest of our days, or even the next few years?

We talked about it that night, but only briefly. Strangely, even though our feelings might've been similar, I resented having them out in the open. It felt like a betrayal of our whole plan, our whole way of life. If we don't have this, what do we have?

I was thankful that Liz wasn't asking to head for home or running off to buy an air ticket. She just wanted me to know how she felt. I saw no point in adding my own feelings to the pile. And anyway, this might be only a passing midnight thought, cleared away in bright daylight, but it would lie in the background for the coming months, something we'd have to deal with eventually.

7. Winter in Spain

We hadn't originally intended to go to Barcelona. Much of what we'd heard about it from other yachties was that it was a crime-ridden, dirty city where it was unsafe to leave the boat, where you were almost sure to get mugged or to have stuff stolen off your boat. But we met a guy in Pollensa who'd wintered in Barcelona and claimed that was all nonsense. He had nothing but praise for the city, so we decided to have a look.

After an overnight passage, we entered the inner harbor and side-tied to the city wall along with a number of other boats. We struck up a conversation with the Frenchman behind us, who seemed determine to confirm all the bad things we'd heard about the city.

"What you must do," he said, in the officious manner that Frenchmen sometimes exhibit, "is use your spinnaker pole to push your boat some distance away from the wall." He showed us how he had his rigged. "That way, nobody can get on board easily." He claimed he had caught people climbing on his boat at night before he'd come up with this strategy. I was skeptical but also a little uneasy. If things were really that bad, I wasn't eager to stay very long.

But a little while later, we talked to Nick and Kirsten, a young British couple on a little boat tied up nearby.

"That's ridiculous," Nick said. "We've been here for a week with no problems. Just take ordinary precautions, lock the boat when you're away from it, and you'll be fine."

I was glad to hear that, but we fretted about it for several days, even left a light on at night to indicate that we were on board and awake. Finally we started to relax. As we'd often found, it seemed that people who were *expecting* trouble were the ones most likely to find it. We were there for nearly two weeks and had no trouble at all.

And Barcelona proved to be a wonderful city. Admittedly, the area around the port was a little seedy: there were parks frequented by drug dealers and a red-light district (this was before the area had been renovated in preparation for the 1992 Olympic games), but in general the seedy stuff was quite confined. We walked down Las Ramblas, one of the great streets of Europe, that extends from the port area for about a mile into the more upscale parts of the city. That was entertainment in itself, for the street was home to bird sellers, flower sellers, street performers of all kinds from musicians to living statues. We wandered through the *Barri Gotic*, the Gothic Quarter, around the Cathedral. One night we watched the *sardana*. the national dance of Catalonia, being performed in front of the Cathedral. It's a strange dance, very ritualistic, with a complicated step. People put their bags and belongings on the pavement in a pile, hold hands in a circle around them; others break into the circle to participate whenever the spirit moves them. A guy took Liz's hand and tried to teach her the steps.

The Metro stop was just a few steps away from our boat, so we could get just about anywhere in the city cheaply and quickly. We took the Metro to the *Sagrada Familia*, Gaudi's fanciful cathedral (begun in 1882 and still unfinished) that's become a Barcelona landmark. Incredibly, they were still working on it—slowly—and we spent a couple hours exploring it and climbing the towers. We went out to *El Corte Inglés* (The English Cut), a huge department store, and to *Servei Estació* (Service Station), a sort of super hardware store. We went to the extremely interesting Picasso museum and to the delightful *Parc Gaudi*. And we'd only scratched the surface.

"This wouldn't be a bad place to spend the winter," Liz said.

"It certainly has its advantages," I said.

There was a lot of coming and going in the harbor though. We were next to the wall, but boats frequently came in and tied up next to us or tried to squeeze into small spaces fore and aft of us. You had to keep an eye on things. One day the city put on a big celebration centered in the port area when they brought the Olympic flag from Seoul, site of the 1988 Olympics, to Barcelona in anticipation of the 1992 Olympics. Throngs of people swarmed over the wall above our boat, though the only downside for us was the array of pistachio shells we collected on deck: that seemed to be the snack of choice for the crowd. The next morning, the newspaper ran a big photo of the celebration, and there was our boat on the front page!

On the wall in Barcelona—the Olympic flag ceremony

A couple of boats about our size came in: *Jakana* with Jack and Anna on board and *Tempo* with Lee and Judy. They'd come from England through the French canals. Jack and Anna were from Newcastle in northern England, and Jack spoke with a thick Yorkshire accent, but he also had a self-deprecating sense of humor; Anna, always well-groomed, was quieter and more deferential. Lee and Judy were Americans from the Midwest who were planning to cross to the States the next fall. We spent several evenings with them telling our various stories over drinks, but they left after a couple of days, while we stayed, still not sure what we were going to do.

As it happened, circumstances made the decision for us. Liz had gone into town to investigate the possibility of getting an

English-teaching job if we should decide to spend the winter in Barcelona when, about 1030, a uniformed guy came by and told me we had to leave in an hour, for "*seguridad*," he said. Security. They were clearing all the boats off the wall because—get this— the Queen of England's yacht was making a stop in Barcelona. Far be it from me to interfere with the Queen's travel plans, but I wasn't going to leave without Liz, and I had no way to contact her. I got the boat ready to go, went to the office and paid our nominal fee, but by 1300 Liz still wasn't back and the guard was asking me when we were going to leave. I didn't bother to try to explain that a little more advanced notice would've been nice. Finally, about 1345 Liz showed up, and we got underway.

It was blowing pretty hard outside, so we put up the reefed main, still not sure what to do. A quick consult with the chart suggested that we might be able to duck into Vilanova, about 25 miles down the coast, so we headed for that, almost directly downwind with 30+ knots on our anemometer. It was just after dark by the time we made the harbor. We couldn't see well enough to get into the marina, so we eased in behind the outer breakwater and anchored in what we hoped was an out of the way place.

In the early morning light, I looked at the marina through binoculars.

"Hey," I said to Liz, "*Jakana* and *Tempo* are in there." They'd left several days before us, so we figured there must be something worth checking out if they were still there. I looked again and saw that *Gavot II*, Nick and Kirsten's boat, was there too. We got in the dinghy and went in to investigate.

"We're staying for the winter," Jack told us. "It's a great deal." All three boats had decided to stay.

It turned out that the marina was brand new, not quite finished, so the rates were low that season; for us, it amounted to just about $100 a month, including water and electricity. Showers too. The water was a little brackish (as it is in many places in the Med), but it was fine for most purposes and we could buy bottled water for drinking. We signed up without hesitation and moved in to a slip. As in Gibralter, it was a matter of tying the bow of the boat to the concrete pier (there's almost no tide in the Med so fixed piers are normal) and the stern to a line leading to an underwater chain. And there we were: set for the winter.

It turned out to be a great choice. Vilanova i la Geltrú, to give it its full Catalan name, was a city of roughly 50,000 people; it had traditionally been a fishing port, and still was, but it now had a modest tourist business (mostly Spanish), the new yacht marina, and a number of educational institutions. We learned later that it had some notoriety for the enthusiasm and fervor with which its residents embraced their various festivals. (More about that later.) A supermarket, a *panadería* (bakery), and a fresh food market were all in easy walking distance. Best of all, it was only 25 miles south of Barcelona; we could hop on one of the frequent trains and be in the center of Barcelona in a half hour.

The only drawback that we could see was that it was a little further north than we liked and was therefore likely to be colder and windier than places further south. We discovered too that a surge would develop in the harbor in windy weather; that wasn't particularly uncomfortable, but it did subject our lines to a lot of chafe. As it turned out, the weather was fine most of the time. The nights were sometimes cold in the dead of winter, but the days usually warmed under clear and sunny skies. Since we had electricity at no additional cost through the marina, we bought a little electric heater to take the chill off. From time to time it blew hard, sometimes very hard, and the beach sand blew all over the boats. But we always felt quite secure.

A nucleus of about 15-20 boats ended up spending most of the winter here, with a few others passing through and staying for various amounts of time. Roughly half-a-dozen of the wintering boats were Brits, three were Americans (including us), a couple were Spanish, and a smattering of other nationalities were represented. It was a varied cast of characters:

Mike and Ann were an engaging young British couple in the slip next to us on a large wooden power boat, *Celerity*. They had limited experience but lots of enthusiasm. I don't know that "naïve" is quite the right word for them, but "cynical" is way off the mark. They walked around the marina holding hands like young lovers. Mike seemed to regret that he didn't have a sailing vessel, and he and I discussed various aspects of cruising at length.

George was an American who'd bought an old steel boat very cheaply. His problem was that he had a lawn-care business back in the States, so he could only get to the boat in the winter and therefore couldn't do much sailing, if any. That didn't deter him from entertaining several lady friends who flew in from the States; the only question we all speculated about was: would one arrive before the previous one left?

Isabel and Tony were a young Spanish couple living on their homebuilt trimaran. Isabel spoke a little English, but most of our conversations with her were in Spanish. We prevailed on her to help us with our Spanish—we'd either trade English lessons with her or pay her for her time. We weren't able to get together as often as we would've liked, but we managed some sessions with her and learned a lot, both language and cultural history.

Manuel and Lia were another Spanish-speaking couple living on a 25-footer. He was from Spain, she was from Argentina, and they both spoke pretty good English. Manuel had just completed a six-year circumnavigation in the boat (which had no engine, not even an outboard). He'd met Lia in Australia, and she'd sailed the rest of the way with him. Their boat wasn't much more than a daysailer—large cockpit, tiny cramped cabin you could barely sit up in—but somehow they managed. Manuel told us he'd finally accepted a tow in the Red Sea after an extended period of time trying to beat his way up it.

Alfredo was an Argentinian on a scruffy little gaff-rigged boat with Spanish girlfriend Nuria who had a job in Barcelona. He'd been bumming around the world for 10 years—not by boat: he was only doing local sailing. He looked like a long-haired bandit, nobody you'd want to meet in a dark alley, and he didn't speak much English, but he'd always make an effort to speak Spanish slowly and distinctly to me. I liked him.

Nick and Kirsten, who we'd met in Barcelona, were the youngest couple in the group—somewhere in their 20s. In November Kirsten announced that she was pregnant, which meant for them going back to England before the baby was due and putting cruising plans on hold.

Lee and Judy from *Tempo*, the other Americans, had been in company with *Jakana* since the French canals, we gathered, and despite differences in cultural background and interests, had become good friends with Jack and Anna.

So those were the people we were to spend five months with. As in TV sitcoms, these were the regular cast members, but there was also an erratic flow of guest appearances to add a little variety as people came and went. For the most part, it was an extremely social time, a nice contrast to the isolation that we'd often felt.

Five months is a long time though, and sitting in one place wasn't ordinarily our idea of the cruising life; it's a lot of down time. It was important to find ways to occupy ourselves. I spent a couple of weeks doing painting in the bilges, an activity that often required me to contort my body in awkward ways. The unhappy result was that I pulled a muscle (or muscles) in my back, and that severely limited what I was able to do for more than a month. I'd been trying to run with some regularity, but that was no longer possible. The amount of discomfort varied, but I had to be very careful not to aggravate it.

On Thanksgiving we had a baseball game on the beach—it seemed appropriate for an American holiday. With half-a-dozen languages floating around and wildly varying levels of athletic ability, it was a recipe for chaos. Naturally the Americans were the only ones who had much of an idea how the game was played or what the rules were, so we had to explain it to everyone else…a job in itself. My back hurt too much to play, so I umpired. What developed was only an approximation of baseball, with rules being made up as we went along, but it was good for lots of laughs. A pot-luck Thanksgiving meal followed, and then a bonfire on the beach. We toasted marshmallows, played around with musical instruments, talked Spanish. Jack got very drunk. We had a great time.

As Christmas approached, the success of our Thanksgiving activities prompted us to prepare even more extensively for Christmas. The British were good at organizing this kind of thing. Nick and Kirsten volunteered to write a "pantomime," one of those semi-satirical, comic take offs on fairy tales or other children's stories that are popular entertainment in Britain at Christmas. We were all assigned parts and had to attend scheduled rehearsals. Mike and Ann organized a scavenger hunt with clever clues. We had a carol sing, which also required rehearsals. Jimmy, one of the guest characters in our little group, also a Brit, took over as chorus director. The differences between the British and American versions of the same carol provided some amusement. When the time came, we all went out on a crisp evening, walked around to the various boats, sang a carol or two at each, and in return had a glass of champagne or other treat at each. As you'd expect, the singing got more and more off-key as the evening went on.

The Christmas dinner the next day was a great success, the whole thing prepared and executed in style. The marina had given us a room to use, we decorated it appropriately, and more than 20 people attended. And the pantomime performance lived up to its promise. Lee and I, both bearded, were the two ugly stepsisters from the Cinderella story, but Jack stole the show with his whacked out performance as Captain Hook, even though he had trouble staying in character. The scavenger hunt on the next day—Boxing Day—was a hit too.

With the new year upon us, my back had improved enough for me to start jogging again. At first I just did a few minutes on the beach, gradually increasing my time as I was able to run without things hurting again. Before too long, I was up to a respectable time and was able to run with Jack. He was older than I was, but he'd been an amateur rugby player and was in good shape after having suffered an injury a year or so before. We made it a point to run at a pace that enabled us to chat as we went along, however Jack always like to keep a half step ahead of me; whenever I tried to draw even with him, he'd pick up the pace a little. In that way he pushed me without appearing to.

We were in the dead of winter now, and though some days were cold and blustery, most days were fine. Jeff flew in to see us for a week in mid-January. We did a bunch of touristy things: went in to Barcelona and visited the Sagrada Familia again; walked down the Ramblas which was loaded with the usual street performers: magicians, sword swallowers, shell games, tarot readers, artists, hookers; took the train to Tarragona south of us to see the Roman ruins there; rented a car and drove up to see the Dali museum in Figueras north of Barcelona, which we all enjoyed; visited Girona and some of the nearby villages. Back in Vilanova we attended the Tres Tombs event, where animals from the surrounding countryside are paraded through the streets –three times around—and blessed by the priest. All kinds of animals are eligible, but the most visually impressive were the horses, some of which were pulling wagons decked out with elaborate harnesses, while others were ridden by men in traditional costumes, all very festive and with roots in the ancient past.

Jeff's stay was short this time, which was probably okay; it was good to see him, do some stuff with him, without getting too much in each other's faces.

A Frenchman named Roger had arrived in the marina sailing

a 38-footer which he was trying to sell. He'd apparently made an Atlantic crossing in it, although that was a little unclear. He succeeded in pissing me off by telling me officiously that you *must* have safety lines rigged on your boat if you're doing offshore sailing. Since I'd done a circumnavigation without such lines (I considered them just something to trip over), I demurred, which only made him more adamant. I should have let it alone, let him believe what he wanted to believe, but something in his manner irritated me, and we got into a stupid argument. I felt embarrassed about it afterwards, as several other people witnessed it, but we can't always act with perfect sanity and moderation. A few days later, when we were on Nick and Kirsten's boat, Roger started expounding on what the regulations were for importing boats into Spain. Kirsten had done some research and disagreed with him. He continued expounding while Kirsten got quietly pissed. It was some comfort to me that he had that effect on other people too.

+

Meanwhile, Liz and I were still snapping at each other too much, and occasionally we'd have a real, senseless fight over nothing. We'd never really played that game before—in the past, if either of us got pissed at the other, there'd usually been a good reason for it. Some of it, I'm sure, was due the "down time" that the winter forced on us. We were lucky to be in a situation with other congenial people around and a fair bit to do, but the situation didn't require the focused attention that sailing does. Maybe we just had too much unstructured time.

When we talked about it, I told Liz that if she wanted to fly back to the States, I'd stay; I wasn't done with the sailing yet. I think that took her back a bit. I don't know how serious I was about it, and I don't think she ever intended to desert me, but I needed to have my feelings out there. I also felt that the whole task of keeping spirits up, of being responsible for having a "good time," and of maintaining a positive attitude about the sailing had fallen on me. I resented that she'd forced me into a cheerleader role, and I told her so.

Of course I was far from blameless in all this. In the first place, I was probably as ambivalent about the voyage as she was, but to admit that openly would place our whole enterprise in jeopardy. I knew I wasn't ready for that kind of upheaval. Nor was I in a place where I wanted to deal with her feelings in any extended discussion when my own feelings weren't clearly defined. I preferred to sweep the whole thing under the table and carry on as if all were well.

The crazy thing was, we'd stumbled into about the best situation we could've hoped for that winter—a great place, a great bunch of people—and if we were unhappy here, well, what did *that* mean? And the last year, in most ways, had been one of the finest we'd spent afloat, with no major problems threatening the voyage. Had this all just become too easy? Were we too jaded? What was going on?

To some extent, I think questions like this arise with any voyaging couple, or at least most voyaging couples have their own similar difficulties. In most cases, one person is more committed to the voyage than the other. Too often, the whole thing is the man's idea and the woman comes along in support. Or sometimes, in these days of easy air travel, she simply flies out to meet him in various ports while he sails the boat with whatever buddies or crew he can scrounge up. In some cases, in all honesty, rather than dragging along an unwilling partner, that may be the way to go. But I think the important thing—and this is the hard part—is to have a clear idea of why you want to do it in the first place. Voyaging is not for everyone. Even a coast-hopping kind of voyaging is not for everyone. If you're going to succeed at it as a couple, you have to have a pretty clear idea of what you want to get out of it and what you expect of each other. It's not like chartering a yacht in the Caribbean for a week or two: there's a much bigger commitment required.

Liz had always been a fully committed crew member. I knew I could count on her, whether on passage or day-sailing, in doing anything that needed to be done. I relied on her so thoroughly that it would've been very hard for me to take anyone else as crew. But I also knew that I needed her to be enjoying the whole thing as much as I was, and I didn't like to see that sense of a shared experience slipping away.

+

In early February, we had the Carnival celebration. This was a huge deal in Vilanova with a full week of festivities. In the tradition of carnival "misrule," the first event was a study in semi-controlled chaos. Various societies and organizations from the town patrolled the streets, each in a distinctive costume, each with a band and a banner. They carried big bags of hard candies, and they hurled the candies at each other, at the crowd, at anybody. Others, often kids, picked them up, but that hardly made a dent in the mess. Soon the streets were covered with candy; it got stuck all over our shoes. They proceeded to the town square where a big candy battle ensued. And yet it was all done in a spirit of good fun, not at all nasty.

That evening, we decided to go to Sitges, the town just up the coast a few miles, to see their carnival parade. Sitges was a well-known center for gay culture, sort of like Provincetown or Fire Island in the US, so the parade promised to be quite elaborate. Like most things in Spain, it happened late. We caught the train at 8 with Jack and Anna, Mike and Ann, and Nick and Kirsten. The parade didn't start till 11, so we walked around, had a beer, looked at the scene, so different from much more conservative little Vilanova. The parade finally got underway with innumerable floats, flocks of dancers with each float, elaborate costumes, female impersonators, the whole bit. It was fun to see but two hours of it, standing there in the cool night air, was a little much. When it was over, the trains had stopped running, so we tried to get a taxi, No taxis either. We decided to walk back with Jack and Anna along the coast in the dark, about three miles; the others decided to stay and catch the first train at 6 am. Luckily, Jack had brought a small flashlight which at least gave us some idea of where to put our feet. It wasn't as difficult as I'd feared, but it did require attention. We got back about 3, glad we weren't still marooned in Sitges.

Carnival in Vilanova

Two days later, the highlight of the Vilanova carnival week was their costumed "paseo" which was quite different from the more formal Sitges affair. Throngs of costumed people flooded the city Ramblas in the chilly night, some in groups with coordinated costumes, some with their individual costumes. The street was virtually solid with people. They milled around, carrying little flexible beaters to hit people with and big bags of rice. We went with some of the other yachties, and hiding behind their costumes the people didn't hesitate to involve us, to tease us, to "beat" us (they were beating everyone), to throw rice at us or even rub it in our hair. But again, it was all done in a spirit of fun—there was no hint of nastiness, no drunken foolishness as there would've undoubtedly been in a similar even in the States. The costumes were unbelievably complex too. We were told that people often spent months working on them. In one group, 10 or 15 people were decked out as dress shirts—just shirts with large stiff collars, no apparent body—so that the impression was of headless shirts floating down the street; they had eyes holes cut in the ties so they could see where they were going. The culmination of the night was the judging of the costumes in the town square, but we missed that as we didn't have the stamina to stay out into the wee hours of the morning.

With carnival over, things quickly got back to normal. The weather continued mostly beautiful. We worked at little boat jobs and started doing some planning for the upcoming season. And then trouble struck from an unexpected direction that was to have a long-term impact on our plans.

On a day in late February, I started having diarrhea. I had to go to the head about every hour. I didn't consider it anything serious at first, just probably something I ate, and I continued functioning okay. Then about 5 in the afternoon, Liz and I started into town to do some shopping. I got down to the end of the pier, maybe a hundred yards or so from the boat, and I realized I wasn't going to make it. I had to go back. By 6 I was having chills and fever. By 7 I was in bed, though I had to get up every hour to go to the head. I had a whanging headache. I'd never had such horrible diarrhea. I started worrying about fluid loss. The next morning Liz got some Gatorade-type stuff, and I drank a lot of that during the day, although I couldn't eat anything. I had very little urine output which suggested dehydration despite the fluid I'd been consuming. I lay in bed all

110

day, half-dozing. I couldn't read, couldn't do anything. I tried eating a little applesauce and toast, just a couple bites, but that went right through me. Finally in the late afternoon, I had an aspirin mushed up in applesauce, and that seemed to help my headache a little.

I managed a little sleep that night, but I still couldn't eat anything the next day. In 48 hours, I'd eaten almost nothing.

By the third day, the diarrhea started to ease off, and I was able to get down some food and retain it. But it was a slow process. More than a week later, I still tired very easily. It was more than two weeks before my digestive system started functioning anywhere close to normal. More disturbingly, I developed a shortness of breath and a cough. I started being afraid to breathe deeply because I knew it would start me coughing. I was aware of a certain tightness in my chest too. The sensible thing to do at that point would've been to go to a doctor, but even though I was vaguely worried, I basically thought it must just be some kind of low-grade viral infection triggered by or associated with the diarrhea. I didn't really believe it was anything serious, and I expected it to get better on its own.

And in fact it did start to get better but at a snail's pace. A week went by, then two, then three, and I could look at my condition and see that I probably was marginally better than the week before, but the symptoms continued to hang on. It was an up-and-down process too: some days were better than others.

By then, we were getting ready to leave. I wondered how I was going to hold up at sea. We only had to make two- or three-day passages as we worked our way across the Med, but they can be tiring. I had to be able to function well enough to be able to deal with whatever came along. It was worrying.

The time in Vilanova had been great in most respects, but we were ready to leave and get on with "cruising," even though the third week in March was still early for the Med. We knew that, but we decided to go anyway. We'd been sitting too long. So we said goodbye to everyone—once again, realizing we'd probably never see them again—and set off with some trepidation.

8. Across the Med

Somehow it never fails. When you've been in port for awhile and had plenty of time to ensure that the boat's in good shape, all systems are functioning well, and everything's set for a season of cruising…something unexpected breaks as soon as you go to sea.

The forecast was for strong northwest winds but "attenuating," We intended to head for Menorca, so strong northwest winds were fine with us. We had some fine sailing…for about an hour. Then the wind died, got very light, and went into the east (the *east*!). We flopped around in the leftover seas, annoyed at having been lured out there by the forecast only to confront this kind of nonsense. The mainsail emptied and filled with some violence as we rolled in the swell, and finally—pop, pop, pop, pop, pop, pop—half a dozen sail slides on the foot of the main broke.

Great. I almost decided to turn back at that point, but when I'd cooled off a bit I realized that was probably more trouble than it was worth. I cut off the rest of the slides on the foot since they were all suspect now, took a length of ¼" line and laced it around the boom and through the grommets in the foot of the sail. That worked so well that we sailed with it like that for some months before we got around to replacing the slides.

After a night and morning of confused and lumpy seas with very little wind, we decided to go into Pollensa on Majorca again, which was about 20 miles south of us at that point, until things straightened out. We had to motor, and the motion was severe in those seas, but as I suppose I should have expected a nice breeze of 15-20 knots from the northwest came up as we entered the harbor. I was too burned out and tired to try set off again, and I had no confidence the wind would last anyway, so we motored in to the anchorage, watching a heavy swell breaking halfway up the cliffs on the south side of the long cape like a slow-motion geyser.

We spent a comfortable night and found the forecast in the morning again promising strong northwest winds. Did we believe it? Not really, but I decided we had to see for ourselves. Out we went, but halfway out the bay an east wind came up again at about 10-15 knots, driving a short sea into the bay. It was tough going for our little engine, but I persisted because I couldn't believe that was the true wind. But well past the mouth of the bay, the wind was blowing directly from 100, our course to Menorca. That was it. We went back in to anchor.

The strain of the last couple of days hadn't done my chest problem any good. I started taking prednisone, a steroid, which we happened to have. I wasn't crazy about it, but I didn't like the tightness in my chest either.

We tried again the next day, and this time the wind was more in the north, so we stuck it out. We found big seas between Majorca and Menorca, but they weren't too confused; we had some fast sailing and ducked into an anchorage on the south side of Menorca just after sunset, having covered 60 miles in 10 hours, our best sail in the Med so far. I was wiped, and the prednisone didn't seem to be doing much.

Next day we got up early and motored around the corner to Mahon, the main city on the island, before the wind got up. When we went ashore to the market we found only a few motley boats at the quay who'd apparently wintered there. We spoke briefly to one British fellow who didn't seem remotely interested in us. What a difference from Vilanova! I spent a quiet afternoon, and I wrote in my journal:

> *I'm too tired, sick, whatever to want to take off for anywhere. I'm getting pretty worried about this affliction. Despite the prednisone, it doesn't seem to be getting any better. Physical activity or just being out in the wind aggravates it. <u>I need to get well!</u>*

We ended up spending a week in Mahon. I took it quite easy and started feeling a little better, but it was only toward the end of our stay that I felt sound enough to walk for any distance ashore.

Meanwhile, we had a minor crisis with our Visa card. Liz had attempted to get a cash advance, and it was twice refused. The teller in the bank had started to look at her suspiciously. Worried, she called her dad and asked him to check with our US bank. He reported that there was no problem on that end. We were puzzled, but we decided to try to ask for *more* money than we'd been asking for. The teller was skeptical, but he tried it and, presto, it went through with no problem. We'd been asking for *too little* money! Apparently it wasn't worth their bother.

+

From this point in the Med on, we relied on Rod Heikell's cruising guides for Italy, Greece, and Turkey. They were indispensible at that time: very detailed with lots of sketch charts and mostly good advice. We could have easily sailed in the Med with only those guides and perhaps a small scale chart or two. (Remember, this was still before the convenience of GPS.) Only in a few instances did we find them wrong or misleading. So in a sense we were not flying blind; we always had some sound advice in our ears. We were headed for Sardinia next, and as the geography of our movements there is a little complicated, the map may help to clarify a little.

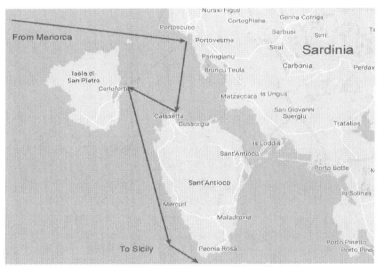

The southwest corner of Sardinia

The weather in the Med in the spring is volatile, as we were learning. Systems move fast, things change quickly, and the forecasts have trouble keeping up with them. Not only that, but conditions are always very local, so that even if the forecasts are generally accurate, they may not have a good handle on what's happening in your precise area. Our primary source of weather was the English-language shortwave broadcast from Radio Monaco which covered most of the western Med; it was reasonably accurate but could still occasionally get caught short.

We left Menorca on a good forecast and had mostly decent

sailing with a little motoring thrown in at night when the wind died. But it came back the next day and gradually drew forward. By evening of the second day, a southeast gale, previously unmentioned, was forecast.

"Just what we need," I muttered, as we struggled to make progress to the southeast.

But it did no good to curse the forecasters: we had to deal with what we had. At sunset, we were about 20 miles from the island of San Pietro off the southwest coast of Sardinia. The wind was light and ahead of us, so with the imminent gale in mind we started the engine. The wind increased as predicted, and we had a real struggle getting around the north of the island, at times able to make good only about two knots. Once we got into the channel between Sardinia and San Pietro, it was a little easier, but as we got further south toward the harbor at Calasetta at the north end of Sant'Antioco island, our intended destination, the seas got so bad we couldn't make much progress. What to do? The town of Carloforte on San Pietro has a good harbor, but it's open to the east and didn't seem like a reasonable alternative in the current conditions. So we headed for the western shore of Sardinia to try to get *some* shelter. Finally, at about 0300, tired, wet, and strung out, we got the anchor down near the breakwater at Portovesme about a quarter mile from shore; it was open to the southeast but sheltered from the east, which is where the wind was at the moment.

I noted tersely in my journal: "Tough night."

In the morning, with the wind down a little, we motored over to Calasetta in the rain. We anchored in the small harbor and flaked out. Later in the day when the rain stopped we debated moving, debated going ashore, decided not to do either. During the night the wind went into the northwest (against all predictions) and drove a little chop into the harbor which made me uneasy, so at first light we moved around the corner to the west side of the fishing harbor where we'd be more sheltered from the wind direction and tried to anchor between the piers. But the bottom there was covered with thick weed (we brought up plenty of it with each attempt), and the anchor wouldn't grip. So we motored over to Carloforte and anchored comfortably there behind the breakwater.

Our only stumbling block now was that we didn't really want to check in. We weren't intending to cruise Italy; this was just a stopping place. Besides the time involved, we'd heard that Italy required all yachts to have insurance…and we didn't. Presumably they'd have some arrangement to sell you some, but it seemed rather pointless to get into that. So the strategy was simply to keep a low profile and hope we wouldn't be bothered. If we were, we could just leave.

We went ashore and found an attractive little town with narrow streets that looked curiously all the same. We changed some money and bought a few groceries. After so many months of listening to Spanish, it was weird to hear Italian spoken, though strangely it was much clearer to our ears than Spanish.

Nobody bothered us, but that night a series of violent squalls came through with strong gusts, thunder, and hail. We were glad we were in a place with good shelter, good holding, and plenty of swinging room. We didn't really intend to leave the next day, but it started to clear in the morning, and the forecast sounded okay though it was still blowing hard. We put two reefs in the mainsail, hanked on a small jib, and left.

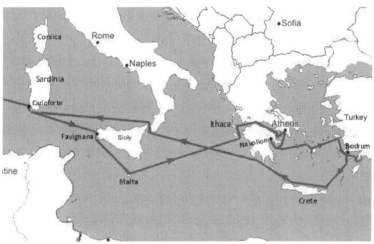

Spring and Summer 1989

As I've said, we knew we were sailing early in the year for the Med: it was only the first week in April, and we had to be prepared for some heavy weather. I was aware too that gales in the Med could be more dangerous to small boats than gales in the open ocean because of the steepness of the seas. We were soon to have all that theoretical knowledge confirmed.

We had a rough trip down the west side of Sant'Antioco as the seas poured in there, but once we turned the corner of the island, heading southeast toward Sicily with a Force 7 wind behind us things got much more reasonable. That didn't last long though: in the evening squalls started to build around us, there was a lot of lightning around, and we began to get apprehensive. As the night wore on, a whole series of squalls came through, and finally in a particularly hard one, I had to drop the little double-reefed main. We put up the trysail in its place, and sailed with that alone through the rest of the night and most of the next day, doing six knots or better. I commented in my journal:

> *Seas steep and confused—not comfortable sailing. Cockpit pretty dry, but we dip the rail into a crest once in a while, and once we took some water over the stern—don't do that very often. Both of us very tired.*

Finally, by late afternoon, the wind was down enough to change back to the main. And—wouldn't you know it—the wind continued to die; we had to motor the last six miles to our destination.

The Egadi Islands are a small group of small islands off the west coast of Sicily. We were bound for the harbor on Favignana, the largest of the group, which was supposed to offer good shelter. However, the harbor is very small with stern-to mooring required, and we didn't relish entering in the dark, so at 0400 we anchored outside and got a couple hours of sleep as we rolled in the swell. In the early morning, we entered the harbor and got ourselves securely tied to the wall with our anchor nearly out the harbor entrance. There were no other yachts there.

+

We had on board a copy of Ernle Bradford's book, *Ulysses Found*. In the 1950s, Bradford, in several small sailing boats, attempted to trace the travels of Odysseus (or Ulysses) through the Med as described in Homer's *Odyssey*. The basic premise of the book is that the places Odysseus visits are *real* places, not just a poet's fantasy, and that they can be identified by clues in the text. It makes for fascinating reading, even though it's all speculation and somewhat fanciful in itself. In any event, this island, Favignana, Bradford suggests, is the island from which Odysseus and his men looked across at mainland Sicily, eventually crossing the five miles or so between them only to encounter the Cyclops. Could be. At least it added to the interest of the place for us.

**The harbor at Favignana and the mountain that deflected
the wind**

Modern Favignana is a fishing and tourist port. There were few tourists because it was so early in the season. Several yachts came and went while we were there, but mostly we had it to ourselves. We were anchored in amongst the fishermen, who didn't seem to mind. The fishermen at that time were still setting big nets by hand, using huge anchors to secure the nets, to catch bluefin tuna in their annual migration. Of course we were still in Italy, still somewhat worried about the officials, but despite the fact that we were, in effect, right in the center of town, nobody bothered us.

Ashore, we found a pleasant little town, a jumble of small shops and restaurants and bicycle rental places looking like they expected a lot of tourists. We took a long walk out to the lighthouse, past little farms and big stone quarries where they cut the blocks for the island houses. We tried to go up the ridge of the Montagna Grossa in the center of the island, but it was a "military zone" and we couldn't even get halfway up. But there's a line in *Odyssey* about the goats descending from the heights, and that made sense in this setting.

Meanwhile, the wind remained stubbornly in the southeast, the direction we wanted to go, and it was often strong, so we were effectively stuck. One day Liz got to talking with a guy on the pier. With our stern to the pier and our American flag on our stern, we were fair game for anyone interested. This guy, Salvatore Tomare, was 56 years old and had lived in the US for a time; he didn't speak a lot of English, but he didn't mind trying. He invited us to come to his house for something to eat. We did. We met his wife who didn't speak any English, though she listened to Salvatore's words with amused tolerance. They served us coffee, then dinner (at noon): spaghetti first, then veal, along with a strong wine which he warned us about but then insisted we keep drinking.

They had a tacky little house with little religious items all over and embarrassingly bad pictures on the walls. He showed us pictures of his dog and post cards he'd received. Some people don't mind baring their lives to strangers. He told us he had a son by another wife in the US, but he'd lost track of him; that seemed to bother him.

"In America," he told us, "the first question people always ask is: what do you do?" He shook his head. "What do you do? What difference does it make? In Italy we don't ask that. That's not important."

I'm paraphrasing his English, but that was the gist of it. He kept coming back to that idea, as if he couldn't believe it. In a way, I'd have to agree with him in some respects, although of course knowing what someone does for a living does give you lots of other information about him.

After the meal, they took us for a drive around the island, pointing out the sights. It's a small island, only about three miles long, not much more than a mile wide, and quickly seen, but it's always interesting to see a place through the eyes of its inhabitants.

Salvatore promised to stop by the next day, but the weather had other ideas. We were about to have a couple of the most miserable nights we've ever had in port. A German boat came in from Sardinia and insisted on mooring next to us, rather precariously because they couldn't get an adequate line to the pier. Rain and squalls started after dark, and we got up around 0130 as the squalls got harder. We suited up in foul weather gear and went out in the cockpit. The gusts were incredibly hard. Our anemometer was pinned at 60 knots—its maximum—for 30 seconds or more at a time. One gust blew the boom out of the slot in the boom gallows to the slot on the opposite side. Another blew our dinghy from alongside us into the cockpit. The whole world seemed to be going nuts. Most disconcerting, the gusts came first from one side of the boat and then from the other—what amounted to a 180 degree shift. The reason for that, we decided later, was the bare peak directly across the harbor from us; apparently this fierce wind would hit that peak, and depending on the exact direction of the gust would accelerate around one side of it or the other.

Eventually the German boat dragged, luckily away from us. We held for a while but eventually we too started to drag, slowly. I hadn't been able to let out as much scope as I wanted to when we anchored because the harbor was so small. We let go our stern line, always the first thing to do when you start to drag when Med-moored. We surged away from the wall on the weight of the chain, that eased the strain on the anchor gear, it got a grip again and we felt better about it. With first light, things seemed to be calming down, so we re-moored to the wall. But in mid-morning we had another hard squall. Liz and I stood in the cockpit with the engine running, getting soaked. The squall passed, we went below for lunch, and then another one hit. This was getting ridiculous. We decided to side-tie to the wall so that we wouldn't have to worry about the anchor dragging. That was a tough operation in the conditions, especially because there were big tires attached to the wall as fenders for larger vessels, but they were just the right height to press against our stanchions, and we broke a couple of welds on the stanchion bases. I finally decided we had to set a breast anchor—an anchor out perpendicular to the side of the boat—to hold us out away from the wall a little. That worked pretty well, and we began to relax.

But we were also starting to feel that we'd be better off at sea than in the confined harbor. where there were things to hit...or get hit by. A second night of hard squalls only confirmed that feeling. We listened to the forecast in the morning and it sound sort of okay—Force 6-7 in Sicily Channel—so we decided to get the hell out of there and head for Malta. We hadn't had much sleep in two days, but I still felt we'd be better off at sea.

We motored out directly into the wind, making slow work of it, and promptly encountered a tuna net that required us to go a mile out of our way to get around it. Once we cleared that and while we were still motoring, I noticed that the engine was overheating. Just what I needed to make my day. I killed the engine and we got sailing under the double-reefed main. I spent the rest of the day working on the engine in appalling conditions while Liz handled most of the sailing. The area around the engine was hot and airless, the motion was severe, and I had to nearly stand on my head to get to the water pump; for one of the first times at sea I started to experience motion sickness and had to come up for air every once in a while.

Under trysail, heading for Malta, wind Force 8-9

I discovered that all the water was gone from the cooling system and the water pump was leaking. I tried valiantly to get the leak to stop but finally had to call it quits without success. Meanwhile, the wind had increased so that eventually we had to go down to the trysail alone. By late evening the wind was Force 8-9, not at all pleasant conditions. We took some heavy water, filling the cockpit once. Another wave entered the hatch and landed on my face in the port quarterberth. In the morning, I noticed that one of our port side stanchions had broken off: we'd reefed the weather cloths (those rectangular pieces of canvas that are supposed to protect the cockpit) but not enough: the sea hitting the canvas had broken the stanchion. We'd lost our boom vang tackle overboard. And we didn't sleep.

Chaotic seas, heading for Malta

I went back to working on the engine. I finally took apart the water pump valve and found the culprit: a broken gasket. I replaced it, got it all back together, and started the engine. It worked! Big relief.

But we weren't done yet. We'd spotted Gozo, the neighboring island to Malta, where we were headed. The Italian forecast acknowledged a Force 8 gale (34-40 knots) but we could attest, conservatively, to Force 9 (41-47 knots). Then—more trouble. A big wave inundated us, burying the deck and pouring gallons of water *through* the dorade vents—which are baffled to keep water out—and into the cabin, landing on the bunks. Clearly we should have closed off the dorades in those conditions. Another wave landed in the corner of our almost-new dodger, tearing out the side panel; the same wave swept away one of our water jugs that we carried in the cockpit.

None of this stuff was particularly serious but it certainly wasn't contributing to our sense of well-being. It wasn't the wind strength that was particularly troublesome: it was the confused nature of the seas. They were steep and basically behind us, but we also had a cross sea that was coming at us from the side: those were the ones causing the trouble.

As we sailed down the north coast of Malta, I got increasingly worried about getting into the harbor. I called Malta Harbor Control on the VHF and asked about conditions there.

They wouldn't say anything. Not their business to give weather reports. Thanks a lot. I started the engine as we approached the harbor entrance. It ran happily for five minutes and then started to overheat again. My heart sank, and I quickly shut it off.

What now?

Nothing for it but to enter under sail. The approach is reasonably wide and clear, but in those conditions anything could happen. We went in under trysail and storm jib. That worked okay, but once past the harbor entrance, we had to turn to windward. With high land around us, the wind was very gusty, and we didn't have enough sail when the gusts relented…and we had too much for the harder ones.

Reluctantly, I started the engine, hoping we could make it into a sheltered spot before it overheated too badly. I nursed it in until we were in 10 fathoms where we dropped the anchor. I quickly shut off the engine. The anchor dragged until we were in 13 fathoms (that's 78 feet) before it caught.

We were sitting in the middle of Marsamxett Harbor, and I knew from the cruising guide that anchoring was not permitted there. I called Harbor Control, told them what our situation was, and asked for a tow. They sent one of their patrol boats, but the guys on board didn't really know what to do. They tried to come alongside us but couldn't control their boat and managed to break off three more of our stanchions. I was silently furious, but I also realized it was my own stupidity that had allowed it to happen: I shouldn't have allowed them to try that maneuver. Finally, after some discussion, they agreed that we could just stay there.

I went back to work on the engine. I removed the water pump and rebuilt it (we did have the kit for that on board): it was a lot easier now that we weren't getting flung around. But to my dismay it *still* overheated. Desperate now, I pulled apart a bunch of water hoses to get to the thermostat. Once I reached it, I saw that there was a lot of gunk in it and around it. Could that be the problem? I cleaned the gunk out, tested the thermostat by heating it in a pan of water on the stove and watching to see if it opened. It did. I put things back together, ran the engine for a good long time, and—I hardly dared hope—all was well. Apparently it was the clogged thermostat, that was the root of the problem; that caused the overheating which in turn caused the waterpump to fail. I might've found the problem sooner if I hadn't had to troubleshoot in the middle of a gale.

Since it was well into the evening by the time I had that sorted out, we stayed where we were till the next day. And what do you know? The weather the next day was ideal: sunny, warm, with light winds. We picked up our 200 feet of anchor chain and moved, as directed, to a berth along the quay.

Boats in Malta Med-moor, but there are some peculiarities there. The harbor is generally well-sheltered, but it is open to the northeast; when it blows from that direction (the wind that's known as the *gregale*—as in much of the Med, the winds have names) it creates a powerful surge in the harbor. It's usually not dangerous, unless you're carelessly moored. Boats staying more than a couple weeks were required to hire a diver to take an anchor line down and attach it to a heavy chain on the bottom in the middle of the harbor. Short stay boats were allowed to use their own anchor, but it was advisable to use very heavy lines to the quay. We had no strong *gregales* while we were there, but even in a 10-15 knot wind we'd surge back and forth 15 feet or so, stretching our lines, which could be unsettling.

+

It was time for us to take stock. It had been just about a month since we'd left Vilanova, and we'd had our share of excitement. We'd taken heavier water than we had since our circumnavigation years ago, testament to the nastiness of the Med seas. And there's no question they were nasty. K. Adlard Coles in his classic book *Heavy Weather Sailing* (1967) notes that seas in the Med are shorter and steeper than in the open ocean, and he offers an account of a sailor in a 40-footer who was swept overboard by a sea with a big breaking crest in winds of only 25-30 knots. As we could now confirm, those seas were nothing to mess with, though thankfully neither of us had come close to going overboard. We heard later, too, that a fleet of a half dozen or so French boats being delivered to a charter operation in Turkey had run into trouble in the same weather between Sardinia and Italy, and a couple of them had been wrecked.

"So what have we learned?" I said.

"We've learned we need to be more conscientious about preparing the boat when heavy weather's possible, "Liz said. "We get a little too careless, I think."

That was true. You get so used to being on the boat and dealing with it in ordinary conditions that it doesn't often occur to you that things can go wrong in an instant when the weather turns nasty. We made a list of things we should've done: close the dorade vents, zip off the side panels of the dodger (we'd had them made removable for just that purpose), remove the weather cloths, make sure the life raft is secure (it had started to shift in its mounts), check for loose gear (the boom vang), keep a hatch door in place, find a better way to secure jugs in the cockpit. These kind of debriefing sessions, if nothing else, helped to keep us aware that bad stuff can happen. We wrote it all down.

But overall I was pleased with the way we'd handled it. Once again, it was clear that Liz and I could work well together in stressful conditions. There was no conflict, no game playing, no nonsense: we both just did what had to be done.

+

We spent most of the first few days in Malta cleaning up and getting stuff repaired. Tony, the guy who had the boat next to us, was Maltese and very helpful. He took me by car to see a welder about repairing the stanchion bases we'd broken. The welder suggested a way of doing it whereby I could removed the bases, he'd weld them in his shop, and then I could bolt them back on. That worked out well. We stitched up our ripped dodger. We bought blocks for a new boom vang. We got a new set of spares for the water pump. And after five days we had ourselves almost back to normal after a 32-hour passage. Such are the joys of sailing.

We ended up spending about two weeks in Malta. The island has a fascinating history stretching back into prehistoric times, through a succession of invaders and rulers, to a terrible bombing attack as part of the British Empire in World War II, to independence in 1964. St. Paul was supposedly shipwrecked here in 60 AD. In Valetta, the capital, we found a strange little city laid out on hills with steep streets, steps going down some of them. We walked up Strait Street, very narrow, seedy, with lots of grubby little bars—a sailor's street. We rode the buses around the island: to the Tarxian temples and the underground Hypogeum, a fantastic temple and burial site carved out of the rock, dating from around 3000 BC, to Birzebugger (love those Maltese names) where we had lunch, then to the cave at Ghar Dalman where thousands of old animal bones and ancient human remains have been found. Another day we went up to the walled medieval city of Mdina with its narrow, curving streets and nice views of the whole island from the walls. We visited St. Paul's grotto where he supposedly lived after his shipwreck (you wonder if this is just legend perpetuated for tourists or if there's any hard evidence for it) and to St. Paul's catacombs, a labyrinth of tombs carved out of the rock. (There's a lot of rock on Malta.) The buses were a convenient way to get around, but the drivers kept giving us the wrong change—deliberately, we think—in the confusing Maltese money. The Maltese were friendly, but sometimes we felt we were being nickel-and-dimed to death.

Liz in Malta, Valetta in the background

The next leg of our jaunt across the Med would be over 300 miles to the Greek Island of Zante in the Ionian Sea. We weren't eager for a repeat of the conditions we'd experienced getting to Malta, so we listened carefully to the forecasts trying to find a couple of days of settled weather. "Is the weather ever settled in the Med?" Liz wondered. It was easy to forget the many long, sunny, windless days we'd experienced the previous summer.

Finally things started to look hopeful, and we decided to go for it. We dithered around in the morning, preparing the boat, double-checking the forecast, getting checked out, so it was mid-afternoon before we got away. And in fact we had reasonable conditions for the first 48 hours or so: the wind was up and down, sometimes strong, but nothing to cause any serious worry.

But with 80 miles to go, clouds started to move in, and just before dark a hard squall hit us—60+ knots, heavy rain—and the rest of the night was thoroughly miserable: we were in and out of squalls and thunderstorms, lightning all over the place, drenching rain. We didn't dare leave much sail up because when the squalls hit they did so with real fury, but that meant we couldn't make much progress in the lulls. We ended up motoring the last 15 miles with just the trysail. Both of us were up all night.

The squalls abated as we rounded the southern corner of Zante and entered the breakwatered harbor on the east side of the island, and the morning sunshine rendered everything sharp and clear and bright, as if the night had been only a bad dream.

We anchored and started to back down to the quay, but the guy next to us said we'd crossed his anchor chain with ours. Maybe. I didn't think so, but in my bleary state I couldn't be sure, so I picked it up and reanchored: a lot of work. The problem in these Med-mooring situations is that things are never as neat as you might think. When the wind's blowing from the side (as it usually is, in my experience), it blows the bow off so that the anchor isn't out in front of the bow: it's off at an angle to windward. So when you're trying to moor, you have to pay attention to the *angle* that the anchor rodes of other boats are making with their bows. With boats at such close quarters, screw-ups are commonplace.

We were secured by 0930 and went to bed. But we woke up a couple hours later to find it had decided to blow again, with some hail mixed in for good measure. Later in the day I wrote in my journal:

> *Things seem to be settling a bit now—thank god. We are so sick of worrying about the boat and the weather. Nevertheless, here we are in Greece.*

And so we were. We'd had our share of difficulties, and we'd made most of the trip from Vilanova in winds over 30 knots, but we were in Greece now, summer was approaching (it was the 30th of April), and we hoped to be able to relax and enjoy ourselves: wasn't that what we were supposed to be doing as yachties?

9. Greek and Turkish Waters

We'd tried to check in on the afternoon of the day we'd arrived, but it was a Sunday and when we went to the Port Office the duty officer said, "Tomorrow." Fine. We went back the next morning only to find the offices closed. We walked around the town for a while, still spacey and tired from the passage. It was a pleasant, touristy little town filled with souvenir shops, tavernas, and mostly-Greek tourists. We walked up out of the town to the top of the ridge where we got a great view of the port area. There were flowers everywhere—roses, honeysuckle, bougainvilla, lemon trees—everything lush and green, a nice island.

Finally, the next day, we managed to check in. Unlike Spain, the process was involved, taking most of the morning. The sequence of events, as we trekked from office to office, was as follows: Customs→Port Authority→Police→Bank (to change money so we could pay) →back to Port Authority→back to Customs. It cost us 3000 drachmas for the Transit Log (the official cruising permit), 160 drachmas for the stamp on it, and 250 drachmas to the port. All that amounted to a little over $20, but the bureaucracy of it all nearly buried us. On top of that, we were supposed to show the Transit Log to the officials in every port, a requirement that we learned to mostly disregard unless we were asked. In the afternoon, a guy came by to seal up our scuba tanks. They didn't want us gathering ancient artifacts from the sea bottom in Greek waters, and there was a heavy fine for removing the wire seals.

We'd learned that Jeff was to fly in to Athens on May 17, so we had only a couple of weeks to get to Piraeus, the port for Athens, which didn't leave a lot of time for exploring the Ionian or the Gulf of Corinth. But we did want to see Ithaca, the island generally accepted since ancient times as Odysseus's home. It's only a day sail from Zante, and for much of the time we were sailing along the rugged, beautiful, green coast of the much bigger island of Cephalonia: it's separated from Ithaca by a narrow strait.

As we entered the port we passed a sign that said: "Every traveler is a citizen of Ithaca," a reference to the travels of Odysseus and his yearning for home that I found strangely moving.   We anchored in front of the town of Port Vathi, where red-roofed buildings squatted under green hillsides. There were a couple of yachts tied up at the quay, but since it was early in the season we had the anchorage to ourselves. In truth, it was a relief to be at anchor instead of at a quay in amongst other vessels with all the resulting noise and confusion that usually entails.

Next day, to explore the island, we rented a motor scooter. Ithaca is a small island, not as small as Favignana but still less than 15 miles long and only a couple miles wide in most places (squeezed down to almost nothing in the middle, almost making two islands out of it), so we figured a scooter was the way to go. The rental shop guy didn't have a lot of English (and of course our Greek was close to nonexistent), but after we'd paid and got ready to ride off, he cautioned us: "Slow, very, very slow." He wagged his finger. "Insurance— no!"

Well, at least he warned us. We weren't about to back out at that point though, and off we went. We drove out to Stavros in the northern part of the island over a spectacular winding road on a sheer cliff above the sea. Luckily there wasn't much traffic. Slow wasn't a problem: the little two-person scooter struggled on the uphills. Stavros is on a ridge above the bay of Polis and is in the general area of the supposed site of Odysseus's palace. A woman in the town asked us if we were going to the museum and said her husband could open it for us. Why not? The man led us a half a mile out of town on a road lined with neat stuccoed little houses set amongst olive, lemon, and fig trees. The museum proved to be a bare room in a little building with a few glass-fronted cupboards holding neatly labeled bits of pottery, stone, and metal from various periods, ranging from 2000 BC to 500 BC. The man hesitantly and in a combination of rough English and pantomime told us about the various pieces. There were vases and bowls, some pieced together from fragments; tiny lamps and perfume vases; obsidian blades for shaving; and a tiny carving of a sex scene. It was nothing special, except when you stopped to think exactly how long ago those things were made.

View of Ithaca from "Odysseus's Acropolis"

We drove around for awhile in the north of the island, passing the site of "Homer's School," a fanciful misnomer, but it is a spot where Linear B (an early form of ancient writing) inscriptions have been found. It wasn't clear where Odysseus' palace had been located, but if you were king of the island you could do worse than site your palace in this landscape, on the height of land with a view over the narrow strait to rugged Cephalonia. As we drove back toward Vathi, we stopped at a spot on the isthmus that connects the two parts of the island, parked the scooter, and climbed a steep trail to "Odysseus's Acropolis" (or so the sign said). At the top of the hill, we found the ruins of big Cyclopean walls, huge blocks of stone that had obviously been placed there by humans. There wasn't a lot left of them but enough to see that whatever they were protecting must have been big. It was exceedingly doubtful that they had anything to do with Odysseus, but I wondered how much excavation or study of the site had been done.

By then our asses were sore, it was getting late, and we returned the scooter to the shop where the guy seemed relieved that we'd made it back without some insurance-less accident to deal with.

The Gulf of Corinth is that long and relatively narrow slot of water that divides mainland Greece from the big peninsula of the Peloponnesus that hangs down from it, connected only by the isthmus of Corinth west of Athens. (And yes, that's the same Corinth, the city on the western side of the isthmus, that Paul addressed a couple of letters to that found their way into the New Testament.) Ancient Sparta was located in the middle of the Peloponnesus, and the whole area is loaded with ancient sites. There's a canal cut through the isthmus which offers a much shorter way to Athens than the tedious multi-day trip around the bottom of the Peloponnesus. That's where we were headed.

We left Ithaca with no wind and motored on a flat sea over to Oxia, the island at the southwestern tip of the mainland. We wanted to anchor—it was a spectacular spot—but couldn't find water shallow enough despite what the Heikell guide told us, so we continued on to Missolonghi and slogged through a long channel, bordered by houses on stilts, into the basin there against a rising wind. This was the place where the poet Lord Byron died in 1824—he'd come there to fight in the Greek war of independence from the Turks—but we were just glad for the sheltered anchorage.

Then it was through the Gulf of Patras and into the Gulf of Corinth; the transition between the two Gulfs is the strait of Rion where the mainland and the Peloponnesus are only a mile apart. For us, It required some attention because of the constant barrage of ferries crossing back and forth (there was no bridge at that time), sometimes six or seven underway at the same time, heedless of our approach. We flew through them white-knuckled at seven knots in gusty conditions. The wind tends to funnel there and accelerate because of mountains on both sides.

Somehow we avoided hitting anyone, or being hit, and I started to relax a little. It was strange to think that I'd been here before, in this area, 30 years ago, when I was a college student hitchhiking through Europe. I'd arrived at Patras from Brindisi in Italy by ferry. From there, three of us (a Swiss backpacking girl, a Dutch artist, and a young Greek guy we'd met in Patras) took a *taxi* to Athens, a distance of about 130 miles. It was a wild trip, drinking wine, music playing from a little spring-mounted 45 rpm record player that skipped occasionally, sometimes stopping for a swim in the Gulf, as thoughtless and carefree as a 20-year-old can be.

A couple days later we were Med-moored to the quay in the attractive little city of Galaxidhi from which we had a view of snow-capped Mount Parnassus. We were here because it was the closest port to Delphi, the ancient site famed in ancient times for its oracle and its often ambiguous predictions of the future. Once we had the bus schedules sorted out the next day, we were off to visit the oracle. The ride took us through huge olive groves, then up the hillside through a picturesque village with tile roofs and tan stucco walls; we could look back and see Galaxidhi, even from Delphi about 20 miles away, with the olive groves looking like a huge green sea. The setting itself was enough to make you believe in oracles: a deep gorge in the mountains, ancient ruins clinging precariously to the hillsides. Sure, there were tour buses and school groups, but they weren't too obtrusive. We bought a guidebook and worked our way slowly through the site reading it as we went, enjoying ourselves thoroughly. It helped that the day was perfect, sunshine with just a few clouds, cool, and light winds.

Then on to the Corinth Canal. We anchored close to the canal in the afternoon to be ready for a morning transit. The canal is very narrow, less than 70 feet wide, so it's one-way traffic only. The anchorage was uncomfortably rolly, but there we were and there wasn't much we could do about it. We motored over to the canal at first light and saw that the red flag was up, indicating traffic in the other direction. We anchored and waited. Another sailboat arrived and anchored. Three small ships arrived and also anchored. After about three hours, a big cruise ship emerged from the canal being towed by a tug. I was surprised something that big could fit through. At last we had a green flag, and our little convoy started through, with us at the rear. It was slow going, only about three knots, but the canal is only about four miles long. The walls of the cut loomed over us. The rocks alongside displayed paint marks of various colors, suggesting that numerous vessels had had some unfortunate encounters.

At the other end of the canal, we had to tie up to pay our fee at the canal office. As we were making our approach to the one vacant spot at the pier that was suitable for yachts, a German yacht about to transit in the other direction beat us into it by about 10 seconds, sort of like somebody zipping into a parking place ahead of you when it's clear you're aiming for it. We dithered around for a while and finally managed a rather precarious tie-up with our stern hanging off the end of the dock. The canal fee was based on net tonnage: we were charged about

132

$80 but the other yacht that came through with us, a 36-footer, was nailed for about $175, which hardly seemed fair. Incredibly, while we were dealing with this, a big cruise ship that was entering the canal got *stuck* just past the canal entrance, an event that no doubt quickly ruined his day. The canal was closed to traffic—obviously—while they worked to free him. I don't know how long it took because we left before they succeeded, but it was clear that the pushy German yacht didn't gain much by all his rush: he wasn't going anywhere till the cruise ship moved.

Transiting the Corinth Canal

So now we were only a day sail from Athens, and we had a few days to kill before Jeff's arrival. We sailed down to Korfus, a well-sheltered little anchorage on the Peloponnesus, and spent the time there being rather lazy. My strange illness was much better but still there. I had a disconcerting tightness in my chest from time to time, and I tired easily. I tried a little jogging and was pleased to see I could do it, but 20 minutes or so was enough.

When the time came, we had a nice sail to Zea Marina in Piraeus, the port for Athens. We saw a few boats at the outer quay as we entered, but we weren't sure where to go till a guy told us to tie up to one of those boats. Once we did, the people on the boat who were Dutch said they'd probably be leaving about the same time we were, so we appeared to be all set. Even better, the charge turned out to be only about $2 a day.

I'd been in Athens and Piraeus in my hitchhiking days and a couple of times when I was in the Navy, but nothing in the port looked familiar. Piraeus was massively confusing, even though they had maps posted around the port area. (Of course all the signs were in Greek, using the Greek alphabet not surprisingly, and therefore not as helpful to us as they might've been.) We finally located the Metro stop so that we could get into Athens, but it was close to a half hour walk from the marina. Athens was a little more familiar, as we walked from Syntagma Square to Omonia, and later to the Plaka with the Acropolis and Mount Lycabettus lording it over all. I still had indelible memories of drunken evenings in the Plaka, the old section of Athens on the slopes of the Acropolis, and a particularly vivid one of sitting outside one of the bars there very late at night with an English girl and a bunch of other people listening to a long-haired American girl playing the guitar. But the kid I'd been when I was last there seemed very far away.

+

Jeff arrived the next day, but as usual not without a certain amount of hassle. We rushed to get out to the airport at 1000 only to find his flight was delayed, expected to arrive at 1230. So we had over two hours to kill with absolutely nothing to do. Somehow the time passed, we saw the plane land but had to wait for nearly another hour watching people emerge from Customs and Immigration before Jeff finally appeared. Then, as we attempted to catch a bus to Piraeus, just like the one we'd taken to get to the airport, we learned that the drivers on that line were now on strike, so we had to get a bus to Omonia Square, then the Metro to Piraeus, then a bus back to the boat. It was 1530 before we made it, but at least it was the same day.

Jeff had just completed his junior year in college and although he was still very young in some respects he was noticeably more mature than when we'd first left him a year and a half before. It was always strange to see him at these intervals of some months, not sure exactly where he stood on the spectrum between kid and adult. He'd be with us for about a month this time, and here we were in Greece after all, with the prospect of plenty of interesting stuff to see and do. We were all looking forward to it.

We felt a certain obligation to spend a day in Athens

seeing the requisite sights. We went first to the Acropolis—naturally—and were suitably impressed by the Parthenon, even though restoration work was going on and the back end of it was covered with anachronistic scaffolding. Tourists swarmed over the place too, but even so it was hard to dismiss the majesty of the site, all that ancient stuff sitting up there overlooking the modern city below. After a picnic lunch in the National Garden, we went to the National Museum. I'm usually a sucker for museums, but I nearly overdosed in there. There was just too much stuff. The guidebook we'd bought was singularly useless: incomplete, poorly organized, impossible to follow. I liked the Mycenean stuff—there was a ton of it—but it might've made more sense to see it after we'd visited Mycenae. We'd been planning to stay in Athens for the evening, but all three of us were too burned out, so we opted to retreat to the boat. Having had enough of cities for awhile, we left the next day.

+

A few comments on weather systems in the Med are in order here. I've already noted that in the *western* Med, between Spain and Italy, a big high pressure system (an anticyclone) settles over the area in the summer. The situation in the *eastern* Med, where we now were, is a little different. As the deserts of the Middle East heat up in the summer, the air rises, creating low pressure over that area. Picture those two big systems: the high pressure over the western Med rotating clockwise and the low pressure over the Middle East rotating counter-clockwise. There's a point where those two systems interact. If you draw it out on a map, you can see that the result is northerly winds, and that occurs most predictably over the Aegean Sea. From early July into September, that northerly wind, known in the Aegean as the *meltemi,* blows with unnerving consistency. In the central Aegean it's particularly strong, sometimes up to gale force. Around the edges of that sea, close to the coasts of mainland Greece or Turkey, it's usually less strong; further south, in Crete, it often loses some force too. But few winds in the world are as predictable, and it pays to take that into account when cruising the Aegean.

We were aware of all that, we knew we had to plan our route accordingly, but the reality of just how much of a factor the meltemi can be hadn't been driven home to us yet. What it boils down to is that, whereas lack of wind is the biggest problem in the western Med in midsummer, too much wind is likely to be the biggest problem in the Aegean. In fact, people who charter yachts in Piraeus and set off to cruise the islands in July or August, sometimes have to pay deadhead fees for someone else to get their boat back to Piraeus when the meltemi's blowing like stink and their vacation time is running out. For now, though, we still had a good month or more before the meltemi was due.

Our first goal was to visit the bronze age site of Mycenae, both because we'd read about it—it was excavated by Henrich Schliemann, the guy who later excavated Troy, in the 1870s—and because it was relatively easy to get close to it by boat. To do that, we'd have to cross the Saronic Gulf after leaving Athens, then round the first big peninsula of the Peloponnesus and sail up the Argolic Gulf to the city of Navplion at its head. All that would take a few days.

As we motored toward the island of Hydra in a flat calm sea, we were passed by a fast hydrofoil from Athens whose wake left a swath of blue-green water on the surface of the darker sea long after it was gone, like the contrail in the sky behind a speeding jet. We avoided the tiny harbor in front of the town which we feared would be far too congested for our tastes, and anchored around the corner in Mandraki Bay where there was more room. It was a 20-minute walk from there into town, but that was hardly a serious drawback.

Hydra is the quintessential Greek island: a colorful harbor, lots of tavernas and tourist shops, white buildings, tons of tourists. We opted for a long walk up to the Prophet Elias monastery in the hills above the town: first on a switchback road out of town, into a pine forest, then up a series of stone steps. The monastery had a beautiful site, but the only sign of life was a few chickens. It took us an hour and half up and an hour down. Most of the tavernas were closed by then as the cruise ships from Athens had left, but we found one to have a drink in. I wrote in my journal:

> *Nice day. Best thing is that I'm feeling better. Maybe the Athens pollution was bothering me. My chest seems a lot better and the hike didn't aggravate it much at all. So maybe I'm on the mend at last. I hope so.*

**View of Hydra and its tiny harbor with fast hydrofoil
approaching**

The next day we motored past Spetses, the island that John Fowles depicted in his novel *The Magus*, and in to Porto Kheli, a well-sheltered harbor that we'd heard might be a possible winter spot. Perhaps, but it seemed a little isolated to us. We tacked up the Gulf in variable winds, a little frustrating but at least we *could* sail. When we reached Navplion, a guy in a white uniform motioned us to come alongside the wall. Since there's usually somebody motioning you to do something in the Med, you have to decide how seriously to take it, but this guy did have a uniform and the wall looked well-fendered, so I went for it. He didn't speak any English, but some people on a charter boat nearby told us we might have to move because a large vessel was due to come in the next day. In fact, we were able to stay where we were, though I did consider moving out to anchor when the wind started driving an annoying little chop against us.

The narrow streets of Navplion were filled with shops and tavernas and the usual tourist stuff. A Venetian fortress, Palamidi, built in the early 1700s, overlooked the town, which has been a port since the Bronze Age. Jeff and I climbed the 857 steps up to the fortress the next day (it took about 20 minutes) and explored the maze of fortifications.

Jeff and Liz and the Cyclopean walls at Tiryns

Then we all went to the Bronze Age site of Tiryns, a 10-minute bus ride away. It was unimpressive as we approached, a little fenced-off hump in a field, not exactly what you'd expect of one of major palaces in the area 3500 years ago. But closer up the walls were huge things, enormous stones closely fitted, and the guide book was excellent, walking us through the details of the site. In one of the vaulted galleries in the walls, the stones were polished smooth by the coats of flocks of sheep and goats that had sheltered there over the centuries. It required a little imagination to get a handle on what it must've looked like in its heyday—there wasn't much left of it other than the walls and the stone outline of some of the spaces—but I found it mind-bending to be tracing the steps of those ancient people. There were a few tourists there, but it wasn't at all crowded, so we could explore at our leisure

The more famous site of Mycenae was an hour away by bus across the Argolid plain, and we went the next day. The site is on a low hill with a mountain on each side and a deep gorge to the south; you can see the Argolic Gulf from the top, the peninsula of Navplion, and probably Tiryns too if you knew where to look. I was disappointed and surprised to see dozens of tour buses in the parking lot—I hadn't expected the site to be quite that popular. But we passed through the famous Lion Gate, just as the Myceneans must have done all those centuries ago, and went slowly again, reading the guidebook, while the tour groups hurried past us. The guidebook wasn't quite as good for this site as it had been for Tiryns, it was all a little more confusing, but we could mostly sort out the major features. There was more here than at Tiryns—the impressive Lion Gate, the cistern (a winding dark staircase down to the water source beneath the walls), the graves, and the tombs outside the walls. Whether or not the citadel had anything to do with Agamemnon, as Schliemann believed, it was still a major force in the area till 1200 BC or so, and apparently some 30,000 people lived in the citadel and the town below. It was hard to picture it as a vibrant community now, just an old stone ruin on a Greek hilltop overrun with tourists, but I still enjoyed seeing it.

+

It was time for us to head out to the Greek Islands, specifically the Cyclades. These bare rock islands are what people usually have in mind when they dream about cruising Greece. With a few exceptions, you don't go to the Cyclades for their archeological sites. You go for the brilliant blue sky, the deeper blue of the sea, the white-washed buildings that stand out against the purple-grey rocky landscape and the blues of sea and sky. And you go for the beaches, the partying, the nightlife—at least some people do. There is a certain sameness to the islands though, which is not to say they're boring exactly, but if you were suddenly transported to one blindfolded, when you removed the blindfold it might be difficult to tell which island you were on. Tourists definitely rule these islands in the summer, and in places there's almost a big city feel as people rush here and there at a frantic pace.

From a sailing point of view, although they're attractive in some respects, they have their problems too. The best harbors are crowded. The charter boats, of which there are many, usually prefer to tie up in the center of town where they can step ashore easily for meals and drinks. But being jammed in at close quarters (and it's *always* close quarters) amongst all the holiday makers never had much appeal to us. We preferred to anchor out, though that often meant settling for a less sheltered spot.

Now, in late May, the meltemi wasn't yet a factor—that would come later—but we still had to contend with katabatic winds in the lee of some islands. The Cyclades were mostly stripped of trees in ancient times, and the wind finds it easy to accelerate over the bare rocky peaks; on the lee side of the islands, the wind is accelerated further by the force of gravity as it rushes down the mountainsides. So, if you're sailing in the lee of an island, although you'd think you'd be well-sheltered there, you can be suddenly hit by terrific gusts, and because the wind force is essentially downward, the heeling of the vessel actually *increases* the force of those gusts on the vessel by exposing more sail area to the wind. That's the opposite of what happens with gusts in a normal horizontal wind, and you can take a pretty good knockdown before you realize what's happening. Of course heading up will spill the wind from the sails, but that makes for tense and uneasy sailing. A further consequence of this phenomenon is that, as you sail along a coast in the lee of an island, you may have gale conditions, while if you go out a few miles, it's just a nice sailing breeze.

We had a fine, rollicking sail out to Kithnos, in seas that got a little nasty as they poured out of the strait between Kea and Kithnos. A couple days later we had to motor out to Siros in a calm, then to Mykynos where we anchored in Ornos Bay on the south side of the island: it's open to the south but otherwise well-sheltered and just a short walk into town. But we wanted to visit Delos, the island a couple miles to the west that's supposedly the birthplace of Apollo, so we motored over there the next day, managed to anchor with some difficulty, and set off to explore the site. At first it was disappointing: tons of stuff but confusing, scattered with no real focus, the guidebook wasn't much help in sorting things out, and the day was blisteringly hot. But it got more interesting when we discovered the houses in the "theater district": they had marble doorways and columns and mosaics on the floors, all over 2000 years old. Hermes House had been partially reconstructed, making it easier to picture people living there.

When we were done, we moved over to the main harbor in Mykynos and tied stern-to the wall. The harbor was busy and noisy. Mykynos is the iconic Greek island, probably the most famous, a favorite of jet-setters (it was rumored), and boasting a "wild" nightlife. Maybe, but we didn't see much of it. We went into town in the evening and walked around: it seemed that's what most people were doing. There were plenty of discos, but they were empty; we were told they didn't fill up till about midnight. There were plenty of gays, but they seemed as subdued as the rest of us. Everyone seemed to be waiting for something to happen. Perhaps it did, later, but for the moment we enjoyed just wandering around in the back streets with their white-washed buildings and unexpected twists and turns.

The next afternoon we had one of those incidents that leaves a sour taste in your mouth. First, a German boat came in next to us, and we helped them tie up with no problem. Then a German charter boat came in on the other side of us, offensively, at full speed, driving their bow into one of our lines, bearing heavily on it. I had to ask them to move back a little to get off our line. I tried to be polite, but I was quietly seething. They didn't want to move back because their bow lines weren't long enough, which clearly was not my problem. I had to ask them several times until they finally did, grudgingly. I probably got more pissed than I should have, but you can't let people get away with crap like that: they were intruding into our space as if they had a right to.

Confrontations like that do happen in Med harbors, but given the crowded conditions, probably less often than you'd think. Most people are reasonable and polite, but, as in all aspects of life, there are inevitably people who think that the world revolves around them and that nobody else deserves much if any consideration. One can only give them as wide a berth as possible.

We sailed down to the island of Paros, one of the bigger of the Cyclades, and anchored off the little town of Naoussa in the north. We took a bus into the main town, Paroikia, and bought Jeff's ferry ticket back to Athens, as he was going to leave from there in a few days. Meanwhile we explored the island. Paros was greener than many of the Cyclades and therefore perhaps more attractive. Grapes and grain were under cultivation, and we watched a woman threshing with a donkey. Naoussa was a nice little tourist village with its own tangle of streets and still, apparently, with its own active fishing fleet. I managed to get in the water for a swim for the first time that season. The water was about 70 degrees, not terribly cold, but I'd been reluctant to get in because of my chest problem. That had been much better the last few days, so I gave it a try and had no ill effects. Maybe I really was getting better.

Then, unexpected trouble. We moved a few miles around the corner of the island to the anchorage off Paroikia so that Jeff could easily catch his ferry. But that evening it started to blow.

The bay was well sheltered from most directions except the west, and as the wind was in the southeast we felt quite secure. Soon it was blowing 30 to 35 knots with gusts to 45, which didn't make for a restful night. I knew the anchor was well dug in—I'd looked at it with a mask—but it's tough to relax with that kind of nonsense going on. When morning came, it was still blowing hard. Jeff had to make the ferry at 1330, so we decided he and Liz would go in about 11, just to be sure, while I'd stay on board to keep an eye on things. The wind was up and down, and after a lull from 1030 to 1100, it kicked up again. Finally, in a brief lull about 1130, Liz and Jeff were able to get ashore in the dinghy and pull it up on the beach.

From then on, the wind continued to increase. Soon we were experiencing gusts to 60 knots, and 40 to 50 knots sustained wind. A Dutch boat behind us dragged and went hard aground. Another smaller boat also dragged. A cargo ship dragged out of the harbor. We were holding fine, but I dropped a second anchor as insurance. Things were getting pretty wild. Liz came back to the dinghy about 1330, but the bay was so rough she couldn't launch it, and even if she'd been able to our little outboard wouldn't have been able to cope. So she waited there on the beach.

Meanwhile, we watched Jeff's ferry come in and attempt to dock. These Aegean ferries are large vessels, more like cruise ships than simple car ferries. As the ferry attempted to enter the harbor, he ended up coming in almost sideways as he attempted to compensate for the conditions. I marveled at the sight of this huge vessel proceeding slowly into the harbor entrance, his wall-like sides now functioning as his bow. It was clear though that the captain barely had control of the vessel, and he finally gave up and went back out of the bay. His strategy at that point was probably the right one: just hang around out there where he had maneuvering room until conditions improved.

After a couple of hours of sitting on the beach getting pelted with blowing beach sand, Liz finally got a guy with a powerful outboard to bring her and our dinghy out to the boat. And finally, about 1700, Jeff's ferry managed to make it in to the dock. We were still worried because his flight was the next day from Athens, and the earliest the ferry could get in now was about midnight. What would he do? Would he be able to deal with it? We didn't know, but it was out of our hands. A cell

142

phone would've been a nice convenience to have in that situation for the peace of mind of all concerned, but cell phones were still a decade or so in the future.

Through the evening, the wind slowly moderated. The Dutch boat finally got pulled off but not before breaking at least one tow line. By 2100 the wind was down to mostly 20-25 with a few higher gusts. The only harm we suffered was to get sand blown into the workings of our outboard; I cleaned it out the best I could, but it was never the same after that experience. And we never did find out exactly what Jeff did when he got to Athens in the middle of the night, but somehow he managed to get to the airport and make his flight. We learned the next day by ham radio that he'd arrived safely.

This whole adventure was an example of extremely bad timing...on the part of the weather. Any other day, we could've simply hunkered down and watched the entertainment in the harbor. But the fact that Jeff had to leave that day made it much more complicated and worrying.

With dawn, we decided we'd had enough of Paroikia, and since the forecast was promising a west wind at Force 6-7, to which the harbor would be open, we bailed out and motored back to Naoussa. The expected wind never did materialize. Instead of anchoring off the town, we chose a spot about a mile across the bay well inside the northern cape of the island, off Monastiri Beach. It was a beautifully sheltered anchorage, a lovely spot, and there we remained for more than a week.

We'd had enough of sightseeing for a while and were simply grateful to be able to be lazy in a beautiful and secure setting. Boats came in and out, but the anchorage never got crowded. The little beach was moderately busy at times. We swam and hiked on trails over the peninsula. We met Rudi and Irma, a Dutch couple on a 60-foot Gulfstar. It wasn't their boat although they were living on it: they were the paid crew. The Greek owner visited only on the occasional weekend. They'd sailed the boat across the Atlantic at about the same time we made the crossing. In a way it was a sweet deal as long as you didn't mind being at someone else's beck and call and catering to him when he was on board. I couldn't do it, but I could see the attraction. We spent several convivial evenings with them.

We finally worked up the enthusiasm to leave. We sailed down to Ios, intending to go to Santorini the next day, but a southerly wind discouraged us. The anchorage at Santorini is dicey at best and I was afraid it would be either uncomfortable or unsafe, so reluctantly we gave up on the idea. Were we getting too cautious? Maybe, but we'd had a lot of rough weather in the Med that season, both in port and on passage, and I was wary of exposing us to more. So, like fearful animals, we scurried back to that anchorage in Paros and spent another week there. Liz summed up our feelings in her journal:

> It is not worth any hassle to me to travel around these islands. I want at least to be in a safe, comfortable anchorage when I get there. On the other hand, I don't want to "not have seen" Greece.

Objectively considered, we wasted those pre-meltemi weeks in June by simply sitting at anchor. On the other hand, we needed a break and that worry-free anchorage was the best spot we'd found. The other factor was my chest, which had started to bother me again. It had seemed to get better, and it was still better some days than others, but it remained a worrying problem. I was starting to regret I hadn't seen a doctor in Spain.

When we finally left, it was only to sail up to Mykynos where we anchored on the south side in Ornos Bay again. I don't much like to offer unasked-for advice, but as I watched a charter yacht attempting to anchor and not succeeding, I was sorely tempted. After about 45 minutes of watching them struggle with it, I finally dinghied over and suggested they let out more chain: they were using about 30 feet of chain in 15 feet of water. What do you know? My suggestion worked. They turned out to be Americans, two couples from Florida, and asked us over for drinks. They were nice people, but they hadn't much of a clue about anchoring. They couldn't understand why their plow anchor kept lying over on its side.

I said, "That's what it's supposed to do."

"It is?" they said. They'd been trying to turn the anchor over by hand in the water so that the point of it faced downward.

"Sure. It'll dig in fine that way."

You can't get wise advice like that for any amount of money.

We were intending to sail over to the Dodecanese, near the Turkish coast, and we tried several times to leave, only to encounter unfavorable winds or no wind at all. I didn't relish motoring the 50 miles or so that we had to go, so we came back each time. That wasn't exactly psychologically uplifting, but we finally got away, stopped for the night at an uneasy anchorage on the island of Fourni, then continued on to Samos.

Samos is not actually part of the Dodecanese (literally, "twelve islands"), but it sits at the north end of the chain, with its southeastern tip barely a half mile from the Turkish coast. The Dodecanese trail off to the south, down to the island of Rhodes, none of them very far from Turkey. It makes for an interesting dynamic since there's no love lost between Greeks and Turks. It would be sort of like have a bunch of Russian islands just off the US coast. There are many more than 12 islands, over 150, though many of them are very small. Still, some are good-sized, have been settled since ancient times, and have fascinating histories. There are good anchorages and ports scattered throughout.

Samos, though, is noted as the stomping ground of Pythagoras of triangle theorem fame, and we anchored in the port of—you guessed it—Pythagorean, on the south coast. There was an inner harbor, but we were content to stay out in the bay with the other cruising riff-raff. The bay had a pleasant aspect, overlooked by green hills and red-tiled roofs, reminding us of the Ionian; ashore we found a nice but touristy little town. The major nearby historical site, according to the guidebook, was the Tunnel of Epaulinos, a marvel of 6th century BC engineering, an underground aqueduct more than a kilometer long constructed to bring water down to the town. We checked with the tourist office to make sure it was open before we trekked about a mile uphill to the entrance; it was, they assured us. But when we got up there, we found it closed with a bunch of sour-looking tourists sitting around. That was enough for us, and we retreated.

My main memory of Samos is of the quantities of archeological junk lying around. Wherever you walked, it seemed, there were broken pieces of marble columns, bits of stone, shards of ancient construction, not part of any designated site, just leftover stuff from long ago. It must be strange, in the modern world, to live amongst such tangible reminders of the distant past.

It was the first week of July, and the meltemi arrived right on schedule. We were well-positioned, though, for sailing southward through the chain of islands. Our first stop was at Agathonisi (locally called Gaidaro), where we witnessed an unfortunate example of just how boorish some people can be. The harbor was small, but there was a substantial pier where the ferries docked. Yachts were allowed to tie up to it with the understanding that they might have to move to make room for the ferry. We anchored out. There was a German boat at the pier, and shortly after we arrived six French boats (a charter group) came in and found room there. Then a big (60 feet?) American power boat entered the harbor. He immediately got on his loudspeaker which resounded throughout the harbor and *told* the German boat to move so he could come into the pier. That wasn't a request—it was delivered as an order. He was obviously another one of those people who's convinced the world revolves around him and wants that to be perfectly clear to everyone in the vicinity. The German was not persuaded and stayed where he was. The guy on the power boat then instructed his crew over the loudspeaker to go ashore and "move the German." The German stood firm despite a heated argument. What the power boat guy didn't realize was that a ferry was due in and he'd have to move anyway. After the boats moved off and the ferry came and left, the German moved back to the pier, and the American managed to squeeze in, though not without backing into the German, luckily not very hard. Comfortably situated and full of himself, he then proceeded to play loud music that echoed over the whole harbor until midnight, and to call further attention to his importance he shot off half a dozen flares. Granted, it was the 4th of July, but behavior like that wasn't likely to endear Americans to anyone. However, I'm sure that was the least of his worries. As a fellow American, I was frankly mortified.

When we tried to leave the next morning and actually poked our nose out of the harbor, we decided it was too rough to make for a pleasant day, so we came back in and anchored in a small cove out of sight of the noise and confusion in the harbor. This was a nice spot, but the only part of it that had water shallow enough to anchor was right up in the corner where there was no swinging room. We dropped the anchor in 35 feet and took a line to shore to hold us in position. That was fine except the meltemi was blowing hard, and the gusts off the hills put a heavy strain on the anchor gear. Then Liz had a brilliant idea:

"Why don't we take a line from the *bow* to the shore?"

Our anchorage at Gaidaro

I immediately saw the wisdom of that strategy. If we let off the stern line and took a line to shore off the bow instead at roughly a 45 degree angle to the anchor chain, then the boat could swing to line up with the wind, easing the strain on the gear while limiting the *amount* of the swing so we didn't have to worry about ending up in shallow water or on the rocks. The only possible problem would be a big wind shift which might cause us to swing over the line, but in these meltemi conditions all the gusts were from the northerly quadrant, pretty much negating that concern. In fact, it worked like a charm, and we felt much more secure than moored fore and aft. It was like having two anchors out, except you could be sure at least one of them wasn't going to drag.

But here we were. There was nothing in the bay. The hillsides were open, so it was possible to walk over to the port or up to the Chora, the main village, following ill-defined goat tracks, but it didn't take long to exhaust the amusement in that. This is the place where Liz decided that the Greek islands were 90% rocks and goat shit.

Every morning I'd climb the hill above the anchorage from which I could look out to sea and get some idea what conditions were like out there. The Greek forecast was for north winds Force 7-8, and it looked like it. We certainly could've safely sailed with the wind behind us, but there was no guarantee that, wherever we went, we'd find a sheltered spot to anchor. So we waited...for five days.

Eventually the wind eased a little, or seemed to, and we left. We sailed first to Patmos, about 20 miles away, where we remained for a few days, mostly because the harbor was large and well-sheltered from the meltemi. There was more to do there than in Gaidaros, though nothing much of lasting interest. We walked up to the Chora with its tangle of streets and presiding monastery whose interior was dark and filled with ornate frescos and other artifacts. We went to the cave where St. John supposedly wrote the book of Revelation, but it was so jammed with tour bus groups that we passed it by. I always wondered how seriously to take these claims of local significance anyway. There were a few other cruising yachts in the anchorage, so we spent much of our time in conversation with them.

One encounter was less amiable: Liz heard a noise shortly after we went to bed, looked out, and found a huge power boat, maybe 100 feet long, on top of us...literally. The guy on deck said his anchor had dragged and his anchor winch didn't work. He'd attempted to anchor in a very small area between the sailing yachts and the shore, which was a stupid move in the first place. And it seemed to me that if you could afford a boat like that, you ought to be able to keep your anchor winch functional. We untangled ourselves and he took off looking for other people to trouble.

We sailed down to Leros, where we found a secure anchorage in Partheni Bay at the north end of the island. There wasn't much of anything there, but we could get into town on the bus. The town was strangely quiet too, for high tourist season. I suspected that Leros wasn't on many people's must-see list. We liked the anchorage, even though it wasn't near any sights or sites. It was about this time that we resolved to go only to anchorages that the guide rated highly for protection. We were happier when we weren't rolling our back teeth out or getting our socks blown off in port. The boats that stopped there tended to be more serious cruisers than the usual charter groups anyway, so we at least we had compatible people to chat with.

Liz on Kalymnos: "I'd give anything for a little greenery."

On to Kalymnos after a few days. We were the only boat in the anchorage when we arrived, and only a few came and went during the week we spent there. For much of the time we were there it blew like stink, regularly gusting 40-50 knots and sometimes more. The anchorage was safe, and once the anchor dug in we weren't going anywhere, but the gusts were unnerving: it was a strain to sit on the boat. We did a lot of walking in the hills, long walks, just to get off the boat. But Kalmynos is as bare and rocky as it comes, and we didn't find the landscape particularly appealing. It started to get to Liz. "I'd give anything for just a little greenery," she said. We slept poorly too, the shrieking of the wind a constant backdrop to our uneasy dozing.

Of course the rocky landscape was part of the reason for the gusty conditions. These were true katabatic winds, accelerating down from the bare peaks. In fact, the true wind wasn't as strong as all that. When we finally gritted our teeth and sailed out, sick of sitting there and determined to take whatever punishment we had to at sea, we found conditions nowhere near as bad as we feared. In fact, once we got a few miles out from Kalymnos, we had just a decent sailing breeze. "Why did we sit there so long?" I wondered.

+

We'd decided to head for Turkey, and to check in we'd have to go to Bodrum, about 20 miles away. Theoretically, we should've checked *out* of Greece before checking *in* to Turkey, but checking into either country is a time-consuming procedure; with the Greek islands so close to the Turkish coast, we naturally wanted to have the option of going into either country without hours of bureaucratic nonsense and endless piles of paper. So we kept our Greek transit log and simply showed up in Turkey. Once we had our Turkish transit log, it was only a matter of pulling out the appropriate one for whatever official asked for it. Others had told us of this strategy, and as long as we presented the right log to the right official there should be no problems.

In fact, checking in at Bodrum took a full afternoon. We went to what we thought was Customs first, but they told us we were in the wrong place and, anyway: "You must go to the Passport Police first." The police told us to get the transit log first at the marina. That was on the other side of the bay. We dinghied over there and bought the transit log, then took it back to the boat to fill it out. That done, we went back to the Passport Police to find out where the doctor was, as we needed his signature. We got directions to the Health office, found it, got the signature, then went back to the Passport Police. There, they filled out some forms and directed us to Customs. We couldn't find the Customs office and had to return to the Passport Police to get clearer directions. When we finally found Customs, we were confronted with more forms. After we got those filled out, the Customs officer took us to another office where a girl stamped a visa form in our passports, then told us to go back to Customs. The Customs officer told us we needed the Harbormaster's signature. Where do we find him? The guy gestured vaguely in one direction and said, "Three hundred meters." We looked but couldn't find it. We went to the Health office where we'd got the doctor's signature and asked. He gave us directions. We still couldn't find it. We asked at the Passport Police office, and the guy said it was on the other side of the harbor. I knew *that* couldn't be right. Finally Liz asked at the tourist office…and by happy coincidence the Harbormaster was there! We got his signature, went back to Customs, where the officer signed it again, and to our shock and amazement we were finally done.

One can only hope that they've managed to streamline the procedure a little since then. Even some prominent signs on the various offices would have been a step forward.

All that took place in the heat of the day—and it *was* hot—so we were relieved to retreat to the boat and take stock of our surroundings. The round little bay where we were anchored was quite colorful, with a whole fleet of varnished wood *gulets*, traditional Turkish sailing craft, moored stern-to, loading throngs of tourists. Most had big engines, with the sails being more of an afterthought, probably a good idea when dealing with tourists and the Med. We would see more of these vessels in the anchorages along the coast. Bodrum, we learned, was in fact the ancient city of Halicarnassus, one of the most spectacular cities of the ancient world. It was part of the sprawling Persian empire and was conquered by Alexander the Great in 334BC. Its inhabitants, living in the lap of ancient luxury, were noted for their decadence. We saw none of that however; in its modern incarnation, it had become nothing more than a bustling tourist port.

Next day I ferried water in jugs out to the boat from the tap by the mosque; that took four trips. We visited Bodrum Castle, which overlooks the harbor, and went into the attractive little underwater museum. And we visited with Bill on *Aloha*, his wife Sherry, and their guest Sally, and ended up going out to dinner with them. They were all big talkers, Bill especially, who told us in detail about various disasters he'd suffered and a head injury that had left him at the mercy of Italian doctors for two years. As with many of these big talkers, you never know quite how much of their story line to believe, as these things tend to grow with the telling and retelling.

When we left Bodrum, we sailed down to Knidos on the tip of the Datca peninsula, a pleasant bay with access to the ruins of the ancient city. We anchored, swam, then rowed ashore where a young girl met us and informed us it would cost 2000 Turkish lire apiece to see the ruins. That wasn't a huge sum but we didn't have money with us which meant we'd have to row back to the boat. She offered to let us see the site and bring the money in later, which was quite decent of her, but I couldn't shake my annoyance at the unexpected charge, so I declined.

Shortly after, as we were just starting supper, Liz and I had a stupid fight, essentially over nothing, and somehow we couldn't stop arguing. We never do that. I got very angry and rowed off by myself in the dinghy, found a beach, and sat on it till it got dark and, hopefully, we'd both cooled down. I mention that only to illustrate the kinds of tension that can erupt when you're living at such close quarters for extended periods of time. In fact, we'd been getting along quite well in the last few months, but sometimes things just boil over. I don't know if that was inevitable or not—people are different—but I suspect it's the rare couple than can live in constant harmony on a cruising boat. We both felt a little foolish the next day.

+

Before we got to Turkey, we'd talked to many people who told us how wonderful it was and couldn't find enough good things to say about it. Our reaction was different.

In the first place, the geography of the area made the sailing conditions variable, to say the least. With lots of inlets and bays and peninsulas, and with the numerous Greek islands just a stone's throw from the coast, the wind could come from just about any direction with just about any force. You'd be sailing along with a nice breeze, and a mile or two later you'd be becalmed or have 30 knots on the nose—you never knew which. It was real garbage sailing, with conditions seldom remaining the same for an hour at a time. That didn't bother the charter boats much: they'd just crank up the engine and only unfurl the sails when conditions were right. That's probably what we should've done. Instead, I just sputtered and fumed.

Further, many of the anchorages were attractive, but they were also crowded with gulets and with charter boats. Med-mooring was often required, which could be complicated when you had to squeeze in to a narrow slot between boats and get a line ashore, either to a pier or to a rock or at least something immovable. You had to allow a couple hours for the anchor drill when you got into port, and that quickly got tiresome. There were a few cruising boats here and there, but for the most part we'd be jammed in with a bunch of tourists or charterers with whom we had little in common.

Another part of the problem was that we'd had too much of this island-hopping kind of day-sailing, which had never been what we enjoyed most. It's okay for a week or so, but a steady diet of it is a weird sort of drudgery, especially when there isn't a lot of difference between anchorages. I can see how this kind of cruising could be appealing to charterers, who have only a week or two to cram in all they can, but it had us wondering what we were doing here. It seemed that most of the things we enjoyed about sailing were missing.

And once again, we often felt isolated. We did meet a fair number of cruising boats, but many of them had been in the Med for years and seemed content with pointless meandering, while those that might've been more compatible always seemed to be headed in different directions; we'd chat for an afternoon, tell our stories, perhaps trade books or have a drink or a meal together, and then we'd go our separate ways, never to see them again. It wasn't the most meaningful way to live.

So we played around in the area between Bodrum and Marmaris for a couple of weeks, with several forays over to the Greek island of Simi, which sits nestled under the Datca peninsula, geographically much more Turkish than Greek. When we finally went in to Marmaris, we found the anchorage area described in the cruising guide had been monopolized by the marina. The only room was outside the moored boats in 60 feet of water, a rolly and exposed position. We tried it but soon picked up the anchor and moved over to the western shore to a spot better sheltered from the wind direction opposite a bunch of hotels. The bottom was thick grass but we finally got the anchor to hold by letting out most of our chain.

That wasn't much of an improvement: it was a really zooey spot: windsurfers, outboards, water skiers, jet skis constantly harassed us—hardly the sort of environment you're most likely to picture when contemplating cruising the Turkish coast. We went ashore in the afternoon. The ticky-tacky resort area left us with not much desire to explore. In the evening and well into the night the discos blared loud music. I hoped the tourists were having fun because I sure wasn't. I wrote in my journal: "Really soured on Turkey."

It's possible we didn't give Turkey a fair chance. We'd plunged into the heart of the resort area at the height of the season: what did we expect? Further north and further south perhaps we'd have found things more to our liking. I'd wanted to visit the site of Troy on the northwest corner of Turkey—that was on my must-see list for the Med. Southern Turkey opposite Cyprus was reputed to be good cruising ground. The marina at Fethiye, about 30 miles to the east, was a prime wintering location for cruising boats. But by then, by the time we'd got to Marmaris, all that was only of hypothetical interest. We'd already decided to go in a different direction.

10. A Change of Plans

I'd been talking on the ham radio with Al from *Sunflower*. They were in northern Turkey, planning to go down the Red Sea in the fall and out to southeast Asia that way. He suggested we come along them. "It's the best cruising in the world out there," he said.

I'll admit I was tempted. It was the sort of ambitious plan that always had some appeal for me. But when I thought about it rationally, I knew it didn't make sense for us. With Jeff and our aging parents back home, a trip like that would just put us too far away. Plus there were other considerations.

I'd broached the subject with Liz when we were in Paros, right after Jeff had left. I said, "I don't think I want to spend another winter in the Med."

"What? Why?" It totally took Liz off-guard. After all, she was the one who'd expressed dissatisfaction back in the winter. Shifting dynamics.

She wrote later in her journal:

Bruce and I talked about summer plans. He wants to keep open the possibility of going back across the Atlantic this winter. This panics me for two reasons: too much sailing and having to face what we're going to do next. I can see that he has been bothered by worries about the winter and by my negative reaction to his passing mentions of going back. I've been enjoying this life more and he's been enjoying it less lately I think. We agreed to keep the subject open and discuss it later in the summer.

I tried to explain. "There's too much down time," I said. "Vilanova was great, but I'm not sure I want to spend another four or five months just sitting. It was fine to do it once. I'm glad we did it, but I have trouble convincing myself I want to do it again."

Liz nodded. "I can see that."

Our plan had always been to spend a winter in the eastern Med, spend the next summer there, perhaps venturing up to the Adriatic, and decide then what we'd do next. Now, in Paros, even though it was barely summer, we'd already been wondering where we'd spend the winter. The cruising grapevine had given us possibilities to investigate in Turkey, Greece, and Cyprus, but I couldn't quite picture us in any of those places.

"I'm worried about my health too," I said."Whatever this thing I've got is, it's still hanging on. I'm definitely better, but I'm not completely well. Maybe this isn't the best time to be wandering around without access to consistent medical care."

"You could go to a doctor."

"I could. Maybe I should've done that in Spain. But now we'd probably be dealing with a language barrier and a lot of uncertainty. I am getting better—I'm just thinking more long term."

"I don't know how I feel about it," Liz said.

"The other thing is, this isn't really our kind of sailing."

"I know. It seems like it's always a struggle to get anywhere."

"The way to cruise the Med," I said, "is with a big engine. And probably the best way would be to fly home for the winter like Al and Beth do, get away from it all for a while, and come back with a new attitude in the spring."

"But we're not set up to do that."

"No, we're not."

In truth, even at that early stage, the Med had started to grind us down. The first summer it was all new to us, we were getting used to the fluky wind conditions and the various anchoring or mooring hassles. We'd coped pretty well initially. But now it was all beginning to seem like too much trouble. There were things of interest to see, but they weren't always within easy reach of a good anchorage. If we spent another year in the Med, I wasn't at all sure it was going to enrich our lives.

By the time we'd reached Marmaris, it had become clear to both of us. We'd sporadically enjoyed some things about Med cruising, but the past couple of months in the Aegean had only confirmed what we'd started to feel: that neither of us found much satisfaction in the experience as a whole. It was time for us to bail out. Rather than spending another winter in the Med, we'd head back across the Med and then cross the Atlantic to the Caribbean in the late fall. It would mean a lot of sailing, but it seemed the preferable option.

So we'd bypass Rhodes with its crowded, difficult harbor (we'd been thoroughly briefed on that and decided it wasn't worth it), and head down to Crete, the first leg of our journey back.

We went out to Simi again, and then sailed down to Alimnia, a little uninhabited island off the western coast of Rhodes. It was a nice well-sheltered spot in a wide bay, only a little rolly from the swell hooking around the point. We went ashore and looked at the drawings made by German soldiers in World War II in the old buildings there. In the morning we got ready to leave for the overnight trip to Crete. We deflated the dinghy, cranked in most of the chain, Liz went to start the engine and: nothing! *It wouldn't start!* The starter turned it over easily, but it made no effort to catch. I bled it, made sure the fuel pump was working, tried everything I could think of, couldn't get it to go.

What to do? There were no facilities at all on the island, nobody to consult with. There weren't even any other boats in the anchorage. I finally decided, in my wisdom, that it must be clogged injectors. I took them out and cleaned them. A deceptively simple statement because it took *hours* and much vile language to get them out. Cleaning them was a fussy job too. They were a little dirty, but when I put them back in the engine still wouldn't start. By then it was three in the afternoon, and I was getting frantic. We started to talk about sailing direct to Malta. We knew we could enter the harbor there under sail, and we also knew we could get help with the engine there.

And then, by some kind of fortuitous inspiration, I checked the stop control, the thing you pull to kill the engine. And found that *the stop cable had broken!* That broken cable was holding the stop control lever in the half-open position, which was preventing the engine from starting. Once I moved the little lever back, the engine started right up.

I felt tremendously relieved but also a little foolish. The obvious lesson was to always check *all* the simple things first. My method in this case was roughly equivalent to attempting to fix a car that won't start by rebuilding the engine before checking to see if it's run out of gas. At least the minor side benefit was that I now had squeaky clean injectors.

We left early the next morning for the 115 mile trip to Crete. It was a typical Med passage with shifting and variable winds, a lot of motoring, and no sleep, but by noon the next day, bleary-eyed, we were anchored in Spinalonga Lagoon near the east end of Crete.

+

Ironically, after making the decision to leave the Med, we found Crete to be quite delightful. True, we had to beat our way along the north coast of the island against the meltemi which had a northwest slant to it, but that was only a moderate bother; at least it wasn't blowing gale force.

We spent three days in Spinalonga, a quiet and restful place, with only one other boat anchored well away from us: it was a relief to get away from the charter boats. We bought a guidebook to Crete and took a bus to visit the Minoan ruins at Gournia. Only marginally interesting, as ruins go, but it did give some substance to the whole Minoan thing.

When we left, we bashed our way to Khersonisos where we were treated to a rolly and uncomfortable anchorage, then slammed on to Iraklion, the capital city. The inner harbor there was jammed with boats, but we'd noted a couple of boats tied to the outer breakwater, so we opted for that. It was a difficult tie-up because the bollards were far apart, positioned for large ships, and the wall was high, but once we were situated it worked out fine and nobody bothered us there.

A whirlwind tour of the archaeological museum in Iraklion proved to be more interesting than I'd expected. Everything was well-arranged and in order so you could follow along with the guidebook. The pottery was beautiful, more appealing than that from Mycenae or the later Greek stuff. We enjoyed it much more than the Athens museum, and it provided a context for our visit to Knossos the next day.

Knossos is the huge Minoan site that was excavated and partially restored by Sir Arthur Evans in the early years of the 20th century. The earliest habitation of the area dates from around 7000 BC, while the first palace complex dates from about 1900 BC, roughly equivalent to Mycenae. At its peak around 1700 BC, some 100,000 people were living in and around the palace complex, so it was a pretty big deal in its heyday. The restoration work has always been a bit controversial—how much restoration is too much?—but there's no question that it does allow you to better visualize what it might've looked like.

We got there when it opened at 0800 and were disappointed to find several tour bus groups already entering. I have no problem with tourists who genuinely want to see stuff, but too often these groups consist of bored people being paraded through, talking and not listening to the guide, probably wondering when they can get out of there and do some shopping or go to a decent restaurant, and generally clogging up the area and diminishing the experience for the rest of us. But there they are, and you have to put up with it. Still, following our usual procedure of reading the guidebook as we went along, we managed to enjoy it. Whether the restoration is strictly accurate or not, the colors and the sense of space in the buildings, particularly in the staircase and throne room area, gave a possible interpretation—Arthur Evans' interpretation, of course—of the findings there. And once again, my mind struggled to understand the time scale involved: people were living here, doing their thing in a relatively civilized manner, 4000 years ago.

The partially restored "throne room" at Knossos

Leaving Iraklion, we continued to bash along the north coast where the scenery looked as if it might've been beautiful except that it was so hazy we couldn't see much of it. After stopping a couple of days at Rethimnon, we plunged on to Souda Bay. I had vague memories of entering there on the destroyer back in the 60s, but they were only that: vague. It's not the usual place to stop for yachts—it's basically a commercial port; most yachts opt for Chania, which is just a few miles around the corner. But we were ready to stop and we suspected Chania would be crowded, so there we were.

We got ourselves tied up at the pier and were told to check in with the officials. I presented our transit log to the Port Captain, and he asked for our passports. That was fine, except that we had a Turkish stamp in there and no indication that we'd ever left Turkey. Anyone who was determined enough could figure out that that Turkish stamp shouldn't be there if we still had the Greek transit log. I sat across the desk from the Port Captain and sweated while he looked at the transit log, then turned to the passport and took his own sweet time, examining it, turning the pages, looking at each visa stamp, as if (I imagined) he took particular pleasure in torturing me. I had plenty of time to picture all kinds of distressing scenarios when our criminal behavior was rudely exposed. Finally, he closed the passport, handed it back to me, smiled, and told me to enjoy our stay. If he suspected anything, he never let on.

We ended up staying there for a week. Only one other yacht came in for a day during that time. Once we had to move back along the pier when a big grain ship came in, but otherwise it was quite convenient. Buses ran frequently into Chania, and as we expected the harbor there was chock full and didn't look very comfortable—the moored boats were bobbing around restlessly while we were sitting in perfect calm in Souda.

Our big excursion from there was to the Samaria Gorge, the premier tourist destination in this part of Crete. We caught an early bus into Chania and from there the bus to the start of the hike through the gorge. It's all nicely set up: the bus takes you up the northern side of the mountain ridge to a height of 4100 feet, and from there you hike roughly 10 miles down through the spectacular gorge to the southern coast where a boat takes you along the coast to a place where you catch a bus back to Chania. Of course we weren't exactly alone doing it. The bus to the gorge was loaded with hikers, but the ride up took us through fantastic scenery: mountain vistas, pine forests, more greenery than we'd seen all summer.

From the height of land, the first part was a fairly steep descent on a winding switchback trail, mostly in the woods through which we caught glimpses of cliffs and ridges. There were lots of people on the trail, but for the first part they were well spread out so that a lot of the time we were walking alone.

Unfortunately, after the first hour, Liz got serious blisters on both feet, which didn't portend well for the rest of the hike. She was in pain, but she toughed it out; there wasn't much else she could do unless she wanted to summon a rescue service somehow, and things were hardly that serious. Besides, the scenery was welcome compensation.

At the bottom of the descent, the trail wound back and forth across a flowing stream. We ate our picnic lunch just past the old deserted village of Samaria, then started into the gorge proper. There, the flow of people was more continuous, and we were more or less hiking in a line. This part of the hike was certainly spectacular, leading between sheer cliffs that rose 1000 feet on either side of us separated at one point by only 10 feet, but it was slightly less enjoyable because of the crowds: you had to hike at the pace of the people in front of you and you could barely stop to look or take a picture because of the people behind you. Most of the hikers were probably in their 20s or 30s, but I was surprised to see a fair number of very young kids and a smattering of senior citizens; it is all downhill, but the path is rocky and 10 miles isn't a trivial distance.

We made it to the little hamlet of Agia Roumeli just in time to catch the 1415 boat, and Liz could finally stop aggravating her blisters. The boat was hot and crowded, filled with people babbling in various European languages—not much English. It's about a 10-mile sea trip to the town of Sfakion where the buses meet the boats. When we got there, we could've jumped right on a bus, but we chose to swim at the beach first and get the next bus back. That was a good move: the water felt delicious after the hot hike.

I don't know how typical our bus ride was, but it had me clinging to the seat in sheer terror. The bus had to go up the central ridge and down the other side, just as our bus in the morning had done. Somehow this driver didn't inspire confidence though. I wasn't the only one who was scared: some of the other passengers were looking around nervously too. Rounding some of the steep switchbacks at a faster-than-wise speed, it felt like the downhill wheels were hanging off the edge and it would take only another inch or two of steering error to send us plummeting down the cliff face. To my amazement and relief, that didn't happen, and the bus even stopped in Souda, which saved us from catching another bus in Chania.

The Samaria Gorge

+

It was time to leave Crete, but we both felt it was a place we could happily come back to, even as tourists: it has mountains, beaches, historical interest, great scenery, friendly people, and we'd only scratched the surface. But for now we had some sailing to do.

Three peninsulas hang off the bottom of the Peloponnesus, as you can see by looking at any map of Greece; we were headed for a little island off the most westward of those peninsulas, primarily because it offered a good anchorage with, we hoped, a minimum of fuss. The only problem was that as soon as we left the harbor, we confronted fluky headwinds and a choppy sea. The winds were never particularly strong, but they were up and down and shifty so that tacking was always a gamble—would the wind shift just after we did so?—which made for frustrating sailing. So although we had only about 150 miles to go, we ended up sailing almost 300 miles and it took us just short of three days. After we arrived, I wrote in my journal:

> *After three days of beating against headwinds, we ended up in a tranquil anchorage. And then the killer bees attacked!*

Literally. We had to close up with screens because of the plague of bees. They weren't much of a problem when we were outside, but they persisted in coming into the cabin if given the opportunity. But the anchorage was nice and calm, and we were the only boat there, which was a good thing because swinging room was limited. It was a lonely spot, with only the lighthouse looming over our heads for company. That, and the bees. We ended up sitting there for three days, waiting for a reasonable wind for the next leg to Italy.

Finally, with the Italian forecast promising winds not *directly* in our face and a favorable shift to come, we left. We were headed, ultimately, for the Straits of Messina between Italy and Sicily, but we planned to stop at a harbor on the toe of the Italian boot, Capo Dell'Armi. We'd heard that this was an artificial harbor, well-sheltered by breakwaters, constructed for some purpose that had never yet materialized, just sitting there now and free for the use of passing yachts. The distance was a little over 300 miles, and once again the wind was far from consistent but at least it wasn't consistently ahead of us. We motored a fair bit though, and were treated to a morning of rain and thunderstorms—it actually hailed a little—on the second day. It was only early September but it seemed that the summer weather patterns were already breaking down.

We had some difficulty locating the harbor—it was far from obvious; we went right past it before we realized it and had to turn around and come back. A few other yachts were in there but there was plenty of room with Med-mooring the order of the day. We dropped our anchor, backed into the wall, and before we had our lines straightened out the officials showed up. I didn't even have time to stew about our lack of insurance or any Italian documentation, but thankfully they just took down our names and that was it. You never know.

I tried to get some sleep (I'd been up all night) but got woken up by a French boat coming in next to us, so I got up and went out to meet the rest of the people here. David and Betty were Australians who'd come up the Red Sea the previous year and were going to Tunisia for the winter. Joachim and Ullie on a German ketch were going to Malta and Tunisia; they'd wintered one year in Souda Bay. George and Gerta had come up the Red Sea this year and were going to cross the Atlantic at the same time as we were. The French couple had a kid on board and another on the way. It was decidedly strange to find this big collection of real cruising boats there in this nothing little harbor. We all walked up the road together to a little fruit stand, the first exercise I'd had in a week.

But the next morning everyone but us left and we were alone there for the next night. Then it was off to tackle the Straits of Messina. Purported to be the Scylla and Charybdis of Greek legend, the straits don't pose anything like that kind of difficulty for modern vessels—you're not likely to get eaten by a monster or sucked into a maelstrom—although tidal currents can be strong there. I remember passing through at night with a carrier group when I was an OOD on a destroyer in the 60s. A bunch of destroyers were spread out in a circular formation around a carrier; I had the watch and as we headed for the narrow strait it was clear by looking at the situation on radar that we couldn't fit through the strait in that formation. But the admiral on the carrier was in charge, and we couldn't do anything until he told us to. He, or his staff, let us sweat until the very last minute, it seemed, and I was on the verge of telling the captain that we had to take independent action, before the signal came over the radio to reorient the formation into a double column of ships. That was a pretty dicey maneuver in a confined space at night, but somehow we pulled it off, and the column passed through without incident.

But now we found a nice flat sea in the straits and made good progress until we hit the narrowest part, where the current turned against us: we motored five miles to make good the last two miles, and we were continually set to the left, but we emerged unscathed. It started to rain. I didn't know what to do. We had no wind. The closest harbor was at Milazzo, about 20 miles down the northern Sicilian coast, so we headed for that. When we got there about 1900, we found that the possible anchorage we'd been told about was ridiculously deep: over 20 fathoms very close to shore. No thanks. We headed out, resigned to staying at sea, and luckily a wind came up.

But the weather situation was a mess. A few comments from my journal, starting with the next day, give a rough idea what we were dealing with:

Wed Sep 6. A wicked swell from the N developed in the late afternoon, making things quite uncomfortable. We're charging along even though there are supposedly strong winds ahead. Monaco says F8. The Italians say F6. More worrying are the thunderstorms supposedly between Sardinia and the Balearics. We may not get that far, although the E wind is supposed to continue till Sat or Sun, according to Monaco.

Thu Sep 7. Another gale! ...We changed to the trysail after supper, which has been giving us 5-6 knots in very rough seas. We reefed the weather cloths and took the side panels out of the dodger [lessons learned on the trip to Malta]. *We haven't taken any serious water yet but it only takes one. Still totally cloudy. Night very dark. We're getting under Sardinia now. I don't know whether to stop or keep going toward Majorca. It's a shame to waste a fair wind, but these conditions are really shitty. Porto Colom* [on Majorca] *is a bit open to the SE. Hard to know where to go. I wish I knew what the weather was going to do. According to the Italians, this is SE 4 increasing to SE 5. Monaco says E 7-8. We've had a healthy F7 since dark, 30 knots on the anemometer, frequently gusting to 40.*

Fri Sep 8. Last night was terrible. Seas remained awful. Morning was grey, damp, rainy. Visibility real bad. The Monaco forecast for the first time promised a westerly wind shift some time today. The Italians were still saying SE 5. Big sail drill about 1300 when the wind increased to a steady 35-40 knots (F8).

It was obvious to us that Monaco had a better handle on the weather for our area than the Italians did. The hardest part of this kind of sailing is often the decision-making. You sift through the various bits of forecast information available, factor in the conditions you're currently experiencing, make your best guess of what's likely to happen, realizing all the while that it's only a guess, and try to come up with a safe and sensible strategy. Should we try to press on to Majorca, or perhaps Menorca? Should we go in to Carloforte? Cagliari on the south coast of Sardinia had also been an option, though we were well past that now. We were ready to stop, and Carloforte seemed like a worthy goal, especially if Monaco was right about the shift to the west, which would be a headwind for us. But I was afraid we wouldn't make it before dark, and I wasn't anxious to be messing around in that area in the dark in these uncertain conditions. I stood in the cockpit, unsure what to do, waiting for inspiration...or a sign.

I soon saw that we'd begun to pick up some current—I could tell by the way we were zipping past the land, the south coast of Sardinia—so I decided to go for Carloforte, which at least was familiar to us from the spring. As we turned north along the island of Sant'Antioco, the wind shifted to the west, as Monaco had predicted, and booted us along. Score one for Monaco. With the help of the current and the westerly wind, we made it into the anchorage at 1830, another chaotic Med passage completed. I was very glad we hadn't tried to tough it out: running into headwinds after the nonsense we'd been through wouldn't have been my idea of a good time.

After a restful day in Carloforte, and once again no problem with the officials even though we did go ashore to buy a few things, we were off for Majorca. And of course the weather messed with us again. A little sailing, a little motoring the first day, then contrary to all predictions the wind picked up from the east, and as soon as it got dark we could see lightning to the north. The storms got closer as the night went on, and we were treated to some spectacular streaks of lightning, but unsettling as that was we sailed right on without being touched. In the morning the wind increased and shifted to the west, heading us, blowing straight from Majorca: I wasn't even surprised anymore. But after only an hour or so, the wind freed again so that we could steer our course. I wrote in my journal:

> *I was really depressed at the thought of having to spend a third night at sea, but the wind shift made everything look a lot better; we may make Majorca tomorrow after all. I wish I wouldn't get so upset. Some of it is due to lack of sleep, I guess. Also the cumulative effect of this Med sailing. We have not enjoyed one night at sea in the Med— it's always such a hassle.*

In *The Odyssey* Homer describes how the ships would get within a mile or two of their destination, whereupon a great gale would come up and sweep them away with no chance of getting back anytime soon. That sounds like poetic hyperbole when you're reading it in the comfort of your home, but it made a lot more sense to me now. I could see how it could happen in the Med, even to us. And those ancient people lacked the benefit on engines. Obviously the weather enjoyed messing with them just as much as it does with us.

However, we did make it into Porto Colom the next evening, so things weren't all bad. We found *Kalona* there, our friends from Central America. I'd been talking with them on the radio occasionally, so I knew they were moving at a more laid-back pace than we were, which was probably not a bad strategy. There were changes in the harbor though: the officials were now charging for anchoring though it'd been free when we'd been there a year ago. It wasn't a lot but it was a hint of things to come and I didn't like the trend. It's one thing to charge for tying up to a pier, quite another to charge for allowing you to drop your own anchor.

We stayed in Porto Colom for a week, getting some much needed rest. I managed to do some running—my chest was definitely better. Then we set off for Gibraltar. First to Cabrera, where we'd spent a week the previous summer, then on in changeable conditions (in the Med?...surely not!) to Espalmador south of Ibiza where we snuck into the anchorage after midnight. Another overnight to the Spanish mainland and after a couple of unmemorable anchorages we rounded Cabo da Gata and made for Almería. But one look at the harbor there convinced us it was no place we wanted to be: there was a mean-looking surge in there, and it was clear if we stayed the best we could hope for would be a very restless night. It was late, but we decided to press on to Almerimar, the marina about 20 miles away that we'd been to the previous year. It was late, but we decided to press on to Almerimar, the marina about 20 miles away that we'd been to the previous year. We got there after dark and anchored outside behind the breakwater; the next morning we went into the marina for another very welcome rest day: this kind of continuous day sailing, always trying to make a good chunk of mileage in whatever conditions you've got, can be grueling.

Then on to Motril; no wind but the forecast suggested a westerly was coming and I wanted to get as far along as we could before that happened so we motored shamelessly. When we went ashore the next day, we were accosted by the officials who asked to see our papers. I went back to the boat to get them and brought them in to their office where we filled out the inevitable forms. There was no charge but, curiously, they stamped our passports, the first time that had happened in Spain...just before we left for good. Once again, the motivation and mind-set of the officials was a mystery to me. One more overnight, mostly motoring, brought us to Gibraltar, and by early morning we were happily ensconced at Marina Bay.

+

It had been a slog. I keep careful records of passage times and engine hours, and totaling it up afterwards I calculated that we'd motored 20% of the time from Spain to Greece in the spring and 30% of the time from Crete to Gibraltar coming back in the fall. (Of course most of the trip in the spring was made in winds of 30 knots or better.) It seemed like a lot of motoring to us, but it was probably considerably less than most boats manage. We worked at it though. My account here only hints at the amount of sail handling we did. With conditions so variable, it was the rare day that we could put up one sail configuration and leave it for more than a few hours. Four or five sail changes in a day wasn't unusual, and sometimes it was more. No wonder we got a little burned out.

As we'd got closer to Gibraltar, we'd started meeting boats who'd just recently entered the Med. When they asked us how we liked it, it was hard to respond constructively without squelching their enthusiasm. We had to keep in mind that there were some fine things about the Med: the historical interest of course, the array of different cultures, some incredibly beautiful anchorages, often the ability to step ashore in an attractive city or town. But you had to be satisfied with a kind of tourist's mentality, and although we could enjoy things on that level for a while, it began to pall as time went on. In the end though, it was the weather and the sailing conditions that ground us down. The effect was cumulative. For a few months it was okay, we could deal with it, but gradually it began to seem like more trouble than it was worth. We weren't alone. While some people cruised happily in the Med for years, others found it hard to put up with. Personalities differ of course, and your attitude can be governed by your expectations and your tolerance for the sort of hassles that the Med provides. Those who were most content were often those who hadn't sailed anywhere else. Maybe if we'd had a big motorsailer, the kind of vessel the Med is noted for, and could power through most conditions without worrying about sailing, maybe then we could've kept our enthusiasm up. Maybe. And it certainly would've helped to be able to get away for a few months in the winter when sailing conditions were at their most questionable. But for now we were mightily glad to be in Gibraltar, contemplating the passage back.

11. In the Wake of Columbus

First we had to haul out. I wanted a clean bottom for the passage and for the Caribbean, and I had some paint bubbling along the waterline again, thanks to the Awl-Grip. So we hauled out at Shepherd's, stayed out for three days and did our work at a flat-out pace. We found *Rainbow Runner* at Shepherd's, last seen in Menorca a year ago: they too had gotten fed up with the Med and were heading for Madeira in a couple days.

We stayed in Gibraltar for 10 days, preparing for the passage. We loaded the boat with fuel and water and provisions. We did our grocery shopping in La Línea, the Spanish town just across the border. The Spanish grocery stores had the virtue of selling cheap table wine in little one liter boxes which stacked nicely in our lockers, maximizing the space. We knew that wine was expensive in the Caribbean, so we took full advantage of that convenience.

When we were fully stocked and ready to go, the next problem was to find the right weather for passing through the Strait of Gibraltar and on to the Canaries. The wind was easterly in the Strait but it was less clear what we could expect en route to the Canaries; it didn't seem like anything serious was in the offing though, so we decided to go for it.

We left on October 12 (Columbus Day!), put two reefs in the main, and headed out. The wind was moderate at first, gradually increasing to Force 8, as predicted, with some higher gusts. But it was behind us and the seas were never bad except for a few tide rips. We did the whole thing with just the double-reefed main, speeding past Tarifa on the Spanish side and passing Cape Spartel on the Moroccan side almost before we knew it.

Once we were well clear of the strait and we started to feel the long Atlantic swells, I felt a huge sense of relief. This was the open ocean. We were free of the Mediterranean, its capricious weather, its short nasty seas, the constant hour-to-hour anxiety about what would happen next. The Atlantic *felt* different. It felt familiar, almost welcoming. Sure, nasty things could happen out here and the weather could certainly provide unpleasant surprises, but I had the sense that out here we could cope with just about anything that came along. I felt that a huge weight had been lifted off my shoulders.

The easterly wind persisted until we were about 25 miles from the mouth of the strait, at which point it started to ease off and by early evening it was gone and we were sitting, rolling in the swell, with all sails down. What the hell: it was fun while it lasted.

But the next few days were a disheartening mess of calms, squalls, rain, thunderstorms, headwinds, and general unpleasantness. We motored some, but I could never bring myself to say the hell with it and leave the engine on. If the swell wasn't too bad, we just sat. One day we had a day's run of 37 miles, two days later we did 51 miles, followed the next day by 40 miles, not the kind of progress to lift one's spirits. But we finally got some decent wind and had a run of 150 miles, thereby exceeding in one day the mileage of those three slow days by 22 miles, which was a little more like it. A huge school of dolphins visited us as we were creaming along, probably a hundred or more of them, and stayed with us for over an hour. We appreciated the company. When at last we slid into Las Palmas on Gran Canaria, it had taken us eight days to cover the 737 miles, and we'd motored 18% of the time. That was certainly no passage to write home about or to sell anyone on the joys of ocean sailing.

+

The harbor at Las Palmas was no beauty either; in fact it was the dirtiest harbor I've ever had the misfortune to end up in. It was nice enough on *land*, quite pleasant in fact, but the yacht anchorage was tucked away in the corner of the commercial harbor, supposedly protected from whatever leaked or seeped into the water from commercial vessels by a floating oil boom. But the oil boom had sunk allowing free access of all petroleum products. Consequently, the whole anchorage was coated with a thick, shimmering sheen of oil. A swell found its way into the harbor too, which wasn't too bad in itself most of the time, but as the anchored yachts rolled, the oil crept up their topsides and stuck there like some slimy monster from the deep. Any boat that'd been there more than a couple days inevitably displayed a wide black swath on its topside paint or gelcoat. It wasn't easily removed either: I went at it once while we were still there, but of course it came right back, and it took a concerted effort to get it off once we got to the Caribbean. There were elements of high absurdity too: I remember watching some locals windsurfing in the harbor; their colorful sails, which dropped in the water from time to time, had turned a glossy black. We almost left when we saw what the situation was, but the harbor had other virtues and we ended up staying more than two weeks.

Las Palmas has been the traditional staging point for the Atlantic crossing for years—even Columbus passed through the Canaries on each of his four voyages—and every fall hundreds of boats gather there making last-minute preparations. We were well away from the charter boats and vacationers now: these were all serious ocean sailors, some of whom we'd seen before, so we had a lot in common. Some were experienced with many ocean passages to their credit; others were new to the game. We traded books, compared plans and strategies, discussed the weather, told the usual cruising stories.

Keith and Tina on *Gooseberry* were commercial artists from Canada who became good friends of ours. They were on their second Atlantic circuit. Keith was stocky, garrulous, with a sort of boyish innocence about him, while blonde-haired Tina, who still carried vestiges of a British accent (she'd emigrated to Canada as a child), could be wildly funny; she showed us samples of her work, including a Canadian ad campaign for...*bull semen!* Enough said. They were planning to go up the Gambia River in Africa, but we'd see more of them in the Caribbean.

Phil and Doris came in in *Jolly II Roger*. We'd seen them last in Fiji in 1978. They'd spent some years in Singapore working—Phil built swimming pools—then two years in Zanzibar, and up the Red Sea a couple years ago. The previous year they left their boat in France, rented a mobile home, and toured Europe. That's one way to do it.

Don Street, the Caribbean cruising guru from the 70s, came in in his engineless *Iolaire* and anchored outside most of the boats. We'd met him briefly in Grenada in 1977, so I dinghied out to say hello. He was going to Tenerife, the Cape Verdes, and then Antigua.

We talked to Jim and Pat on *Anna B*, a wooden schooner. They'd spent a year in the Azores, during which time they bought and fixed up an old stone house. I envied them: one could do worse than own a house in the Azores.

Two Dutch couples came in, both on steel boats: Karel

and Cris on *Briney Maid* and Theo and Jeanine on *Bricket*. Theo came over to ask about US charts, and we gave him some to photocopy. (Photocopying charts was a frequent activity on the world-cruising circuit in those pre-GPS days.) One evening we got together with them on *Briney Maid* and talked into the wee hours of the morning. Karel was very serious, almost studious, and had read a lot about sailing; Cris, who was actually Belgian, was a little shy about her English skills (which seemed perfectly fine to us). Theo was black-haired, athletic-looking, and spoke the best English; Jeanine was a short-haired blonde, very articulate and thoughtful. Theo and Jeanine were more interested in traveling than sailing and intended to leave the boat in Venezuela and travel in South America.

Americans Dawn and Dave on *Blackberry* came over one afternoon. We'd seen them briefly in Malta. They'd been out for eight years cruising northern Europe and taking the boat down the Danube to the Black Sea after which they spent two years in Turkey. Dave was now recovering from heart surgery but they still planned to do the crossing.

These and many more were part of the group in Las Palmas, all of them braving the oily water, all of them with different goals and different backstories, and for the most part it was a reasonable place to pull oneself and the boat together for the long passage coming up. Keith had the unfortunate luck to have his dinghy stolen though: someone cut the line and made off with it. He did get it back, minus the outboard (a Seagull, like ours), a more serious outcome than our incident in Isla Mujeres. He was convinced it was someone in the anchorage rather than a local.

I managed to do some jogging on the promenade that ran along the harbor. We went to the beach, which was well away from the oil, thank goodness. We topped up on water and made numerous trips to the grocery store to be sure we had the boat as crammed as full as we possibly could. And then we waited for the weather. Keith and Tina left heading for the Gambia River on the African coast but came back because the wind was too much in their face. Some people said it was too soon to go—it was early November—for the conventional wisdom suggested that the trade winds would be better established and the threat of hurricanes less in another few weeks. But I figured the hurricane threat was minimal: there were no indications of any disturbances moving off the African coast, and it was late in the year for those kinds of systems anyway. Most hurricanes that form in November do so in the Caribbean or the Gulf of Mexico, and we wouldn't get there till almost December when the threat was even less. And as for the trade winds, well, that was sort of a lottery anyway—no telling what they'd be up to—so we resolved to go as soon as conditions looked reasonable locally.

+

And on November 5 we left. We didn't know it then, and it didn't appear so in the first few days, but this was to be our best passage ever. The Canaries sit outside the tropics at roughly Latitude 28N, about the same latitude as central Florida, so the idea is to get south well into the tropics where the trade winds should be more consistent. We had a decent breeze as we sailed down the east side of Gran Canaria and turned to the southwest, but thereafter things got decidedly less settled: the wind was up and down and shifty, it was rainy and squally at times, we even had headwinds for a while, and I was unhappily contemplating three or four weeks of garbage sailing. Progress remained adequate though, even if we had to listen to the sails banging when the wind got light. And because of the banging, with the sails slamming around as they spilled the wind and then filled with some force, we put a five-foot tear in the bottom of our genoa. We repaired it with stick-on sail cloth, but we didn't fully trust it after that. Still, even in those conditions we managed to average 120 miles a day for the first six days, and after that as the trades really kicked in, things only got steadily better.

A few comments from my journal:

Day 7: Just nice consistent sailing continues. Hard to believe it can be this nice. Steady wind, clear skies, zinging along at 5-7 knots. Reasonably rested.

Day 8: Good sailing all day---beautiful sunshine. Electricity is a problem. We haven't been running the refrigerator the last few days. We've had no need to motor so we aren't charging that way.

Day 11: Really nice day: clear with lots of wind. F6-7, just about E. Zinging. Did 150 miles last 24. Not much happened today (the way it should be!). Didn't make a sail change or touch a sheet all day.

Day 12: *Another good day, pretty much a rerun of yesterday with another 150+ miles.*

Day 13: *Day follows day without much change. The wind is still ENE, F6.*

Day 14: *Everything continues pretty much as before. Run of 168 miles today—best so far.*

Day 16: *Our routine goes on day by day without much change—we haven't even had to change a sail in days. Wind did get a little lighter last night—mostly F5 now instead of F6, so I'm thinking of unreefing but haven't done it yet. Lots of flying fish on deck every morning—the deck is littered with fish scales. Other than that, not much life. A few petrels, A bosun bird yesterday. A few gull-types. No dolphins. Nothing else.*

Eating up the miles

This was the kind of sailing where you basically work through a simple routine that doesn't vary much day after day, and the miles add up. With only two people on board, we were always a little short of sleep, or at least short of the kind of sustained sleep that really refreshes, but we worked into a groove where that didn't matter too much. We were getting enough sleep to allow us to function without much trouble and, sometimes, to actually enjoy ourselves. We were so used to our routine and to each other at sea, that we functioned smoothly together. There was little tension or argument, and we both knew we could count on each other if anything had to be done. It was a good feeling.

Not much happened. One of the bigger events occurred when we turned the chart over. I had a chart that showed the whole North Atlantic that I had to fold in half to fit on the chart table. Each day I'd plot our noon position on the chart, and the little circled dots showed our progress across the empty ocean. But initially I could only see how far we'd come from Las Palmas. The Big Day occurred when the dots reached the fold and I could turn the chart over to see our destination—we were no longer sailing toward the edge of the world: there *was* some land out there, and it was getting closer each day.

We never felt quite as alone out there as we had on some of the longer passages during our circumnavigation, for ham radio gave us at least a tenuous link to the outside world. We talked to Trudi most days on the Transatlantic net and to a few other yachts. We even managed to talk to Liz's dad and Jeff a couple times by means of phone patches. But our electricity was limited, so I didn't spend a huge amount of time on the radio. The solar panels helped, but the amount we got out of them depended on cloud cover and whether or not they were shaded by the sails, which seemed to be often. We did run the engine out of gear a few times to charge the batteries when they were getting really low.

On Day 18 we had a crisis, the only one of the passage. With the wind a little lighter, we dropped the yankee to change to our nylon genoa. That sail had been up for more than a week, and we were startled to find the halyard almost chafed through. No problem: we cut off the offending end and the halyard was as good as new, though we realized we'd have to monitor it more carefully. We put up the genoa, but then about sunset as we were gybing due to a wind shift, we somehow got the sail seriously wrapped around the forestay. Pulling on the sheet did nothing. I tried pushing the clew around with the boathook (it was up above my head), but that was futile. I tried to unwrap the bottom but it wouldn't yield. There's nothing like a nice tight wrap to ruin your day.

I didn't know what to do. I was beginning to think we'd have to cut it off—if we even could—or lose the use of the forestay. In desperation, I grabbed a sheet and pulled *down* hard on it. It seemed to yield a little. It looked like that was our only hope, so I positioned a block under the sail, took a line to the clew of the sail, through the block, and back to the sheet winch. We might rip the sail, but I couldn't see another alternative. I started cranking on the winch and with much protest the sail started inching down the stay. When I'd got it down a couple of feet, I found that that had disturbed the wrap enough that we could begin to work it around and get it loosened up. Thank goodness. When we finally got it down, I bagged it and put the yankee back up. We were a little too slow under that rig, but I didn't want to deal with the other sail again that night. As it turned out, the wind increased the next day, so it wasn't an issue.

In fact, Day 19 was squally and rainy, the first such weather we'd had in a couple weeks. We heard from Trudi that this was a small tropical wave, and the Barbados radio which we picked up the next day was complaining about the heavy rain and the "cold"—it was only 79 degrees. But by then our weather had improved, and we were really getting there. We sighted Barbados at 0800 on Day 20 at less than 20 miles away, and sailed in toward it on the backside of that tropical wave in absolutely beautiful weather.

We'd already decided not to stop. We'd been to Barbados after we'd come up the South Atlantic on our circumnavigation, and we knew the anchorage wasn't great—it's basically an open roadstead—and we also knew if we stopped we'd have to make another overnight to get to Bequia, where we were headed and where we intended to spend some time. It made more sense to just tack another day onto the long passage, which was no great hardship, and then we could forget about night watches for awhile. So we sailed in toward Barbados, passing within two miles of the south point, inside the "Shallow Ground" indicated on the chart. It was exceedingly strange to be so close to land after nearly three weeks at sea. We sat in the sunny cockpit staring sat it, half-mesmerized.

"Sure you don't want to stop?" I said to Liz.

"No, I want to get to Bequia."

"Me too."

So we kept on sailing, soon dropping Barbados astern. The night was clear and starlit and wonderfully settled. A star fix at twilight showed us a little south of our track, so we steered a little more north, and on Liz's watch, before midnight, she picked up the loom of St. Vincent, the island just about five miles to the north of Bequia. At dawn, we were headed into the channel between the two islands, just a few miles to go, and by 0800 we were anchored in Admiralty Bay.

What a passage. We'd covered 2858 miles in just an hour short of 21 days. That means we'd *averaged* 5.7 knots for three weeks! We hadn't done under 140 miles a day for the last 10 days. Even better, we'd motored only a total of eight hours in the whole passage, including leaving and entering port, though we'd run the engine out of gear for battery charging a few more hours. That's pretty good going for a small boat with a two-person crew. Columbus on his second voyage on much the same route also took 21 days for the crossing from the Canaries to Dominica, his fastest by far.

Of course it's largely a matter of luck, for us as well as for Columbus. We had consistent trade winds the whole way after the first few days, mostly Force 6 to occasionally Force 7, which is perfect for downwind sailing. Boats that left a few weeks after us, closer to the time normally recommended, had no such luck. They encountered light airs and inconsistent wind. We talked to people on boats 40 feet and over that had times of 30-35 days, and some boats took even longer. It's the rare sailing vessel that carries fuel to motor over 500 miles, so no matter what you do, on a long passage like this you're going to have to *sail* about 2500 miles of it. If the wind isn't there, you aren't going anywhere no matter how fine your vessel or how skilled your crew. Even with today's more sophisticated weather forecasting, you never know for sure what you're going to get. But we hit it just right this time. For us, after so much lousy sailing in the Med, it was a real treat to have a passage like that. Maybe there was some justice in the world after all. At times anyway.

12. Caribbean Winter

It'd been nearly 10 years since we'd last been in Bequia, but it still looked familiar and welcoming.

"It's so green!" Liz exclaimed.

After all the rocky, bare islands in the Med, Bequia looked like a tropical Eden. Of course we'd just had three weeks of nothing but blue and grey and white, no scenery but the endless procession of ocean swells. Dramatic as they can be, they aren't particularly colorful, and it was magical to be suddenly awash in tropical technicolor. Bequia looked much the same: sure, the boats in the harbor were a little more modern, there were more little businesses catering to them, most of the locals' boats in the harbor now had outboards rather than sails, and the tradition of going after whales in open boats was mostly a memory now. But the people were still smiling and friendly, even the Rastas who sold produce on the beach.

In my journal, I wrote:

I feel really glad to be here. I love this climate and the water and the tension-free atmosphere. First chance in a long time to relax....It's great to have the boat relatively steady for the first time since early October.

Bequia is one of the those places that everyone shows up in sooner or later. The bay is large with plenty of room for anchoring. It's open to the west, but that's seldom a problem in the winter when the winds are virtually all from some easterly direction, so you can settle in quite comfortably. We'd end up spending the next couple of months in Bequia with a couple trips down to the Tobago Cays about 25 miles away, and then we'd move on to Grenada for another few weeks. We were more than ready for this slowed-up pace, for it seemed that we'd been constantly on the go since the previous March.

We started meeting the current crop of people in the anchorage. Frank on *Schedar* was anchored nearby and stopped by to say hello. He'd just completed a circumnavigation and complained about how expensive it was: he said he'd been spending $40,000 a year. I had to wonder how he was doing that in a boat not much bigger than ours. We'd been spending less than a quarter of that and considered ourselves living quite well.

But one person's luxury is another person's necessity, and on a boat many different living standards are possible.

Doug, a guy we'd heard the radio, came by. He said he'd been in Bequia for six years. I found that sort of depressing; living on a boat if you aren't going somewhere just seems sort of wrong to me. But Doug's chief concern seemed to be how to pass the time until the bars opened.

We talked with Mal and Roz, a British couple on *Elizabeth I*, a fancy and well-maintained 40-footer. They'd worked some years for The Moorings, a charter company, and made enough money to buy this boat which they now operated as a charter vessel. Mal said it was much more like running a hotel than a sailing enterprise. You're on duty 24 hours a day, always at your clients' beck and call, no time to yourself. Liz and I both realized we could never do that.

I stopped by to say hello to the people on a Dutch boat because I saw they had gooseneck barnacles growing on their hull: that was a sure sign they'd just completed the Atlantic crossing. I don't know why those pernicious thing only thrive in the open ocean, but that seems to be the case. They'd made the crossing from Gomera in the Canaries in 22 days, although they'd had to motor quite a bit in the middle.

There were many other people that we'd seen before in various ports, or who had seen us, or who we'd heard on the radio. Often people we didn't know would approach us and say, "We saw your boat in...wherever," our yellow boat being particularly memorable. With more human contact than we'd had in a while, we both started to enjoy ourselves more. It was good to get lifted out of our own narrow little environment and our predictable responses and listen to other people's adventures, enthusiasms, and problems.

There was no airport in Bequia at that time (that was to come in 1992), so the only way to get to the island was by private boat or by ferry from St. Vincent. The wooden schooner, *Friendship Rose*, was one ferry option. Built on the beach in the town of Friendship on the southern side of Bequia in 1969, this vessel made scheduled trips across the channel between the two islands for many years. It had a good (and loud) engine assisted by patched canvas sails. We took the trip across one morning and watched while the crew of six hoisted the two big gaff-rigged sails and a jib by hand—no winches on that vessel. When we got out in the channel, the bow of the boat dipped and rose in the short steep seas, throwing water back over deck and passengers, most of whom scurried inside. The sea smoothed out as we got closer to St Vincent, but that channel can be rough when the trade winds are blowing hard. The *Friendship Rose* handled it well.

Handling the jib on the Friendship Rose

We strolled around Kingstown, which had an unsavory reputation, as we remembered from 10 years before. It was still a grubby little town with lots of idlers just hanging around, a very different atmosphere from Bequia, but we weren't hassled and the shops did have things unavailable in Bequia. It was no place we had any wish to linger though, and we caught the schooner back in the early afternoon. There was a more modern ferry, the *Admiral*. that was strictly a motor vessel, but why take that when there's a much more colorful and traditional option?

We left Bequia and sailed down to the Tobago Cays. Although the anchorage gets crowded at times, it's still a special place that held fond memories for us. The little islets don't provide much shelter: it's basically the large encircling reef that provides protection, so it's usually a very windy place, 20-30 knots much of the time in the winter as the trades do their thing. That can get a little wearying as a steady diet, but it only raises a slight chop in the anchorage and the holding in thick coral sand is excellent: the anchor buries itself and disappears almost immediately. Several boats parked themselves there for days at a time to enjoy the great windsurfing conditions; you get pretty skillful if you're windsurfing eight hours a day, as some of these guys seemed to be doing; we watched them zooming back and forth, executing thrilling turns effortlessly, some of them even venturing outside the reef into the open ocean. Great entertainment.

We contented ourselves with snorkeling and doing a couple of dives, filling our tanks at Union Island just a couple miles away. The coral and the sea life was nice in places but not as spectacular as it had been 10 years before. One day we took the boat out to World's End Reef, which lies east of the Cays. You can really feel like you're at the edge of the world out there, as there's no land in sight and nothing between you and Africa. The anchorage was a little rough and the current was strong so we couldn't explore as much as we would've liked to. We snorkeled around the boat and tried to investigate a pass through the coral, but the current was too strong to make it through the pass. The coral in the spots we found wasn't much, and we didn't see much sea life either, although three medium-sized barracuda tagged along behind us—every time we turned around, there they were, just waiting to see if anything interesting happened. Later, an Australian guy we talked to who'd been out there told us he'd seen a couple of big sharks out by the pass. We missed those. It wasn't a place to spend the night in the conditions we had, so we retreated to the Cays.

After a week, we went returned to Bequia. The trip back from the Cays is normally a boisterous sail hard on the wind and sometimes you have to tack. It looked like we were going to make it okay, but in the last five miles we got set and ended up about a half a mile off the west end of the island. We continued on past it, and one tack gave us a good course right into the center of Admiralty Bay.

We got caught up in the Bequia social life immediately, as a number of new boats had come in. Most were Americans who'd taken two or three years or more to get this far from the States, but boats from Europe were beginning to trickle in. We went with a bunch of people to hear a string band at one of the local bars. The band was great, playing an impressive variety of music. The singer was a short little guy in a baseball cap who sat in the back playing a tambourine and drinking rum, except when he stepped up front for three or four songs and sang with very deliberate gestures and a certain amount of body movement. The showpiece number was a rendition of "Elvira," the Oak Ridge Boys hit ("…heigh-yo silver, away…"). Country music in the Caribbean. Who would've thought?

Gooseberry came in, 22 days from the Gambia. We were glad to see Keith and Tina again. Keith and I started running in the mornings before breakfast and before it got hot. We'd get out at 0600, dinghy ashore, and jog around the harbor and up the hill on the north side. When we got back we'd jump in the water to cool off. The four of us often walked together in the afternoons, to Hope Beach on the windward side, a beautiful deserted beach at the head of a coconut plantation with nice waves for sometimes-rough body surfing, or over to Friendship and along the south coast to Paget Farm near where the airport would be sited. When we got back we'd stop at the Frangipani, a harborside bar, for a beer. It wasn't a bad life.

But I also spent a lot of time hassling outboards. Our Seagull had been fussy about starting ever since that episode in Paros when it got sandblasted. Sometimes it started but it would quit at arbitrary times. I took the flywheel off (with great difficulty), cleaned out its innards (there was still a lot of sand in there), put it back together and…it was no better. The obvious solution was to replace the sealed ignition package and its lead, but the outboard shop in town didn't carry that, though they could sell me a new Seagull for about $525. I said thanks but no thanks. Nevertheless it was becoming increasingly clear that if I wanted an outboard I could rely on, I'd have to buy one.

Of course Keith needed one too, after losing his in Las Palmas. The shop had a couple of small three horsepower Evinrudes and Keith ultimately bought one. I might've bought the other, but I didn't like the way it sounded when we started it up so I passed on it. Eventually I bought a two horsepower Yamaha that had never been used from a German guy in the anchorage for $400. Neither outboard was going to allow us to go screaming through the anchorage at high speed, as some people found it necessary to do, but they pushed us along reliably at a sedate pace and they were easy to deal with.

I was quite happy with my purchase for about a month. Then one evening when a squall came through and it started gusting hard, Liz and I went out to take down our awning and saw that our dinghy, tied to the stern, had flipped over with the outboard on it! A salt water drenching is probably not the best way to improve outboard performance. I got the motor on board, filled the cylinder with oil, rotated it to distribute the oil, drained the oil, and tried to start it. Nothing doing. Here was a depressing turn of events: it began to look like I'd paid $400 for the privilege of having a second outboard with the same problems as the old one.

I struggled with it for the next couple weeks with Keith assisting. The details aren't important (they involve trying different coils and condensers in various combinations), but I finally got so fed up I said to Keith, "I don't want the damn thing on board. It's ruining my life. You take it. If you can get it to run, send me a hundred dollars." I don't know if he took me seriously or not, but he took it and after some effort managed to get it running. Most of the time. So I thanked him, took the thing back, and hoped for the best. If I had any more trouble with it, I resolved to buy a new one in Grenada.

As Christmas approached, our social life increased. There were always new people to meet, and everybody had a story. One of the most dramatic stories belonged to Ed and Jean on *Tropic Moon*, a steel boat in the 40-foot range. They were crossing from Europe the previous year when they were hit by a tanker. It wasn't exactly clear how it happened, but Jean was on watch at night and admitted that she got confused—easy enough to do at sea at night (I'd been there myself). The collision dismasted them and put a big dent in their topsides maybe 15 to 20 feet long. They managed to motor 300 miles back to the Cape Verde Islands. They were so shaken by the incident that they left the boat there for a year before setting out again and successfully completing the crossing. The boat still had the big dent in it, graphic confirmation of their story. It seemed unlikely to me that a fiberglass vessel would've survived that encounter. But the really strange thing about it was that Jean said she'd had a lifelong fear of ships and frequent nightmares about being run down; it wasn't something that developed as a result of being at sea—it had gripped her in childhood, way before she started cruising. Was this a case of a self-fulfilling prophecy? Did her fear in some way help to *cause* the incident? Or was it just uncanny coincidence? I'd probably be inclined to vote for coincidence, but it surely was a strange one.

Keith was outgoing and sociable enough to enjoy interacting with the locals, often asking them aboard his boat and chatting with them. Theft was never much of a problem in Bequia at that time, but one day after he'd had some kids on board, Keith noticed that a line was missing. It wasn't anything very valuable, just something he had sitting on deck, but he knew right away who had taken it. He got in his dinghy, went into town, found the kid, and confronted him. A crowd gathered, the kid admitted his crime, his mother showed up and started berating him too, a very public shaming. Keith got his line back, which he probably would've given to the kid if he'd asked for it, and—the best part of it—the other kids started calling the thief "Rope," a nickname that I suspect stuck with him for quite some time.

We had our Christmas dinner on *Gooseberry* with several other couples: Doug and Ann from *Arion*, who were intending to go to the Pacific, and another Canadian couple that Keith and Tina knew, who happened to know *Xanth*, the boat that had such a long passage from Bermuda to the Azores. The cruising world seems like a very small place sometimes.

Liz and I aren't much for New Year's eve celebrations, but we did go over to *Gooseberry* again for what we expected would be an early night. We brought the last of a case of champagne we'd bought in Spain. Ed and Jean from *Tropic Moon* were there, and we all got a little giggly. Tina as usual became very funny with a couple of drinks in her. Then a French boat came in in the dark and tried to anchor very close to us. Keith stepped up on deck, irate, and started yelling at them, cursing freely. I sympathized but thought he was probably overreacting, emboldened by the champagne. Nevertheless, the Frenchman decided he didn't want to be next to the crazy person and moved away. Jean got upset at Keith's behavior and wanted to leave.

Keith stopped yelling immediately when he realized Jean was bothered. He said, "I wasn't really angry—I was just acting that way to drive them away."

He had a point. Lots of people don't realize how close is too close in an anchorage, or what can go wrong. Admiralty Bay is quite safe and comfortable, but it does get gusty in there at times. Some days later I had an incident with a French boat too. A 40-footer had anchored in front of us, quite close. As it happened, nobody was on board that boat when its anchor let go and it dragged into us, ending up against our bow. I fended him off the best I could while screaming for help. A bunch of guys from nearby boats came over to help. But we soon discovered that our nylon anchor snubber had gotten jammed in his rudder assembly so that the boat was held up against us—we couldn't get him away from us. I let out more chain, but that didn't help. Finally I went in the water with mask and fins, and after working with it for a while I eventually got the snubber free. Meanwhile, the owner of the French boat had returned, and we managed to get the boats separated. It was a big drill resulting from careless anchoring. The owner said he'd "tested" the anchor with his engine. I tried to tell him if he's going to anchor that close to somebody, he should look at the anchor to see if it's set or at least put a heavy strain on it with the engine. I didn't get nasty with him, as he was clearly abashed, but I made it clear I wasn't happy. Luckily, we suffered no damage, but if we hadn't been on board, the outcome might've been different.

So maybe Keith's strategy of being thoroughly obnoxious to anyone who anchors too close was not so out of line after all.

Jeff came to visit in January for a couple weeks. We went over to St. Vincent on the *Friendship Rose* to meet his flight, which happened to be right on time. He brought all sorts of goodies with him: mail, slides we'd had developed but hadn't yet seen, a model airplane magazine for Keith (a special request). We hadn't seen him in six months. How had he been doing? Well, he'd been spending too much money—careful budgeting had never been his strong suit. He was somewhat adrift in his courses; he'd changed his major from physics to a combination of physics and English: that would allow him to graduate but was unlikely to do much else for him. Once again, I felt some twinges of guilt for leaving him on his own so soon: maybe he would've been better off with some closer parental guidance. Maybe, but it was questionable whether we would've been able to do much even if we'd been there looking over his shoulder. At some point he'd have to take charge of his own life anyway, and on the positive side he was decent kid, not messed up with drugs or other temptations to which young adult males often fall prey. I could only hope he'd find his way eventually.

Meanwhile, we went down to the Tobago Cays again. *Gooseberry* came with us. It was more crowded than the last time and windier too. But we managed to snorkel several times a day, exploring the whole reef system, and we did a couple of scuba dives. We dove on a wreck off the nearby island of Mayreau too, then, after a week or so, it was back to Bequia. We took Jeff over to Hope beach, went to see the string band again, and suddenly his two weeks were up and it was time for him to go. There were lots of complex feelings associated with having him with us. I was glad that we still fit easily into the familiar pattern of the three of us on board, but I was also aware that the bonds between us were looser now, that we had less influence now over the direction his life would take, and I couldn't help wondering if we'd abdicated responsibility too early. We gave him some more money—a loan, we emphasized—and hoped he'd be a little more careful with it. I was sorry to see him go.

+

On January 26, I realized we'd been there for two months. We'd enjoyed ourselves, but I was starting to feel it was time to move on. But moving on raised all sorts of questions we had yet to confront. The past two months had provided us with a much-needed reminder of some of the reasons we were doing this. It was great to be in this beautiful setting on a welcoming island with plenty of interesting people around, both serious offshore-sailors and those with more modest ambitions; and unlike many places we'd been there was the opportunity for continuing friendships. It was great to have good wind if you wanted to sail and wonderfully clear water for snorkeling or diving. We'd felt burned out when we left the Med; here, we felt at least partially restored.

But at the same time, I knew it wasn't enough. Neither Liz nor I would be content to meander from island to island for years, as some people were doing. And great as the social situation had been in Bequia for us, as much as we'd enjoyed meeting people and hearing their stories—and of course telling our own stories—a regular diet of that sort of cocktail-hour amiability begins to pall after awhile. We'd had the same reaction to the Caribbean on our first cruise, way back in 1977. It was great for a couple of months, delightful in fact, but as time went on we started to feel that something was lacking, that we needed a new challenge, a new goal, or at least a change of scene. Some people don't feel that. Some are happy to be on permanent vacation and are quite content with the fun-in-the-sun pleasures of Caribbean life. I don't mean to imply any judgment. People are different. But for us the pleasures of the Caribbean would always be a temporary thing. In the larger sense, I knew that Liz wanted something more from life, a more settled existence, the chance to put down some roots or at least establish more permanent connections than were possible as "transients" on a cruising sailboat. I was probably nursing less discontent than she was, but I felt a certain emptiness as well, except I was less sure what I wanted to replace it with.

We'd avoided a serious discussion of future plans—where do we go from here?—since we made the decision the previous summer to come back across the Atlantic. But the time had come to confront it.

"We need a plan," I said to Liz.

"We do," she said. "I guess it's time to talk about it."

"I know I don't want to stay in the Caribbean for the summer, so that sort of limits our options."

Our options had been limited, we both knew, as soon as we'd returned to the Caribbean. There were only three realistic possibilities. We could head for Panama and the Pacific—a far bigger commitment than either of us was ready to make. We could head down the South American coast, but the whole South American thing, which had been my original thought back when we were first contemplating a second cruise, was no longer on the table: we realized now that it would inevitably involve too many of the things we *didn't* like about cruising: isolation, tension, cold, severe weather, and various third-world problems.

That left returning to the States as the only realistic option, and our subsequent cruising plans would likely be limited to the East Coast and Caribbean area.

In a way, that was a tough pill for me to swallow. I think one thing we hadn't fully realized when we set off on this voyage was that we weren't quite as free as we'd thought. Even if we'd been up for it in other respects, taking off for remote areas of the world didn't seem to be in the cards for us. On our circumnavigation our ties to land life had been minimal; we'd been a self-contained family, and concerns about parents were secondary. Now those ties figured more prominently: we weren't quite irresponsible enough to simply say "Screw it" and take off for parts unknown. Even the eastern Med had seemed a little too far away.

"So what do we do?" Liz said. "Go back to Florida? Or New England?"

"I don't think I'm ready to stop for good. Are you?"

"We've been having a good time here…and it's scary to think of what's next. Until we know where we want to live or have some idea of what we want to do…I guess it makes sense to keep things open."

There were two other factors that played into our decision. One was concern about money. The cost of our Major Medical insurance policy was skyrocketing. That took a big chunk out of our savings and injected a healthy dose of uncertainty into our whole enterprise. We still had money, but with bigger and bigger bites taken out of it each year, it was hard to budget with any conviction.

The other factor was my health, one of the big reasons we'd decided to leave the Med. The strange affliction I'd had in Europe had all but disappeared by now. I no longer felt the tightness in my chest that had plagued me for so long, and I seemed to be getting reasonably fit again with all the running and walking and diving I'd been doing. But I still felt it was important to get checked out, to see if a US doctor could discover any cause for my problem, to make sure I really was healthy again. Wherever we spent the summer, that would be a high priority.

I said: "I'm starting to think we ought to go back to Connecticut for the summer. We'd be close to Jeff, we could see family, we could start thinking about next steps. Then unless something wonderful comes up, we could come back to the Caribbean for the next winter."

Liz nodded. "That seems reasonable to me. And it gives us more time to decide what we want to do and where."

I liked the idea too. It would give us a break from the Caribbean and time to consider what the next steps in life were. At the same time, it left our open-ended cruise open for a little longer.

"Offshore to New England then?"

I nodded. "It's a lot quicker and easier than slogging up the waterway. We could go to Puerto Rico, maybe have a chance to work on our Spanish, then go from there to Bermuda and New England from there."

"It's sort of a relief, not having to make any big decisions just yet."

"Yeah." I grinned. "There's nothing like procrastinating."

"Maybe we're just not quite ready to give up on this sailing business."

"Maybe not."

We both felt better about it, I think. We hadn't solved any of the background problems or come to grips with any force about the difference in our attitudes, but we had some idea of what we were going to do in the short term. The rest of it could wait.

+

Nice as it was, we were getting a little bored with Bequia, so by the beginning of February we were ready to leave and head south to Grenada.

As we sailed out of Admiralty Bay, I had the sense that a phase of the voyage was over. We'd done what we set out to do—cruise the Mediterranean—and in the process we'd crossed the Atlantic twice. We'd had a couple of months to rest up, recover, and reflect. And now we'd scaled back our ambitions for a combination of reasons. Our time afloat from now on, for as long as it lasted, would be a sort of footnote to the voyage as a whole. We'd be in familiar waters, and with a few exceptions we'd be visiting places—or at least areas—that we'd been to before. If that seemed a little tame (certainly tamer than the Patagonian channels!), it was also comforting in a way. Maybe we could benefit from a slightly less demanding schedule.

We stopped once again in the Tobago Cays for a few days,

and did more snorkeling and diving. But I had a new problem that was starting to worry me, and in fact it was to have long-range implications: my shoulder had started to bother me. That doesn't sound like a big deal, and that's what I thought at first. I thought I'd just pulled a muscle or perhaps slept on it in an awkward way. But it persisted, off and on, and it didn't seem to be getting better the way you'd normally expect from a pulled muscle. It was only a mild annoyance now, but it was to get worse. After all my struggles with the infection (or whatever it was) in my chest for the past year, this was a low blow.

Meanwhile, we sailed down to Tyrell Bay on Carriacou where we spent a few days. John Bedeau, a local entrepreneur, came out to the boat and gave us a mangrove oyster to try—raw. Not my thing but Liz tried it. John had apparently made it his mission to visit as many of the new arrivals as he could and entice them to try and perhaps buy a bunch of oysters. *Gooseberry* came in the next day, and we had a pot-luck supper on their boat. John brought some oysters out and had a glass of wine with us in the cockpit. He was articulate and interesting; we enjoyed his conversation and admired his initiative.

Then on to Prickly Bay, Grenada. We sailed down the windward side of Grenada to avoid having to motor in the lee of the island. As we turned the corner to sail along the south coast, Liz and I had another stupid argument; it was probably my fault because I was feeling tired and cranky, but her comments only succeeded in egging me on. The whole thing escalated unpleasantly. I mention that because it's something that can easily happen on a cruising sailboat: it's not always easy to be tactful and cheery 24 hours a day, and when a couple isn't in the same mood or the same psychological space things can tip the wrong way. The immediate cause soon fades—at least it did for us—but I realized it was a sign that our fundamental differences were still with us, that even though we'd mostly ignored them in Bequia by keeping busy and interacting with other people, and even though we'd managed to discuss future plans quite rationally, we were still very different people with very different perceptions and feelings about what we were doing.

Prickly Bay is another of those harbors that everyone seems to gravitate to sooner or later. It's reasonably secure although it tends to be rolly at times. A longish walk out to the main road gave bus access to St. George's, the main town on the island, for groceries and other stuff. We met a lot of people in the anchorage but didn't feel much rapport with any of them. Mostly they tended to be the typical Caribbean island hoppers. Maybe we were getting a little jaded or more likely it was just matter of the chance dynamics of the group of boats that happened to be there at the time. Or maybe part of it was that my shoulder continued to bother me and that soured my mood.

We stayed there for almost three weeks though and managed to do some interesting things. We attended a performance of Mighty Sparrow, a calypso group billed as "best in the world." That was probably a bit of a stretch, but they weren't bad at all and the lead singer was charismatic. We rode the buses all over the island. The Grenada buses were mostly minivans, usually packed tight with locals, with calypso-reggae music blaring; they were always fun to ride. We went up to the rainforest at Grand Etang, tropical valleys and scenic vistas through low clouds, a dripping microclimate much different from southern Grenada. We thought about climbing Mount Qua Qua, but the mud on the trail was too slippery and oozy and disgusting to make it a pleasant excursion. Another day we took the bus to Grenville on the east side of the island, a pleasant town with a good market, caught a bus to Sauteurs in the north, and another down the west side of the island to St. George's. The whole island was incredibly lush and green, a riot of tropical fecundity with flowers everywhere adding startling color to the green backdrop. Tons of people about in colorful clothing too, most living pretty basically, doing laundry in the streams, much of their lives taking place outdoors. Keith and Tina had guests from Canada, and we all took a bus out to Concord Falls. From where the bus stopped, we walked about three-quarters of a mile to the upper falls, a beautiful walk lined with nutmeg, cocoa, and banana trees. We swam in the pool at the base of the falls, delightful fresh water, cool but not cold.

The next day we left for Puerto Rico.

+

We'd decided to sail directly to Puerto Rico rather than involve ourselves in tedious island-hopping. With a good wind in the northeast, forward of the beam for us, the nearly 500 miles took us just a little over three days. There's nothing like a good trade-wind passage in the Caribbean when the weather's fine. The only sobering part of it was that my shoulder continued to bother me, aggravated by the motion and having to pull on lines. The green bulk of Puerto Rico showed up at first light on the morning of the third day, but it was difficult to determine which little bump was which on the island outline until we got a sun line—it wasn't a fix but knowing we were somewhere on that line, which sliced across the island in a more or less north-south direction, gave us some idea of what part of the coast we were approaching. Soon we had things sorted out visually and were able to head confidently in toward Ponce, the major city on the south coast.

The anchorage at Ponce off the yacht club was comfortable enough, but it was the weekend, there was a lot of noisy runabout activity, and in the evening loud disco music for our listening pleasure. Friday night, very tired, I slept through it; Saturday night I wasn't so fortunate. Liz went shopping in Ponce, but my shoulder was bothering me so much I didn't want to walk around—that seemed to aggravate it—so I stayed on board.

After a couple of days we left to sail down the coast to Salinas. It was only about 10 miles, but we broke up the trip by stopping for a couple of nights at Isla Caja de Muertos—Coffin Island. It's a nature reserve, and when we were there a helicopter brought in a bunch of people that Gustavo, the resident biologist, told us were the advance party for a group of visiting US Congressmen. What Congressmen hoped to see on this tiny little island I have no idea. Maybe they wanted to do a little snorkeling.

The entrance to Salinas when we got there was a little confusing and shallow as well. The murky water and mangroves reminded me of Belize. But once through the channel we found a well-sheltered lagoon with a bunch of other boats, some of which had been holed up there for quite some time. I could see why. It was a comfortable spot with plenty of anchoring room, a marina, enough facilities ashore within walking distance that provided basic supplies, and Ponce only a short ride away by "público."

The públicos were more like shared taxis than buses, and in fact many of them were just cars. Some had fixed routes, more or less: the Salinas to Ponce route was fairly well-established. The fares were quite cheap, the only catch being they didn't leave until they were full. That meant you could be sitting there for some time before the driver scrounged up enough people to make it worth his while, and then you'd often be jammed in uncomfortably close with other strangers. For us, though, it was a reasonably convenient way to get around.

We stayed in Salinas for about five weeks. One interesting feature of the weather there was its consistency. Every day the wind would pipe up from the east or southeast, often getting up to 20 or 25 knots in the late afternoon. This was apparently a reinforcing effect of the sea breeze on the trade winds as the land heated up during the day. But during the evening the wind eased off, and as the night went on a north wind developed as the land cooled off and the cooler air started sinking down the mountains. Day followed day with that pattern. It was of interest to us particularly because when we left we intended to head east against the trade winds, and it appeared that if we went at night and our observations held true, we might benefit from that northerly slant to the wind, or at the very least the trip might not be quite as much of a wet slog as it was likely to be in the afternoon.

Boats came and went with regularity, including some we'd seen in Bequia or other places, but some had gotten stuck here for various reasons. Fred and Jo on a 51-footer had been here for 15 months. Fred had a huge array of solar panels which he dutifully reoriented several times a day to maximize their electric output so that he could run his refrigerator without running the engine. Seemed like a lot of trouble to me, but we all have our priorities. They were "getting ready to leave." Another guy was rebuilding his engine. The plus side for us was that the regulars had lots of local knowledge. Through them, Liz got a lead on someone to help us with Spanish.

Angela was a teacher at the local school, a speech therapist who'd been at it for many years. The bonus for us was that she spoke very clearly and distinctly; not only that, but she seemed delighted to help us and agreed to meet with us three days a week. We offered to pay her, but she dismissed the idea. She proved to be a real gem. Not only did she speak Spanish with us, she also seemed to consider it her mission to give us a favorable impression of Puerto Rico. She invited us to her home where she always gave us cold fruit drinks (much appreciated), drove us around to see the local sights, explained much about conditions and problems in Puerto Rico. We couldn't have had a better guide, and it was all in Spanish.

The only downside for me was that my shoulder was not improving. It had seemed to get better for a while, but it now seemed to be getting worse and worse. I had to miss a Spanish lesson because I was too uncomfortable. I finally rigged up a sling to wear when I was walking around (that seemed to aggravate it the most), and that helped some. I had no firm idea what the problem was—it no longer made sense to consider it a pulled muscle: it had been troubling me far too long for that. I began to suspect it might have come from scuba diving, perhaps some reaction to pressure changes or even, possibly, a mild case of the bends, nitrogen bubbles in the blood, though how I could've gotten that I don't know, as I was always very careful to control my rate of ascent (coming up too fast is one of the chief causes of the bends). I never nailed down a sure diagnosis, but I was in acute discomfort much of the time in Salinas.

Rainbow Runner came in—we'd met them in Menorca and last seen them in Gibralter. They took 30 days on the passage from the Canaries. Then to our surprise *Gooseberry* came in. They didn't have a radio, so we had no means of keeping track of one another. It's always a treat to meet up with friends again, especially unexpectedly.

We immediately began planning an excursion with Keith and Tina. First we went in to Ponce and, among other things, visited the art museum. The highlight there was the Victorian masterpiece, "Flaming June," by Frederic Leighton. It depicts a reclining woman in an improbably bright orange dress that surrounds her and clings to her as if threatening to consume her in orange fire. It's a startling and arresting masterpiece. Reproductions are everywhere: you can look it up. And there was the original, right there in Ponce, of all places. It had been purchased very cheaply for the museum by a Puerto Rican businessman in the 1960s when Victorian paintings were out of favor.

Then we rented a car for a couple days. We drove to San Juan on the north coast, parked at a mall outside the city, and took a bus in to Old San Juan. Playing tourists for a day, I was reminded of doing much the same thing with Jeff back at the beginning of our first cruise in 1977. On the way back to the south coast we took the scenic route from Caguas, driving curvy roads lined with bamboo and tree ferns and jungly grass. The next day we drove up into the mountains, had a nice walk in the

Toro Negro reserve where the whole forest floor was covered with the red dots of impatiens flowers. I was gulping aspirin and keeping my arm in the sling to keep the pain down. We had lunch in a nice little restaurant in Adjuntas, then wended our way back, once more on s-shaped roads, weathering a downpour that obliterated all scenery, including the road, for a few minutes. Despite my troubles, we all found the mountainous interior of Puerto Rico to be surprisingly beautiful. Today, it's sad to think how badly that lovely island has been ravaged by hurricanes in recent years.

By the middle of April, it was time for us to leave. Naturally I was worried about my shoulder and how I'd do at sea, but I reasoned that I'd done it before and could probably rally. We had a farewell dinner with Angela and her husband at their house. We gave her a bouquet of flowers but it seemed too little: she had been incredibly nice to us. We were sorry to say goodbye. We also said goodbye to Keith and Tina, as they were following a different route back on a different schedule. We would see them again, but not for a long time. We'd enjoyed our time in Salinas—it'd probably exceeded our expectations—but if we were going to avoid getting stuck there, we had to make our move. We had a long way to go.

13. Retreat to New England

A string of little cays extends eastward from Salinas, and there's plenty of room and deep enough water between the cays and the Puerto Rican shore to take the boat. During Hurricane Hugo the previous fall, boats that tied up to the mangroves in this area made out fine, unlike boats who chose to go into Culebra, as we were soon to see. It is true, however, that the center of the storm did pass to the north of Puerto Rico, and there was a lot of high ground between the storm and the southern coast to disrupt the wind.

We left Salinas and proceeded along the coast behind the cays, intending to anchor there and leave in the evening, hoping to take advantage of the wind off the land at night instead of bashing into the full strength of the trades in the afternoon. We didn't have that far to go to the southeast corner of Puerto Rico, only 20 miles or so, but there was no point in beating ourselves up if we didn't have to. The weather in the late afternoon looked unsettled though, so we decided to wait it out and leave the next evening. We sat there through the next day, debating whether to leave or not since the wind was still pretty strong, but we finally convinced ourselves it was a good idea and left about 1800. We went out through the Boca de Infierno, of all things: it was hardly the mouth of hell, though the pass was quite narrow with reefs on both sides, but clearly visible even in the evening light. Still, I probably wouldn't have wanted to attempt it from seaward unless I knew it well.

We never did get the breeze off the land we'd hoped for. The easterly did ease off a bit, down to 20 knots or so, but it was a slog, slow going against seas and current: it took us 9 hours, tacking our way tediously along, to cover the 20 miles to Punta Tuna. We were treated to some nasty little rain squalls too with frustrating wind shifts in them, thankfully without much additional wind force. My shoulder bothered me the whole way, and of course we got no sleep. In the morning we found ourselves sailing between Puerto Rico and Vieques, having made a less than impressive 30 miles in 14 hours, for a rousing speed made good in the desired direction of just a smidge over 2 knots. It was abundantly clear at that point that we weren't going to make Culebra, the island between Puerto Rico and the Virgins which had been our goal, before dark. So we headed for an anchorage behind Isla Pineros, an island at the most easterly tip of Puerto Rico, had a comfortable night, and left for Culebra the next morning. Luckily the wind was more in the south then so that we could almost lay the course, and we entered Ensenada Honda in the late afternoon, glad that all our windward work was now behind us. Or so we thought.

For simplicity's sake, we slipped into an anchorage behind the reef just west of the harbor entrance, had another peaceful night, and moved over off the town in the morning. Culebra was a sobering sight—nothing quite prepared us for it. The center of Hurricane Hugo, a strong Category 3 storm at the time, had passed very close to the island the previous September. The bay had been considered by some as a "hurricane hole," whatever that means exactly, but it was way too big—nearly two miles long—to be secure in a serious blow, as had become only too evident. Boats that tied to the mangroves did okay, but those who chose to remain at anchor came to grief. The shores of the harbor were still littered with wrecked boats after seven months. I don't remember how many we counted, but I suspect it was between 30 and 40, many of them in the 40-50 foot range. There are few things sadder than a wrecked sailboat lying on its side out of its element, at least from a sailor's point of view: the sight effectively screams: "This could happen to you!" One boat bore on its stern the sadly ironic name "Our Dream."

Wrecked boats in Culebra

We'd visited Culebra 12 years before and had always

considered Flamenco Beach on the north side of the island, the place where we first snorkeled in tropical waters, as the most beautiful beach in the Caribbean, and when we walked over to take a look at it again, that impression was confirmed. I had earlier memories of it too: back in the 60s on the destroyer we'd practiced shore bombardment there, steaming back and forth along the north coast and lobbing shell after 5" shell onto the hillsides. I don't remember if we were actually shelling the area of Flamenco Beach, but signs along the way over warned of unexploded ordnance. The beach remained breathtakingly beautiful.

We were waiting in Culebra for the right weather to start north for Bermuda. Ordinarily that shouldn't have been much of a problem, for our course was north and the wind should have been easterly. But the wind had settled obstinately in the north or just a little east of north, and it made no sense to start off with a headwind like that. So we waited. We swam and snorkeled a little, but my shoulder was still acutely painful and a little of that was enough for me. We chatted with people in the harbor without coming up with much of anything of interest. One day we took the boat around the corner to the east side of the island and anchored behind the reef in Bahía de Almadóvar, a beautiful spot and well-protected but nothing much to do there. We spent the night and then returned to Ensenada Honda. Because I was limited in what I could do with my shoulder plaguing me, I began to get bored.

Finally, after more than a week, with the wind almost in the east in the harbor, we decided to go for it, even though it was cloudy and unsettled-looking. Unfortunately, once we got clear of the islands, the wind settled into the northeast, which meant we'd be hard on the wind if we could even steer the course. Which, it soon became clear, we couldn't.

It turned out to be a supremely frustrating five days or so. The line I drew on the chart connecting our noon fixes showed us heading approximately for Beaufort NC instead of Bermuda. We could've tacked, but the course we were on was still more favorable, and as I told Liz with more than usual resignation: "We *could* go to Beaufort." I didn't want to though, and I fully expected the wind to shift to the east eventually. Of course it was rough. It's always rough going to windward in the open ocean. But most of the time the wind wasn't *too* strong except in brief squalls and we weren't *too* uncomfortable, although all such things are relative.

Our masthead light quit working the first night. That was inconvenient because it meant we didn't dare doze on watch unless we could make ourselves visible in some way. We had some little strobe lights that we'd attached to our life harnesses so that we'd be visible if—god forbid—we went overboard at night, and I took one of these and hung it as high up on the backstay as I could reach and set it pulsing. A big argument against using a strobe light instead of a regular navigation light (besides the fact that it isn't strictly legal) is that it's more likely to *attract* ships, which isn't exactly what you want: they see something flashing and want to find out what it is. And sure enough, about 0400 in the morning a ship approached us to see what all the fuss was. I talked to him on the VHF where he identified himself as a US Navy warship. I assured the officer on watch that we were okay and explained why we had the light on. He was courteous and went on his way without troubling us further. At least I knew the strobe worked...in the sense that it rendered us visible.

The one plus in all this was that my shoulder seemed better. Maybe the ultimate cure for whatever it was I had was to take it to sea and abuse it. Whatever the reason, I was surprised and relieved; I'd been worried that even if I could do what I had to on the passage I'd make things worse. The opposite seemed to be happening.

On Day 5, the wind began to free a little, and by Day 6 we could actually steer for Bermuda, even though we still had to sail close to the wind. On Day 7, with less than 300 miles to go, the wind shifted into the south, and I started to believe we might actually make it.

And in fact we did. We'd covered the 900 miles in just over eight days, hardly a record passage but acceptable given the conditions.

+

Bermuda. It was almost exactly two years since we'd last been here. We were in the approach channel at 1230 and by 1330 we'd cleared in at the customs pier and were out at anchor. Greece and Turkey could learn something from that. We were the 131st boat to clear into Bermuda that year, one official told us, though at the moment there were many fewer boats than last time.

We'd been talking to Frank on *Deborah* on the radio (his ham call sign was KP2BP, which earned him the nickname Big Papa) who'd also been heading for Bermuda a few days ahead of us. He had a 51-footer and wasn't above motoring—in fact that seemed to be his preferred means of travel, the sails being just an added attraction for nice days. Frank and his wife Debby asked us over for drinks when we first arrived. They were interesting people in their mid-60s, planning to go to the Med. They'd bought a derelict dairy farm in upper New York state in the late 1940s and operated it while raising six girls. Later they'd operated a tug boat business the details of which I don't now recall. But they'd consistently run against conventional expectations and made a success of it, not the easiest thing in the world to do.

My shoulder was definitely better. I could still feel it at times, particularly if I overexerted, but it was nothing like it had been in Culebra and before. I felt sound enough to go up the mast and fix our masthead light—I found that it had jiggled a little loose and once I tightened up the connections it worked fine. I was able to start jogging too and be generally more active; that boosted my spirits.

Boats were coming in every day now. We visited with Bob and Sandy, a South African couple sailing *Altair*, a home-built 38-footer (gaff-rigged with galvanized rigging wire) who'd left Cape Town in December and were planning to winter in Malta. We tactfully tried, without being outright discouraging, to give them a more realistic sense of what they'd find there than they seemed to have. Martin, a single-handed Californian in another 38-footer was also heading for the Med, and we sold him all our cruising guides and some charts. I suspected I'd probably regret that later, and I did, but I was too soured on the Med just then to care.

The harbor at St. George's is pretty well sheltered, but it can get rough when the wind pipes up. When a front was forecast with winds in the 35-40 knot range, we decided to move to Smith's Sound, a nearly land-locked body of water to the south, more for reasons of comfort than safety. *Deborah* also moved down there, and Frank and Debby asked us to dinner. Their daughter Emily was visiting, and she brought a Jeopardy game with her which we played and which I happened to excel at (to Liz's sometime annoyance). Frank had an electronic keyboard so we rounded off the evening singing, a very pleasant time even if some of the family dynamics weren't crystal clear to us.

The expected gale never materialized, so after a couple days we moved back to the main harbor. We anchored behind an Israeli boat that we'd seen in Iraklion on Crete. I asked the guy if he'd had a good passage across. He said, "No!" with surprising vehemence. And then explained. His forestay had broken and his skeg (the fin-like supporting piece in front of the rudder) had fallen off so that he had no rudder and no means of controlling the direction of the boat. He'd *drifted* for 600 miles before he finally got a tow into Antigua. Some days nothing goes right. I thought about some of the passages we'd had that we considered bad and concluded that our difficulties were small potatoes. Certainly bad things can happen at sea to anyone, but thoughtful preparation beforehand can eliminate a lot of trouble.

Spirit came in, a boat about our size that we'd seen in Grenada. Jack and Barbara were headed for Connecticut, as were we, and they had ham radio too, so it looked like we'd be able to talk on passage. We were ready to leave, but the weather situation looked messy with various fronts doing this and that. Frank had a weatherfax and was showing me the daily maps. Jack was anxious to leave, but I wanted to see a little more clarity to the weather picture before I made my move. *Spirit* decided to go for it. Jack showed me the packet of weather information he got from the Navy when he cleared out. It was very impressive, satellite photos, five-day forecast maps, a wealth of pictures and data. But when you come right down to it, it's still weather forecasting, with all the errors that's prone to. As we were soon to see.

I decided to stay put for at least another day on the off-chance that things would get a little clearer. Sitting on the boat that afternoon we watched *Dolphin*, a huge toy-ship boat come in and anchor a boat length in front of us...*our* boat length. There was absolutely no need for that, as there was a ton of empty space behind us. They had six guys on board, and they proceeded to run their generator and play loud music while they cleaned up. I stewed about it for awhile (they were *real* close), then decided we'd just go ahead and move. When we got up close to them as we were picking up the anchor, I said, "I think it was very discourteous of you to anchor so close."

The captain (apparently), a mild-mannered young Englishman, said in full innocence, "Are you moving because of us? You should have said something."

I said, "You knew you were too close when you came in."

What I *should've* said was, "I didn't think it would do any good to speak to somebody dumb enough to anchor that close."

Anyway, we took ten minutes to move and felt better about it. More evidence that Keith may have had the right idea.

+

Next morning we talked to *Spirit* on the radio. They'd made about 80 miles and had no complaints about the weather. We decided to go. By the time we'd cleared out and taken care of a few other details, it was noon. We had more weather information than we'd ever had at the start of a passage: we had Frank's weather fax printouts, the packet of information from the Navy giving the long-term outlook, and confirmation from *Spirit* that all was well out there. What more could we want?

It started out okay. The wind was light and we motored awhile to be sure we got well clear of the northern reefs. Thereafter we had light winds for most of the first day, but by evening it was blowing Force 7 from the southwest. I wrote in my journal the next morning:

> *Wind still in SW (just forward of the beam) but forecast promises a shift to the W then NW, lasting through Saturday.* [It was now Thursday.] *Sounds grim. We're making good progress but it's not fun. The foredeck is very wet—heavy spray—so you get soaked up there. And it's going to get worse. After the wind shift we won't be able to steer the course and it'll get colder. Anticipating that doesn't thrill me. My shoulder is all right. Just looks like an unpleasant few days.*

And it was. The essence of it was that we had a series of very local gales. The first one came the next morning:

> *Sitting here with just the double-reefed main with 40 knots of wind, waiting to see what happens, looking at this huge weird black cloud that seems to be generating the wind. The rest of the sky is crystal clear. Seas chaotic. Forecast is for West 20-25.*

As we sat there, we saw several funnel clouds. A couple touched down as waterspouts. Clearly things were riled up. I knew waterspouts weren't usually as fierce as tornadoes on land; nevertheless, it wasn't relaxing to have them frolicking about us. The seas had startled to build too, and when we got underway again I sat up in our bubble for a while to keep an eye on things. It seemed that anything could happen in this weather.

Squall clouds passed over us several times that day, each bringing impressive bursts of wind. We talked to *Spirit* a day ahead of us, and they weren't experiencing anything like this weather: they were having a pleasant passage. All my caution about picking the day to leave hadn't worked out well. The forecasts made no acknowledgement of the gale conditions, but if they'd asked I could've assured them that they existed. They were right about the wind direction though: it was northwest, the direction we wanted to go.

We were tired—it was hard to relax enough to sleep in these conditions—but I wasn't particularly uptight. I found myself in a fatalistic, "whatever" frame of mind. If the weather was going to behave like this, screw it, there wasn't much we could do about it. We'd stick it out somehow. That's about all that could be expected of us.

Gradually, during the following day, the wind died. We started motoring. The only notable event of the day was that we crossed the inner wall of the Gulf Stream. It brought about a dramatic change: after passing through an area of confused seas, things suddenly smoothed out, the water color changed from that deep transparent offshore blue to dull greenish grey, and the water temperature plummeted from the mid-70s to 64 (I measured it). That all happened in the space of an hour. We were in New England waters now. There was more trash in the water and more sea life too, birds, dolphins, welcome company.

We motored all night. With no autopilot, we had to steer (the wind vane, of course, was useless with no wind). Not only was that tedious, but the morning brought rain, fog, drizzle when it didn't happen to be raining, and cold. The temperature was in the mid-40s. I sat inside and steered, somewhat awkwardly, with lines from the tiller. Luckily not much effort was required to keep the boat on course, just a touch every few minutes, but it was clear that our inside steering arrangement needed improvement. Or we needed an autopilot for times like this.

Conditions were unpleasant enough and the outlook was far from auspicious. The barometer was dropping all day. The forecast promised more strong winds. Whatever. I just wanted to get this nonsense over with. *Spirit* had arrived, having had a good passage. I found myself quietly resenting them, with no justification whatsoever. Who would have thought that 24 hours would make such a difference?

The wind came up and started increasing in the early evening; it shifted to east of north too, which was good for our northwest course. But soon we were getting gusts to 40 knots so we dropped the staysail and continued on with just the double-reefed main. It got colder. By morning the temperature in the *cabin* was 48 degrees and the water temperature was 58. We weren't in training for these conditions: we were fresh from the tropics. Nothing seemed to last very long in this area though, and things gradually improved throughout the day: it got sunnier, the wind eased, the sea smoothed out, and we got more sail up. We started seeing fishing boats as we got up on the continental shelf. At one point when Liz was on watch, she yelled, waking me out of a sound sleep. I rushed to the cockpit; she pointed: there was a *submarine* on the surface proceeding toward us at high speed. Talk about bizarre sights. Of course he wasn't really headed for us, he was off on his own business, but it was an unsettling moment.

In the afternoon it clouded up and the wind started to die. We were near enough to Block Island to have some chance of making it before dark if we cranked up the engine and ran it full bore. We discussed the situation and decided *not* to motor but to keep on sailing slowly, even though that meant we wouldn't get in till the next morning. A half hour later the wind totally died, making the energy we'd expended making that decision wasted. On went the engine. We motored on with determination in a cold drizzle. Despite the drizzle, visibility remained reasonable and Block Island appeared right where it should be just before dark.

We still had a ways to go of course, and we motored on in the dark, damp, and cold, for some hours, using the radar to pick out the channel as we got closer in. We'd been to Block Island several times over the years, and we both remembered a well-lit and easy entrance channel. Not quite. A large scale chart of the island would've clarified the situation, but we didn't have one with us. The entrance buoy, when we found it, had a flashing red light on it, but contrary to memory none of the other channel buoys were lit. So with Liz up on the foredeck with our hand-held searchlight picking out the buoys, we proceeded slowly in. I don't like night arrivals, but I wasn't about to sit out there in the cold drizzle either. Once safely through the channel, even the harbor was confusing in the dark, especially because it was clogged with moorings; few had boats on them—it was too early in the season—but it was a challenge to find a spot clear of them. We finally got the anchor down about midnight. With 58 hours on the engine and an interesting variety of weather, to say the least, it had not been one of our finer passages.

+

We spent more than three months in southern New England. At first we didn't know where we were going to base ourselves, but after checking with a number of marinas on Long Island Sound and finding that they either had no room or were too expensive for us, we decided to go 20 miles up the Connecticut River to the marina in Portland where we'd originally launched the boat. That meant foregoing any opportunity to go out for the odd sail that summer, but that didn't matter much to us: we'd had plenty of sailing. The marina had the virtue of being closer to family and friends in the area around Hartford, and it had its own do-it-yourself yard where we could haul the boat to work on it. In the yard were several people who'd built their own boats or were refurbishing old ones, so that made for a congenial environment.

But it was strange to be back in a land environment again, or at least to have one foot on land and one on the boat. It was like living with a weird kind of schizophrenia or alienation, as it wasn't clear at any given moment which world we belonged to. People in the land world, even those who owned boats, generally had little idea of what was involved in the voyaging life and were hard pressed to know what to make of us; similarly, it was often hard for us to relate to their interests and concerns since we'd been removed from that sort of life for nearly three years. We were still living on board of course, and we were on a mooring out in the river rather than at a dock, so in that sense it felt like we were still cruising. But we needed a car to get around, so we rented an older car quite cheaply from "Rent-a-Wreck," figuring that was safe enough because we'd just be driving it locally. That was certainly convenient but it could also be seen as a symbolic step away from life afloat. At the very least, it was a reminder of the encroaching complications of land life.

One of my first priorities was to get myself checked out by a doctor. Accordingly, I had a physical, explained the symptoms of the illness I'd had in Europe—now almost totally gone—and the more recent shoulder problem, had all the usual tests, and the doctor found...not much of anything. He did say he'd noted a certain darkness in the X-ray of my lungs which made him think of emphysema, but he didn't seem too worried about it. Since I didn't smoke and jogged whenever I could, I wasn't worried either. It never showed up again on any X-rays I've had, and the chest problem I'd had never bothered me again. Maybe his X-ray films were dirty—who knows? I felt relieved but also a little baffled that I still had no explanation for that protracted period of feeling lousy.

Then on to family stuff.

Jeff had just graduated from college. He had no idea what he wanted to do, and he had no job at the moment. He was talking vaguely of going to grad school in English. We saw a lot of him that summer, gave him what advice we could, but we also felt he had to take responsibility for his own life now. Maybe we should've done more for him—it's hard to know. Parental guilt is common enough since kids seldom turn out the way you envisioned them, and perhaps we had more reason than most parents to feel some of that guilt. Jeff was a good kid though and we had to believe he'd eventually find his way. In fact he did, but it took awhile.

A more serious problem was posed by my mother, and that was to have consequences for us. She was 75 at the time, in mostly good health physically, but she was starting to have mental problems. My father had died when I was two, and she'd never remarried. She'd never been a particularly easy person to deal with, and frankly I'd almost given up trying. We hadn't been close for years, although we hadn't been actively hostile either. Now she'd started having hallucinations of a kind or at least she was starting to believe things were happening that weren't, which may be about the same thing. Her doctor was so concerned she prevailed on me to have her see a psychiatrist since my mother wouldn't do it on her own. ("There's nothing wrong with me.")

Somehow I got her to go and took her there myself. He prescribed her an antipsychotic drug. But my mother researched the drug when she got home (she was never stupid), found out what it was, and said: "I'm not taking that."

There was much more to it than that. I spent many more hours than I wanted to trying to persuade her to take some positive action, but it was like talking to a stone. I was helpless to do anything, and yet I had to deal with her. I couldn't wait to leave. I asked the psychiatrist what we could do if she wouldn't take any medication. He said she'd probably remain about the same, living happily with her delusions, or she'd become a nuisance to somebody who'd finally turn her in. I had to be content with that. I wasn't particularly impressed with the psychiatrist, but I didn't see any recourse. That's where things stood when we left, but it wasn't to be the end of it.

Luckily, Liz's dad was sane and supportive, although his wife (his second wife, not Liz's mother) didn't judge us very kindly for the way we were living our lives and the way we'd "abandoned" Jeff. It all depends on how you look at it, I suppose, but it's true that when you choose an unconventional path in life, some people will always resent it.

We spent most of the month of August with the boat out of the water working on correcting the paint problems along the waterline. That required multiple coats of paint, which was why it took so long. But by the time we were back in the water near the end of August, the boat looked good and I considered it time well-spent. And by then it was almost time to go.

Liz and I were in different psychological spaces throughout most of the summer, but we were both trying to find a way to picture ourselves when we finally did move ashore again. It wasn't at all clear to either of us, and nobody seemed ready to step forward and offer either of us our dream job, so we'd both accepted that we'd head back to the Caribbean for another winter. I think we both felt okay about that. We'd had a small taste of land life—enough to remind us what was involved—and I don't think either of us was quite ready to take that plunge yet. I'd always found a seductive simplicity in ocean voyaging: certainly there are always problems and worries and frustrations—you can't escape those in any life—but there's less extraneous noise, less people wanting this and that from you, less time spent on nonessential trivia; in many ways, it's a more focused way of living, or it can be.

Jeff had found a temporary job at a book dispensary, we'd loaned him some money to tide him over, and it looked like he was set for awhile. I'd done what I could with my mother's situation. So we returned our car—the last link with land—said goodbye to everyone and set off down the river on the day after Labor Day.

+

We had a nice sail out to Block Island. It felt good to be moving again, even if it was only to retrace our route of three years before. Several other boats in the anchorage at Block were also headed south, including *Pendragon*, a 32-footer sailed by Peter and Pauline, a Canadian couple. They'd met Keith and Tina in Sandy Hook, New Jersey last spring when *Gooseberry* was headed home. We were all waiting for the wind to shift out of the southwest so that, if all went well, we could make the 200-mile hop to Cape May with only one night at sea and still arrive in daylight.

We did, but it was tight. The wind in the harbor shifted to the north in the middle of the night and blew like hell. It had eased a bit in the morning and the forecast sounded okay, so we left and had a super downwind sail all morning, eating up the miles. We left *Pendragon* in the dust—*Horizon* is a very good downwind boat. Things were fine at night too, with the wind slowly moderating, until about 1100 the next morning when it died away altogether. We were close enough to make it in daylight, so on went the engine, and we motored for the last eight hours. The sun was starting to sink as we made the inlet at 1900, but there was still enough light to see to anchor (always a bit of a challenge in Cape May harbor). Surprisingly, *Pendragon* came in about half an hour later. Somehow they'd made up a lot of ground on us, maybe while we were motoring.

We hung out in Cape May for a few days, enjoying the company of Peter and Pauline. They came from Timmins, Ontario, way up in the frigid north. Peter had been a teacher, Pauline a tax accountant. We liked them both.

We soon met another Canadian couple, Helen and Erik on *Eventyr*, a 38-foot steel boat that they'd completed from a bare hull. Helen had done all the woodwork and carpentry while Eric had handled the electrical and mechanical stuff, a neat division of labor. They were from British Columbia and had sailed the boat out to Hawaii and then to Alaska and down the inland passage to Vancouver from there. Then they'd had the boat trucked to the east coast to avoid the tedious trip down the coast to Panama. Erik, a former RCMP officer, was Norwegian and they intended to sail across the Atlantic to Norway.

With the two Canadian boats, we left and proceeded up the Delaware with no wind to help us: we motored the whole 52 miles and anchored behind the breakwater at the entrance to the Cape Cod Canal. I hated to motor all that way, but at least it was over with and we all got together on our boat for a cold beer. Next day it was through the canal into the Chesapeake and to an anchorage in the Sassafras River.

+

So there we were in the Chesapeake, looking forward to a few leisurely and untroubled weeks as we wended our way south. It didn't quite work out that way. Instead, things rapidly turned chaotic for me from an unexpected direction. Or perhaps it should've been expected.

We all decided to head for Baltimore, and we stopped for the night at an anchorage near the mouth of the Patapsco River before heading upriver to the city. In the morning I happened to be listening to the Waterway Net on ham radio, a longtime feature of east coast cruising serving mainly boats moving up and down the Intracoastal Waterway. I usually didn't check in to that net but I did listen occasionally. On this occasion I heard my call sign, and when I responded I was told I had an emergency message: "Call home!"

Luckily we were near a marina that had a pay phone (in those pre-cell phone days), so we rushed ashore and called Liz's dad. He told us that my mother was in the hospital. He didn't have any more information than that, so I called my uncle, my mother's brother Harlan, who lived in Vermont. His wife, Eleanor, filled me in. The essence of it was that my mother had apparently acted on one of her delusions. She'd called 911 and told them that her cardiologist, for whom she'd developed an unhealthy obsession, was all alone in his house and needed help. The 911 operator dispatched medics to the surprised doctor's house. The sequence of events isn't totally clear, but somehow my mother got in her car and started driving toward Vermont. She was found some hours later wandering around on the highway near her parked car in Northampton, Massachusetts. It sounded like the script for a bad movie.

Harlan and Eleanor drove down from Vermont, took her back to her home, and when they got the full story they took her to the psychiatric hospital in Hartford. There she was committed for 15 days. What a mess. I called the hospital asking to speak to the doctor responsible but could only get the social worker, who told me to call back on Thursday. It was now Tuesday. I resolved not to do anything until I talked to the doctor. So for the moment, we continued with our plans.

Still in company with the Canadians, we motored up the river to Baltimore and anchored in the inner harbor in the tiny anchorage area under the World Trade Center building. If the anchoring was a little dicey, it was a great location and not crowded just then. My next step was to call Jonathan, my ski school director from ski-teaching days in Vermont. He was now the General Manager of Roundtop Ski Area near Hersey, Pennsylvania, an hour's drive or so from Baltimore. He'd recently become interested in sailing, and we'd been corresponding on sailing matters. He'd asked me to call him when I got in the area, and when I talked to him he said he'd drive down to see us on Friday.

Meanwhile, with everything up in the air for the moment, we explored the city with the Canadians. We were right downtown. A short dinghy ride took us to the landing in the renovated port area, numerous city attractions close by. Over the next few days we went to the Walker Art Museum, the Lexington Market (a huge European style produce market), Fort McHenry; we walked around Fells Point and Little Italy, went to the science museum, and generally had an active social time.

On Thursday I finally reached Doctor Jain at the hospital and had a long talk with him. He said he couldn't give my mother medication unless she consented or unless the court ordered it. He wanted me to call her and try to convince her to stay in the hospital voluntarily. I did about an hour later, but to my relief he'd already gotten her to sign something, and she was starting to feel comfortable there. Were we out of the woods with this? I hoped so. Everybody was expecting me to come racing back, but I couldn't see what good it would do other than make everyone else feel better. It made more sense to me to wait and see.

Jonathan and his wife, Vicky, showed up on Friday afternoon. We hadn't seen him in nearly 20 years. He took us out to dinner and invited us to come visit him next week at his ski area. He'd show us around and give us a car to do some sightseeing if we wanted to. Why not?

I made more phone calls. Doctor Jain said my mother would probably remain in the hospital for at least six weeks. All the more reason for me to bide my time. But when I talked to Eleanor again, she was surprised I wasn't coming back. For the moment, though, I intended to carry on with my plans. If that made me a bad person, so be it, but going back just to satisfy other people's perceptions of what I *ought* to be doing wasn't an appealing alternative.

So after a week we left Baltimore and went down the river to the anchorage at the mouth. This was a safe place to leave the boat at anchor while we visited Jonathan. *Pendragon* came down too, but *Eventyr* was waiting for a part they'd ordered, so they remained in Baltimore. It looked like we'd be splitting up for awhile, but *Eventyr* had ham radio, so we'd be able to keep in touch.

Jonathan picked us up and drove us to his house, a big chalet-type on the ski area property. In the evening he took us for a tour of the area. It wasn't a big mountain, but being close to population centers it did a good business, and keeping things running smoothly meant that Jonathan had big responsibilities. He was proud of his accomplishments, but I got the feeling that he wasn't getting as much satisfaction from it as he used to. He was interested in what we had done and were doing, but I also got the feeling he didn't quite understand the degree of commitment required.

We took him up on his offer of a car and drove through the rolling green hills of southern Pennsylvania to visit the Civil War battle site at Gettysburg. The day was warm and sunny, the area very pleasant, making it tough to envision the bloody battle here. Neither of us were exactly Civil War buffs, but we enjoyed the site.

The visit with Jonathan and a couple nights away from the boat made a nice break, but we were glad to get back and find everything okay. We started working our way down the bay, mostly against light southerlies. We spent time at St. Michaels on the eastern shore and at St. Mary's City, a low-key historic village near the mouth of the Potomac.

Meanwhile, I continued to struggle with phone calls. Life

would've been so much easier with a cell phone, but such conveniences were still years in the future. The biggest problem was nobody could call me, so if I couldn't reach somebody all I could do was try again. And I had to be near a phone booth (remember those?). I talked to my mother again, who now said she wanted to go home. I talked to the social worker, who said they were considering letting my mother go home with assistance from visiting nurses. She asked me to call the visiting nurses to see if they could help. I did. They said: "That's what we do." I talked to Harlan and Eleanor again, who still thought I should come back. I talked to Sandy, my mother's neighbor, who put a guilt trip on me for not being there, even though I couldn't see that she'd done much to help. Some people are judgmental without knowing the full story.

It wouldn't have been a big deal to rent a car and go back for a few days, but the more I thought about it, the less I liked that idea. By now, my mother had more or less accepted that I wasn't there. It seemed clear to me that my leaving had at least partially triggered this whole thing. If I went back now, it was only going to send the wrong message: it would say that if she wanted me to come running, all she had to do was flip out...or pretend to. Harlan thought she might be pretending to be better just to get to go home. He may have been right.

And then we had a hurricane scare. We were in Mobjack Bay when they issued a hurricane warning for Hampton Roads. Hurricane Lily had passed south of Bermuda and was taking aim at us, a rather unusual course. We retreated up the East River on the north side of the bay; it wasn't as sheltered as I'd have liked, but Lily was only a Category 1 storm and it didn't look like we were going to get a direct hit. We tied things down, got additional anchors ready, hoped we were sheltered enough. Shortly afterwards, they discontinued the hurricane warning, changed it to a tropical storm warning. And as it developed, Lily made a sharp right-hand turn before reaching the coast, proceeded northward, and never affected us much at all. Just a little additional dash of stress to add to the already considerable pile.

We carried on to Norfolk, and by the time we'd anchored off the Navy Hospital in Portsmouth, inside Marker 1 of the Intracoastal Waterway, I'd changed my mind and decided that I'd have to go back. Things were just too messy. It was starting to look more doubtful that my mother would be able to live alone. If she couldn't, we needed to find a place for her. Harlan would help, but I reluctantly concluded I needed to be there.

The anchorage was quite safe, so I had few qualms about leaving Liz there by herself. *Pendragon* and *Eventyr* were up in the St. Michael's area, planning to be in Norfolk in a few days, so she'd have some familiar company. It was easy to get ashore for shopping or anything else. We'd had our hurricane scare, the weather looked reasonable: Liz would be fine.

So I rented a car and drove the 500 miles to Connecticut. Harlan came down from Vermont. We stayed in her house; at least we had a phone there. What followed was one of the most depressing weeks I'd ever had. First, I visited my mother and found her eerily subdued, meek, without affect, a huge contrast from the loud and often hyper woman she'd been before. I assumed it was the drugs they were giving her: they'd turned her into a colorless, passive old lady. It was sad in a generic sense, but I felt little personal connection; rightly or wrongly I'd given up on her a long time ago. Maybe I should have felt guilty about that, but I didn't. I'd spent too many years trying to work out some way to relate to her, and she'd always refused to see me for who I was. Much of the problem, I think, was that she lived entirely too much in her own head.

But now we had two practical problems to contend with: to find a place for her and to dispose of her furniture and belongings in some way if she wasn't going to return to her house. The details of what we went through aren't important here. Briefly, Harlan and I visited a number of "rest homes" that ranged from truly horrible to fairly decent. Trouble was, the decent ones didn't want her because they were worried about her disruptive tendencies. In the process of doing this, without much help from the social worker, we received an education in the mechanics of caring for the elderly. It wasn't pretty. We finally settled on the best of the facilities that would take her, though neither of us was real happy about it. We rented a storage unit for her belongings and hauled them all over there in Harlan's truck, just in case she was ever able to use them again. And having done about all we could do for the moment, Harlan left for Vermont, and I drove back to Norfolk.

As it turned out, she didn't go to the home we'd found. Harlan and Eleanor found a more suitable one in Vermont, and even though she wouldn't be near friends in Connecticut, she'd at least be where they could visit her and keep an eye on things. It was probably for the best, and it took some of the burden off me. If I hadn't had that kind of help, things might've turned out very differently. At least now I could get back to the much more straightforward problems of our cruising life.

More or less straightforward anyway. Liz had been fine while I was away, but our refrigerator had quit. You get attached to whatever conveniences you have and are reluctant to part with them. We'd lived three years without refrigeration on our circumnavigation, but now we were unwilling to do that. We'd have to get it fixed somehow, but we had one more obstacle to deal with first.

We set off down the Waterway toward Beaufort, but a couple days later the wind increased as we were crossing Albemarle Sound and ominous black clouds started rolling in. Not liking the looks of the weather, we turned into the Little Alligator River (as we'd had to do on our trip through here three years ago) and felt our way in through six-foot depths watching the depth sounder carefully because we were off the chart. We eased over toward the northern bank in seven-foot depths and anchored, well-sheltered from the northeast wind. Four or five other boats came in to get shelter from the worsening conditions. By evening it was blowing hard, and after midnight it was blowing hard enough, 40-50 knots, that I felt compelled to get up and get a second anchor ready to go, just in case. It blew hard all the next morning, pinning our anemometer at 60 in the harder gusts. At least one of the other boats dragged. There's a lot of strain on the anchor in shallow water because it's much easier to straighten the chain out than in say, 20 feet, but using a nice long nylon snubber, as we did, can ease a lot of the strain as the nylon stretches. The weather broadcast claimed it gusted to 92 knots on the Chesapeake Bay Bridge—nothing to spit into. I turned in for a nap after lunch, and when I woke the wind was down, it had backed to the northwest, and the sky was clearing. Not a hurricane, but not a very pleasant weather system either.

At a marina in the little town of Oriental a couple days later, we got a guy to look at our refrigerator. He found a hole in the evaporator unit, meaning it would have to be replaced. We called the manufacturer in Connecticut, and they were able to send us a new one by next day shipping. I installed it, the guy in the marina recharged it, and after just three days we were all set to continue chilling beer. And the next day, we proceeded to Beaufort where we caught up with our Canadian friends again. It hadn't been an easy month, but here we were at last.

+

So where did we stand now? We both felt the pull of land life, which is probably not the best way to set off on an extended cruise. The past few months had been a further reminder to me, that all the complexities of "real life" were still very much there, waiting to be dealt with. More than ever, I felt we were living on borrowed time. It was sort of like dreading an upcoming surgical procedure, realizing it's necessary, but attempting to put it out of your mind until the moment actually arrives. If this was to be our last winter afloat, I hoped we could make it a happy and successful one. I think Liz shared the same hope, but for her there was also a strong desire to get this sailing business over with so she could get on with her life as she now envisioned it. There was obviously the potential for conflict there, but I hoped we could keep it arm's length.

Liz still enjoyed a lot of what we were doing, probably at least as much as I did. But the actual sailing had become less meaningful to her. Maybe we'd just had too much of it. Certainly the novelty had worn off long ago, and an ocean passage now was simply X number of more-or-less uncomfortable days. I felt that too. But it was also true that over the years the activity had become much more *my* thing than hers. Because I was the one who had to deal with maintenance and repair issues to keep all systems functioning, and because I assumed the role of "captain" in most of the sailing and maneuvering situations we dealt with, Liz often saw herself in a secondary, helper sort of role. I didn't really see it that way. I knew how vital she was to the success of our voyages, but perception is everything, and a role in support of *my* activities wasn't particularly fulfilling to her.

Now, the upcoming cruise was more of a coda to the past three years of voyaging than an integral part of it. It was something we'd tacked on because we weren't quite sure what else to do. I knew we could do it—that wasn't in doubt—but would we enjoy it? Could we make it work? Or were we inhabiting such different spaces that it would just become a protracted ordeal for one or both of us?

In fact, it worked out better than we could've hope

14. An Ideal Caribbean Cruise?

Once again we were poised in Beaufort in late October, waiting for the right chance to leave. From what we could make out of the weather situation, it looked like it might be awhile. There was a "disturbance" in the western Caribbean that they were watching for tropical development, so it was no time to be hurrying off.

We had the Canadians over for a beer, along with a couple other Canadian friends of theirs, Ron and Yvonne, on a boat called *Full and By*. They'd been at anchor in Oriental when that blow we'd had in the Little Alligator River came through. They'd dragged and their boat had gone up on the breakwater. They'd managed to get off with little damage and seemed philosophical about it. The other Canadians were sympathetic but couldn't resist renaming the boat *High and Dry*!

A boat called *Summer Breeze* was anchored nearby, a 41-footer sailed by two guys, Harold and Dale. Harold owned the boat and Dale had been a fighter pilot in Vietnam. They were headed for the Virgins too, on their first offshore passage, and we'd see more of them there.

+

There are basically two ways to get to the Caribbean from Beaufort. The first is the offshore route. It's just about 1200 miles to the Virgins, which for a normal cruising boat usually means a passage of 10-14 days, depending on conditions. The other way is the day-sailing route: down the Waterway to Florida, through the Bahamas to the Turks and Caicos and on to the Dominican Republic, Puerto Rico, and the Virgins. That route can take months. The downside to it is that beyond Florida it's virtually all against the wind. For most people, that usually means lots of motoring. And once you get to the Dominican Republic and turn due east you'll be motoring into the teeth of the northeast trades. There are strategies you can use to make it all a little less onerous, but it's still a slog. We'd met people in Puerto Rico who were so burned out by the time they got there that they'd decided to go no further. But depending on your boat, the reliability of your engine, and your temperament, it can be a satisfactory way to avoid an offshore passage, and people do it all the time.

The offshore route has its own problems. The weather in the fall, after the hurricane threat has passed, can be boisterous, as the fronts moving off the coast plunge further south. You're likely to get gale force winds at some point on this passage. Theoretically, the weather is quieter in the spring, mid-April to early June, but a passage at that time gets you to the Caribbean just in time to start worrying about hurricane season, so relatively few boats choose that option.

Beaufort is probably the best place to leave from. The coast trends to the southwest the further south you go, so you're not gaining much in terms of miles to sail and you're putting yourself in the position of having to make more easting against, most likely, easterly winds. Some boats leave from the mouth of the Chesapeake, but that means you'll be bucking the Gulf Stream longer with the ever-present risk of strong winds against the Stream, which can be very nasty. Some boats leave from New England and sail directly to Bermuda and then south from there. That can be a reasonable option, but starting that far north at that time of year (November) entails more of a risk for heavy weather. If you leave from Beaufort on a good forecast, you can be across the worst of the Gulf Stream current in 24-36 hours— the western wall of the Stream is only 50 miles or so from Beaufort—and you're in warm water as well. It's still sometimes a struggle to get east though, so it often pays to take a more easterly course for the first few days if conditions permit.

We were in a slightly different situation than most of the other boats in Beaufort. First of all, we'd made this passage before, twice before if you count the trip to the Turks and Caicos, which, admittedly is a little easier. Second, for most of the other boats, this would be the adventure of a lifetime, something they probably wouldn't repeat, and once they got to the Caribbean they'd be likely to spend a good chunk of time there, often a couple of years or more. By contrast, we were planning to make this a whirlwind cruise. We had no desire to stay in the Caribbean for the summer, so we'd be heading back in the spring. That meant we had only about six months to spend.

We'd discussed that and come up with a strategy. We knew enough about the area to have a realistic idea of what was possible. Instead of day sailing down the whole chain of islands from the Virgins to Trinidad, as most people do, we'd pick out a few places we wanted to spend some time, sail directly to those places and spend a few weeks at each. That way we could have a fairly leisurely cruise. When you don't feel like you have to see everything, and when you're willing to make a few offshore jumps, it opens up lots of possibilities.

+

We only had to wait about a week. The disturbance in the western Caribbean fizzled, and the weather looked settled enough to give it a go. We got up early (0330), made preparations, waited till we heard the weather at 0600 just to be sure, struggled getting our two anchors up, and went out the channel in the dark using the searchlight on the markers. *Pendragon* left a couple hours later; *Eventyr*, for some reason, didn't leave until a couple days later: I was never sure exactly why. We'd made no arrangements to keep in radio contact. It was unlikely we'd stay in VHF range (about 20 miles) with *Pendragon* for very long anyway, and I knew we could keep track of *Eventyr* by ham radio on one of the nets.

We had a rousing start on a perfect day. The wind was behind us for awhile, then shifted to a little east of north, a beam wind for us. Everything was beautiful during the day. Things got a bit rough after dark as the wind increased to 20-25 knots, Force 6, but we were through the worst of the Gulf Stream current by midnight, and things started to smooth out.

Much later when we were in the Caribbean, we learned that *Pendragon* had bailed out and would be spending the winter in the Bahamas. They'd apparently had a tough night, had broken three halyards, and Pauline had started getting blurred vision, to the point of almost going blind, probably from the seasickness stuff she was taking. We were sorry to leave them behind—we'd enjoyed their company.

The wind died, as it has a habit of doing, and we motored most of the next 24 hours. After that, the wind returned, and while I wouldn't characterize it as *consistent,* we did have decent wind much of the time. In squalls it would often pipe up to 40 knots or more, and though that could quickly get your attention it never lasted very long. We didn't have any prolonged periods of adverse wind direction either. It did go southeast for awhile—the direction we wanted to go; that could still get me cursing and bemoaning my fate, but that didn't last too long either; it soon shifted to the southwest and finally to the northeast with a frontal passage. In other words, we had pretty typical weather for this passage.

One night we spotted the lights of a ship that looked like he was going to be close. I called him on VHF. In broken English he said that he saw us. Later he asked what course I was steering, but he continued on his course apparently oblivious to us. When he got inside a half a mile—which is very close for a big ship at night especially when you're not sure of his intentions—I had to tack. All the evidence suggested he would've hit us otherwise. Needless to say, I wasn't happy about it, nor was I impressed with his seamanship. But like drivers on the Interstate, there are always a few that behave like idiots.

On Day 7 we lost the wind again for awhile, and as we were motoring in a glassy calm we came upon a sailboat just sitting with two jibs up hanging there uselessly. That was indeed a bizarre sight, 500 miles from anywhere. We called him on VHF but got no answer. We saw nobody and since there was no evidence of any problems, we didn't bother to investigate further. I'll admit to being a little wary and perhaps excessively cautious, but when you're that far away from anything, caution is only common sense. In fact, I suspected the crew was probably sleeping: no other explanation made much sense.

My goal was to make it to 25 degrees north, 65 degrees west, just a little dot I made on the chart where those latitude and longitude lines crossed; at that mid-ocean point, I'd figured, we could logically expect the northeast tradewinds to be making themselves felt with some insistence, and our course to the Virgins would be due south from there. We got near enough to that goal to have the desired effect, and we were soon careening along in a Force 7 breeze from the east, headed due south. The only problem was there was a wicked northwest swell, about 10 feet high, that with the east wind blowing against it made things mightily uncomfortable. The forecast spoke ominously of an approaching front. We had 190 miles to go at noon on Day 9, so it didn't look like we'd make it before dark the next day, but I still held out some hope.

The night was grim though, raising memories of our first offshore passage 13 years before. The wind increased just after dark and we started getting squalls, dark black things with lots of rain and wind and lightning, approximately one an hour through the night. Just when we'd think it was settling down a little, another one would hit. Some had 50 knots in them. We hung on, using just our double-reefed main. Neither of us slept. It's nights like that you wish you were somewhere else...*anywhere* else.

But the squall activity let up in mid-morning, and enough breaks in the cloud cover allowed me to get a pretty good fix. Squall clouds moved in again in the afternoon while I was trying to sleep, but they lifted about 1530 and suddenly Virgin Gorda was visible, then Tortola, and finally the whole chain, about 30 miles away. We raced in toward the islands, lost the wind for awhile, had another squall for which we had to drop the jibs, and shortly after dark we were within seven miles of Jost Van Dyke. We were both too tired to try to thread our way into an anchorage just then, so we hove-to, had a comfortable night in the shadow of Jost Van Dyke (so to speak), and managed to get some sleep.

The last day had been a little less than ideal, but overall the passage hadn't been too bad. And in the morning the sight of the high, green, improbably beautiful islands sitting there in the sunshine filled us with a sense of promise and excitement. Somehow, you never get tired of moments like that.

+

The Virgin Islands (17 Nov-13 Dec). By 1000 we were anchored in St. Thomas harbor near *Summer Breeze* who'd got in the day before. In the afternoon, after we'd had a nap and emerged on deck to survey the scene, Phil and Doris on *Jolly II Roger*, last seen in Las Palmas in the Canary Islands, stopped by. They'd spent the winter in St. Martin and were having a power boat built in South Africa. It's always nice to encounter familiar faces when you enter a harbor after a passage, and it happens more often than you'd think.

I made phone calls and found that my mother was now in Vermont and, apparently, doing well, or as well as could be expected. In any case, I was beyond easy reach now; only the direst emergency could induce me to go back. There was some satisfaction in that.

We only stayed a couple of days in St. Thomas, just long enough to pick up a few supplies and visit the Pueblo supermarket. Then it was off to Christmas Cove, one of our first tropical anchorages 13 years before. I was glad to see that it was still every bit as lovely as I remembered. *Summer Breeze* came over too. Liz and I did a scuba dive on Cow and Calf Rocks, about a half a mile to the west. Harold and Dale came along to

220

sit on the boat so we didn't have to worry about it. It was a great dive: tunnels and arches to go through, lots of fish, lots of color; best of all, for my first scuba dive since the trouble I'd had with my shoulder, I was glad to see that I had no problems at all.

We moved over to Leinster Bay on St. John, and a couple days later we had Thanksgiving dinner on *Summer Breeze*, a delightful affair. Harold had prepared a turkey; Liz brought rolls and mashed potatoes. She was impressed by Harold's culinary skills.

"My wife has trained me well," he said. Apparently she was scheduled to fly in in a few days.

We sat around eating and talking and drinking for a good chunk of the day.

I finally made contact with Helen on *Eventyr* on ham radio when they were a day or so out. They had quite a story. I only got the brief version of it on the radio. Their engine had shifted on its mounts in that front that had bothered us as we approached the Virgins. Of course because they were a couple days behind us, it got to them first. Erik had a strange reaction when things started to get nasty. He began to think, irrationally, that they had to get out of there, to get away from the nasty weather. So he started the engine and attempted to *motor* away from it. In a way that sounds screwy, and in a way it is, but when you're short of sleep, your mind can do strange things, your sense of reality can become distorted. I knew. I'd been there before. Anyway, the result of running the engine in those conditions was that it shifted on its mounts, which meant it became badly misaligned and would vibrate frighteningly if they attempted to use it.

They made it in to Jost Van Dyke by running the engine very gingerly as needed. We went over to see them. Erik admitted he'd lost it out there. "I'm not going to Europe," he declared. "That passage convinced me that I don't want to do it."

"What will you do then?" I asked.

"Probably just stay in the Caribbean for a year or two, then go back to Vancouver through the Panama Canal."

"Give it some time," I said. "Don't make any decisions yet. You've just had a nasty passage but it doesn't mean you have to scuttle your cruising plans. I'll bet you'll be looking at things differently in a week or two."

I was thinking of what had happened to us the first time we'd made that passage. Things can look awfully bleak when you've just been through something like that.

At any rate, I spent the better part of a day helping Erik get his engine realigned. I'd had some experience and knew how to do it, but the problem was the flanges—the connecting plates, one on the prop shaft and one on the engine transmission, that have to mate—weren't easy to get to: it required standing on your head and contorting just to get the feeler gauges in between the flanges to check how well they were mating. But we finally got things within acceptable limits so that most of the vibration was gone.

"That's probably the best we can do for now," I said. "I'd get it double-checked by a mechanic though, just to be sure." For the moment, Erik had a functioning vessel again.

+

We'd always liked the Virgins, even though they're overrun with charter boats and have been for many years. The area still offers everything that tropical cruising should: great scenery, both above and below water; plentiful anchorages; consistent breezes; mostly sheltered waters. It's a great place to unwind from a passage.

Summer Breeze came over and we had everybody on board for dinner with wahoo that Erik caught and cherry pie that Harold made as we discussed our respective passages. With the soft tropical breeze playing around us in the night, it was hard not to feel a sense of contentment.

We spent most of the next couple weeks at Trellis Bay on Beef Island, which is sort of an eastern extension of Tortola. It seemed to be a favorite of cruising boats, as opposed to charter boats: there were buses to Road Town and a little beach bar called the Loose Mongoose. *Eventyr* settled in with us, and we spent a lot of time with them. Incredibly, *Ta-Tl*, Don and Ann and the their kids, last seen in Turks and Caicos three years before, were in Trellis Bay waiting to make the hop to St. Martin. More proof that the cruising world is surprisingly small. They'd been to Venezuela while we were in the Med, and had lots of information for us on that area.

Meanwhile, there was plenty to do to keep us amused. We did a scuba dive on the Rhone, a UK mail steamer wrecked off Salt Island, a few miles to the south of Beef Island, in 1867, of all things, and now a colorful dive site, encrusted with coral and serving as a habitat for a ton of sea creatures: rays, lobsters, octopus, barracuda, as well as the usual crowd of smaller fish milling about. With Helen and Erik we visited the Baths on Virgin Gorda again and found it to be as enchanting a spot as ever, with all its rock formations and pools and tunnels, even if it was overrun with tourists. The days passed quickly, and before we knew it was mid-December and time to move on.

Our plan was to sail directly to Bequia and spend time once again in the Grenadines. That meant bypassing a slew of islands, some of which we might've enjoyed visiting again, but it also meant relieving us of the work of daysailing, of motoring in the lee of the high islands, of the necessity to check in and out of each island, and it meant that we'd get to what we considered the most appealing part of the eastern Caribbean all the sooner.

We left the Virgins through Round Rock Passage, and everything was fine for the first 15 miles, whereupon a squall came through and shifted the wind to the southeast—the direction we were going of course. We considered going back, but we were already too far along to make that an attractive alternative. So we stuck it out, and eventually the wind freed enough to make the course viable.

Several other things happened that first day to spice up the passage. First, a Coast Guard vessel approached us from the stern, trailing us like an annoying dog. Not as frightening perhaps as having a searchlight trained on you out of the black, but still a little unsettling. Finally I called him on VHF and asked him what his intentions were. He ran through the usual list of questions, and I was afraid we were going to be boarded again, as we had been in the Windward passage, but no, he was apparently satisfied and let us go. There was another yacht ahead of us, and he went through the same routine with him. I'd like to know how many criminals they actually catch by harassing yachts that way, as the whole exercise—and the boardings too, when they occur—seemed rather pointless to me, especially when there's absolutely no reason for suspicion.

Then after dark we had a couple of additional encounters with ships. The first *appeared* to be with the Coast Guard ship again and he *appeared* to be exercising a remote helicopter, though it was hard to confirm exactly who he was or what he was doing in the dark. As he approached us, I called him VHF. He claimed not to see my lights at a range of half a mile, and he was real snotty about it. We tacked to get out of his way. He told us what course he was steering. We tacked back when we should easily clear him if he stayed on that course. He didn't. He altered course again so that we were closing him again. We had to tack once more. I noted in my log, with some bitterness: *a real asshole*. When we finally got clear of him and his private part of the ocean, we found another ship headed for us in a meeting situation. I called him—he at least could see us—and we agreed on a starboard-to-starboard passage with about a half a mile between us, an altogether saner response.

So after the traffic cleared we were at last free to enjoy a rather raucous passage for the 400 miles to Bequia. We weren't hard on the wind, but we were close to it, and I wanted to be sure we stayed up to windward so we wouldn't get headed. Mostly we used the staysail and double-reefed main. It was rough, lots of lurching and swooping and darting, lots of spray flying, but we made good progress. Good progress excuses a lot.

On the morning of Day 3, we had St. Vincent in sight, almost lost in the clouds and the glare of the sun. But as we got closer, the rugged green peaks emerged, and we marveled at what a lovely island it was, even if its capital city, as we remembered, was a little seedy. By 1330 we were anchored in Bequia, well satisfied with our three-day passage.

+

The Grenadines (Dec 16-Feb 4). We stayed in Bequia for two weeks, until just after New Years. It was strange to find some of the same people there who'd been there the year before. One guy who recognized us said: "Ah, they always come back." In the time we'd been gone, we'd sailed to New England and back; the furthest the regulars in the anchorage had gone was Grenada. Not that there's anything wrong with that. Still, I did feel a little smug.

As usual, we enjoyed Bequia. We had an active and social time, but it wasn't quite the same as it'd been the previous year. We met a lot of people, but we missed the company of Keith and Tina. I talked with Helen on the radio. They were still in Trellis Bay intending to go to St. Martin. After New Years we moved down to the Tobago Cays, for some snorkeling and diving.

To amuse ourselves one day we sailed up to the southern end of Canouan, about four miles to the north. We looked at two bays on the south side but they were exposed and rolly, so we rounded the southeastern point and proceeded up inside the windward reef under power. One of our cruising guides suggested there was great shelter here. Maybe, but the channel heading north was very narrow with coral on both sides, a hairy entrance to say the least. We edged slowly northward, and although there were some open areas, there were lots of coral heads too, all uncharted of course. Nor was it well-protected. We were there at low tide and there was a sizeable chop in the whole area: it would only be worse at high tide when the reef would offer even less protection. No thank you: no place to spend the night if you were looking for a worry-free environment. It was tough getting out too. Even at 1100 with the sun quite high, the glare made it tough to see the coral. Still, once we'd safely cleared the area, I considered it'd been a worthwhile excursion; in sailing, as in life, sometimes a few steps off the beaten path can be an adventure in itself, as long as you don't take stupid risks.

After a week in the Cays, we sailed down to Tyrell Bay on Carriacou, stopping first to clear into the Granada Grenadines at Hillsborough, an annoyance in itself. It was 1210 when I arrived at the Customs office, filled out the usual forms, and was informed there was an "overtime" charge of $20 EC (the local currency). Then to immigration where I filled out their form and was informed it was another $20 EC for overtime. If I'd arrived during working hours, *before* 12 or after their lunch hour, there would've been no charge. Obviously I should've asked if they were "open"—they certainly weren't about to tell me. They were just sitting there hoping some clueless yachtie would stumble in. A pretty slimy group, but I'd learned a long time ago not to judge a country by its customs officials.

Eventyr finally caught up with us. They'd been planning to island hop their way down, but what would've been strong headwinds going to St. Martin discouraged them, so they made the same hop from the Virgins that we did. We had a fine time with them. We took long walks in the hills, lovely rolling countryside with friendly people. We talked with John Bedoe, the local entrepreneur who remembered us from the previous year. He was concerned that not enough was being done in Carriacou to encourage tourism, even simple stuff like cleaning up the beach and providing a dinghy dock. I appreciated his point of view, but I also knew that tourism was often a double-edged sword: tourists in numbers were very good at destroying the things they'd come for in the first place.

One night the four of us went to local bar not far from the waterfront to hear a steel band. It was more of a practice session than a performance, very informal, but the guys were good. The band leader, Matthew, had lived in Miami for 15 years and was personable, funny, talented, a real showman. Yachties and locals of all ages drifted in and out, grooving to the music. There wasn't a lot of drinking, just a general good time, and the locals appreciated seeing us there.

After a week in Tyrell Bay, longer than we'd originally intended, we left with *Eventyr* for Grenada, sailing down the windward side again and then along the south coast to Prickly Bay. But after a night in Prickly Bay, we both relocated to the anchorage behind Hog Island, a couple of bays over, which was a bit less rolly. We could still get into St. George's—or anywhere else on the island—from there, by catching a bus at the head of Woburn Bay, a longish dinghy ride away. We ended up doing that frequently.

The Hog Island anchorage was a favorite with some cruising boats, but it was a very ingrown little community, as sometimes happens in these popular well-sheltered spots. For the most part, the boats there appeared to be those who had settled in for the season, or at least a good part of it, and had little interest in or use for intruders. A few days after we arrived, we attended a barbecue on the beach. Nobody paid us the slightest attention: we were totally ignored, as if we'd committed some terrible offense that no-one wanted to deal with (which, as far as I know, we hadn't). The only guy I managed to strike up a conversation with claimed he was just back from a 12-year circumnavigation, but he was so negative about everything that I saw no potential in that direction. We stayed for a little while, finally figured it was a lost cause, and left. What a downer. Perhaps it was just a function of the boats that happened to be there at that particular time, but thereafter, any social gathering that threatened to be boring or unrewarding in any way we termed a "Hog Island Barbecue." At least we took something away from the experience.

So, since we'd been effectively ostracized (or so it seemed), the four of us spent most of our time there together. We'd go into town, or explore the island on the buses (always a treat), or go for walks in the local area. At the end of the day we'd get together for a sundowner and snacks as the tropical sunlight faded and the mild night air took over. Shortly after we'd arrived, the Gulf War (the *first* Gulf War, though of course we didn't know that then) had started. We both had little TVs—ours had a 4" screen—so we could watch the coverage of the bombing with a combination of fascination and horror; it seemed far removed from our peaceful setting.

We moved back over to Prickly Bay for awhile, starting to think about leaving. *Eventyr* would be heading up the island chain; we'd be going to Venezuela. We'd enjoyed our time with Helen and Erik. When we had a chance to talk with Keith and Tina from *Gooseberry* about them, Tina called them our "replacement Canadians." I suppose they were. Though we talked on the radio now and then for awhile, we never saw them again after we parted in Prickly Bay.

[As a footnote, they finally did make their Atlantic crossing, very successfully. They went to Norway, fulfilling Erik's dream, spent a winter in Holland, another winter in the Shetland Islands, of all places. About four or five years later, after we'd moved back ashore, we got a phone call from Helen. At least Liz did—I didn't happen to be there. She was calling from Portugal.

"Erik *died*," she said.

Liz was stunned: "What happened?"

He hadn't been feeling well, just sort of tired, so he went to a doctor in Portugal. The doctor diagnosed leukemia, and within two weeks he was dead. He was only about my age.

Helen was then sitting there in Vilamoura, Portugal on the boat, wondering how she was going to get it back. She was calling to see if I'd consider helping her sail it back. "He's one of the few people I'd trust to do it," she said to Liz.

Liz didn't know what to say. They agreed that she'd call again in a few days. When she did, she told us that she'd found another couple, as I remember, on a boat in Vilamoura who were very experienced and agreed to sail the boat across. So there was a decision I didn't have to make. We heard later that it all went well.]

+

Venezuela (7 Feb-6 Mar). We sailed overnight to Los Testigos, a group of little islands between Grenada and mainland Venezuela. These are dry, cactus-covered islands with no very secure anchorages, although by moving around you can usually get reasonable shelter in ordinary weather. We checked in with officials on Isla Iguana but found the best anchorage under the western point of Los Testigos, the biggest island of the group. There we were able to take a line to shore to keep the bow headed into the swell and be fairly comfortable. We stayed a few days exploring the islands and snorkeling, then took off for Isla Margarita.

After reading about Venezuela and talking to people who'd been there, we decided not to bother with the mainland. We'd stay in the offshore islands as we worked our way toward Bonaire. The water gets colder and murkier as you get toward the coast, and it seemed that the people who enjoyed it the most were the ones who took their boat to a marina and traveled inland. We had no plans to do that.

We arrived at Pampatar on Isla Margarita after a fast sail and settled in to the lousy anchorage which held quite a few other boats. It was lousy, not because it was particularly dangerous but because it was subject to an annoying swell that could, at times, threaten to roll your back teeth out. We set a stern anchor the first afternoon, as had many of the other boats, and that helped but didn't totally eliminate the rolling. For some reason that escapes me now, we stayed there two weeks.

I guess one reason we stayed was that we welcomed the opportunity to use our Spanish again. It was easy to get into Porlamar, the main city, on the frequent buses. Porlamar was a real city with a good variety of stores and bustling atmosphere, and we liked listening to Spanish and speaking it—in a limited way—when asking directions or dealing with people in the shops. Other than that, not much remains in memory of our time there. A note in my journal indicates that we didn't find much of interest among the boats in the anchorage either, nor did they seem interested in us. Some places are like that.

When we finally got ourselves together to leave, I went in to collect our passports from the little agency that handled all the bureaucratic formalities and other services for the yachties. Gary, the guy who ran it, said, "Now you have seven days to get out of Venezuela."

That wasn't what I'd understood, and I told him so. I had a document that seemed to say, in English, that there was a lot more flexibility than that.

Gary shrugged. "Well, you might get by with two or three days more."

I hate that kind of indefiniteness. If I know what the regulations are, I'll structure my plans around them and do my best to abide by them. When it's all "maybe this, maybe that," which is the way third-world countries prefer to do business, then you never know where you stand. Theoretically, if I was still in the country after I was supposed to leave, they could seize my boat or fine me or make life very difficult for me in any one of a number of different ways

The problem was, as we were heading for Bonaire, we'd planned to stop at other islands along the way. It was going to be at least five sailing days including one overnight to get to Bonaire, so it looked like we weren't going to have time to see much of anything along the way.

"Maybe we'll have to give up on Bonaire," I said to Liz.

"Or we could just go and see what happens."

"I don't know. It sounds risky."

We decided to sail around Margarita to the town of Juangriego on the north side. We thought maybe we could clear back *in* to Venezuela there to give ourselves more time to think through our options. No such luck. Liz went to investigate and found that we'd be subject to various fines if we tried that. Juangriego didn't hold much attraction for us, so we left early the next morning, heading for the island of Blanquilla to the north. Meanwhile, I'd talked to a guy on the radio who was in Bonaire: he said it was the best place in the Caribbean. It pays to be skeptical of claims like that—it depends on what you want, after all—but it was one vote in the positive column.

We had a great sail of 60 miles, good wind all the way, and pulled into an anchorage on the west side among a bunch of local fishing boats, no yachts. I always feel vaguely uneasy in a situation like that, but there we were. The island itself looked flat and uninteresting, although there was a sandy beach in the bay. The fishermen ignored us.

In the morning we went for a walk over low brown hills, through rock and cactus, to American Bay, so named because an American had built a house there some years ago; it was now wrecked and deserted with only the steel framework remaining. When we got back, we were getting ready to go in the water and scrub the bottom a little before leaving, when a guy came out to us in a little fishing boat and said he had orders to take us to the "Commandante."

A little apprehensive, wondering what regulation we'd unwittingly violated, we went ashore, climbed into his waiting jeep, and were driven about four miles to the neat little army post. The drive was anything but scenic: the whole island looked about the same.

Our worries were soon dispelled. Far from threatening us with fines or even paperwork, the Commandante was surprisingly gracious. He took us into his office, served us big cold drinks of Kool-Aid with ice cubes, most welcome in the dry heat, and seemed disposed to chat as he wrote down our particulars. He almost apologized for dragging us out there: it was something he was supposed to do, he said. All this was in Spanish of course. When we'd finished our drinks, he had another guy drive us back to the boat, accompanied by the Commandante's wife and two kids, apparently just out for a ride. It looked like that might've been one of the most exciting things to happen on the island in some time.

We left about noon, heading for Los Roques, an island group about 130 miles to the west, which meant an overnight sail. We had a nice strong wind and a clear, moonlit night, ideal conditions. The only thing we had to watch out for was the island of Orchila which lay directly in our path. There was a Venezuelan military base on the island, and you were supposed to keep well clear of it. The night was so nice and the moon so bright, I attempted to get a star fix by the light of the moon. You need to be able to see the horizon clearly for sextant observations, so star sights are normally only possible at twilight. I could *almost* see the horizon in the sextant and was able to get a sort of iffy fix; it placed us well north of the island and agreed pretty well with the depths we found as we passed over an area of shallower water. Close enough.

At dawn, with the "high" island of El Gran Roque (180 feet) in sight, we headed for an anchorage on Cayo Francisqui, which was a little confusing because we had no chart, only a rough sketch in a cruising guide, and the island seemed to spread all over the place. We rounded a small islet not shown on the sketch, slipped in between two patches of reef, and found an absolutely idyllic anchorage, completely sheltered, flat water. We slept a bit, went snorkeling, sat back and enjoyed the scene.

The Los Roques group consists of some 60 cays, most of them low and flat, some with palms on them, spread out over a large area. It reminded us of the Bahamas but without the convenience of cruising guides or even accurate charts, not much in the way of settlements, and far fewer boats. With clear water, an abundance of sea life, lots of anchorages, and unobstructed trade winds, it was somewhere we could happily explore for a week or two...if we hadn't been worried about the officials. We half-expected to be boarded in the anchorage by officials from the settlement on El Gran Roque, only about a mile away but they mercifully left us alone.

We decided to risk another day in the anchorage, and the next morning *Star*, a plush 35-footer with Tom and Bonnie on board came in; we'd met them in the Grenadines. They were headed for Panama at the start of a circumnavigation. We enjoyed having the company, and the next morning we both left, headed for the anchorage at Lanqui-Carenero, reputed to be one of the best in the group. On the way we passed several other anchorages that looked beautiful and well-sheltered, an embarrassment of riches. Carenero was every bit as good as advertised, but that was no secret: there were nearly a dozen other boats in there, at least some of them apparently based in El Gran Roque where an airport allowed easy access from Caracas.

Star left the next morning but we stayed another day, unwilling to leave such a fine spot. The next stops were Los Aves islands: Los Aves de Barlovento (Windward) and Los Aves de Sotavento (Leeward), roughly 20 miles apart. These are each fairly extensive reef systems with some small cays as part of them but not much else. When we got to the first one, we anchored inside the little mangrove-fronted cay at the southern end where hundreds of birds, mostly boobies and pelicans, sat in the branches watching us, vaguely disturbing as if they'd just flown in from the Hitchcock movie. The islands are appropriately named. We took the dinghy into the mangroves among the birds, escaped untouched, and went out to snorkel on some reef patches.

Again, we stayed another day before carrying on to the second island. On approaching the southern end, we noted a Venezuelan Guardia station on the little cay, so rather than making it easy for them to harass us, we continued on about four miles in the shelter of the reef to an anchorage at the northern end which proved to be a quiet spot. There were several other boats in the area but so spread out that everyone kept to themselves. We took the dinghy a couple miles out to the outer reef and looked at some colorful reef patches out there: nice but not spectacular. There was enough deep water en route that it would've been possible to take the boat out there in good light.

We had already overstayed our allotted time in Venezuela. Or maybe we hadn't: who knew? It was all a little muddy. But with nothing special to keep us, we left the next day for Bonaire.

+

Bonaire (7 Mar-28 Mar). An easy sail took us to Bonaire. We rounded the southern point and sailed up the west side to Kralendijk, the main port. Bonaire is the "B" of the Dutch "ABC" islands, though they're actually in the order B (Bonaire), C (Curaçao), A (Aruba) when approaching from the east. It might've been interesting to visit them all, but we figured anything further west would put us too much against the wind sailing back across the Caribbean to Puerto Rico.

We had to jill around at the customs dock because the only space there was taken up by an unfriendly Dutch boat who wasn't about to let us in or alongside in any way. Finally someone ashore suggested taking a bow line to the dock and letting the boat stream off with the wind. I wasn't crazy to do that, but finally did as there didn't seem to be any alternative. In any event, we eventually got cleared in and went off to anchor.

Anchoring at Bonaire is something of an adventure in itself. There's a narrow strip of sand along the shore that drops off rapidly. We put the anchor in in 15 feet of water uncomfortably close to shore. With 100 feet of chain out, the boat was sitting in 70 feet of water; our dinghy trailing off the stern was probably sitting in 500 feet. That's all fine as long as the anchor is well dug in and as long as the wind doesn't shift (which, given the narrowness of the shelf, would probably deposit you ashore). Like the anchorage in Grand Cayman, the anchorage at Bonaire is wide open to the west, though winds from that direction are not likely in the winter. Theo and Jeanine, the Dutch couple we'd met in Las Palmas, were working as cooks in Bonaire now and had been for some time. In the previous October, the wind had gone suddenly to the west, very strong, causing havoc in the anchorage. Their boat was blown ashore and almost wrecked.

In another instance of what could happen, we were sitting in the cockpit one afternoon chatting with Theo with a good view of a 70-footer that had come into anchor that morning. As we admired her from a distance, it gradually became clear that she was dragging. A boat that drags off the shelf there would either end up wrecked on Klein Bonaire, the little island to the west, or be off on a crewless voyage to Panama, neither a desirable outcome. Nobody was on board, so while Liz went ashore to try to find the crew, Theo and I went over to the boat, jumped on, and hurriedly let out more chain, hoping the anchor would catch. Luckily Liz encountered the crew, the captain and two girls, at the landing, and they soon arrived, somewhat abashed, got the engine started, and re-anchored. The four-person owner's party was still ashore and none the wiser. Theo and I got a beer for our efforts. It might've been less reward than one might expect for saving a million dollar yacht from drifting out of the anchorage, but we didn't complain.

There was one other memorable feature of the anchorage. A guy on a nearby boat had a penchant for playing *bagpipes*! Every morning he'd step out on his foredeck, bagpipes in hand, and pipe away for half an hour or so. I could understand why he chose to do it outside rather than in his cabin: bagpipes are *loud*! The result was the whole anchorage was treated to his melodies, if that's the right word, whether they wanted to listen or not. (And really, who does?)

The day after we arrived we rented a car with Tom and Bonnie from *Star* and did an island tour. Most of the island is flat and cactus-covered, but the northern end, where there's a national park, is hilly. The park was nice: lots of parrots, flamingos, lizards. We ate lunch at a little bay where the snorkeling was delightful, then drove to the southern end of the island, the chief characteristic of which is the salt pans, salt being the reason the island was settled in the first place. After an expensive beer at a hotel bar, we had dinner at a Chinese restaurant. We enjoyed Tom and Bonnie, who'd both been lawyers in real life, but they clearly lived at a different level than we did. As Bonnie said, they'd been DINKs—double income, no kids—which gave them a hell of lot more disposable income than we had.

The real reason to go to Bonaire though, probably the only compelling reason, is the diving. The dives sites all had mooring buoys, and at that time there was no objection to our using them. What we liked best about it was that there were many dives that we considered "intermediate," suitable for our level of skill. In other words, without going much deeper than 60-70 feet we could have a beautiful and interesting dive, plenty of bottom time (the deeper you go the faster you use up your air), and minimal worries about decompression. Many of the moorings were in well-sheltered positions too, which made them easy to access. We did half a dozen dives there, and I always found it fascinating to submerge and be suddenly in a totally different environment, visually stunning and teeming with life, and with that dreamlike feeling of floating through it, hovering like some silent ghost, suspended in a transparent blue ether. There's nothing quite like it.

+

Boquerón, Puerto Rico (1 Apr-15 Apr). The passage from Bonaire to Puerto Rico started off quite blustery. We were close to the wind, trying to be sure we didn't lose too much ground to the current, which would be trying to sweep us to the west. For the first couple days the lee rail was in the water much of the time, the motion was bad enough for Liz to feel sick, and I couldn't sleep. But we were rushing along, which was some compensation. Things moderated on the third day. I wrote:

> *Things settled down in the afternoon. It cleared up, the sea went down, and I got some sleep. Was able to take a star sight at dusk. After several days of rough, you forget it isn't always like that. Liz feels better. Got good sleep last night. Now at 0700 we have Puerto Rico in sight, probably about 25 miles.*

It took quite a while to get in, as the western point, Cabo Rojo, kept receding, or so it appeared. But by 1400 we were anchored in Boquerón on the west side of Puerto Rico. Boquerón is another one of those Caribbean anchorages that's totally open to the west but otherwise well-protected, so it's normally fine in winter weather. We found several boats that we knew from various places sitting here, got the number to call for Customs from one of them, and managed to clear in with a lengthy phone call. Then we fell into bed, tired but glad we'd survived the windward bash with no problems.

The time we spent there was restful, pleasant, with little of note happening. The town was just a low-key, unpretentious beach resort, which suited us fine. Boats came and went regularly, most either on their way back to the States or just arriving in the Caribbean. We chatted with people in the anchorage, but the social situation there was low-key too, which was also fine with us. I'd go in for a run early in the morning, swim, do various little boat chores…and not much else. Liz went into Mayagüez, about 10 miles up the coast, a couple of times, but I didn't. I did spend an inordinate amount of time hassling our outboard, which had never been right since the dunking it'd received in Bequia. It would work fine for a while, then decide to get finicky about starting, or just plain quit at inconvenient times. Such is the price we pay for mechanical conveniences.

We were both aware that we were really headed back now and that we had no clear idea what we were heading back *to*. We had several passages to make before we had to confront that reality, and though we talked about it a little, it seemed best to wait till we were back in the States before we confronted it with any urgency.

We'd decided to head directly for the Abacos, the northern Bahamas, bypassing the rest of the group, which would mean a passage of about 800 miles. At this point we just weren't up for daysailing our way through the whole Bahamas chain, even though we'd probably have the wind with us most of the time. It's a hell of lot easier going in that direction than it is headed *for* the Caribbean, but we'd done it before in 1980. We'd never been to the Abacos and figured they were worth a look.

+

Abacos (22 Apr-7 May). The passage started off fine. The Mona Passage (between Puerto Rico and Hispaniola) was calm. The wind gradually picked up from the east-northeast as we got near the corner of Puerto Rico. It blew a little harder as we got out into the open ocean, but the wind was well in the east, edging toward the southeast, so with our course due north or thereabouts there was little to complain about. There followed four days of delightful sailing (something I don't get to write very often), with moderate, favorable winds and nice weather, the sort of conditions we'd hoped for the previous year on our passage from Culebra to Bermuda. On Day 3, I managed to talk on ham radio to Helen on *Eventyr* (in St. Martin), to Harold on

Summer Wind (in Grenada), and to Tom on *Star* (just heading into Colon in Panama). A scattering of friends.

But there was a front coming, one of those that slide off the US and pass through the Bahamas with an accompanying wind shift. And according to the weather gurus there was another front behind that one. So it looked like our benign weather was about to come to an end. On the Waterway Net, we heard it was raining hard in the northern Bahamas. And sure enough, on our fifth night at sea a wind shift to the northwest came through with some force which put an end to our fun. With it blowing over 30 knots from the direction we wanted to go, we decided to heave to and wait to see what happened, especially since things appeared to be changing quickly.

By 0900 the next morning we got moving again, though still about 30 degrees from our desired course. That day and following night we struggled with winds that shifted back and forth between southwest and northwest, presumably just to mess with us. But gradually, the wind crept around toward the south again, settled in with some prospect of it staying there for a while, and allowed us to head where we wanted to. There was some question as to where we were, as sights had been difficult the last 24 hours, although I knew we were approaching Abaco. By the time I got that sorted out with the noon sight, the wind had disappeared and the sea had gone glassy calm, so we started the engine to ensure we got through the pass through the reef in good light.

I was tired and the hot sun was enervating. It was easy to slip into a trancelike state motoring like that, especially when not much effort or attention was required. But eventually we made our landfall on the low islands and watched the sport fishermen who were rushing this way and that just off the coast. Once we figured out what was what, we headed in toward Little Harbor pass and made it through without incident at about 1630. We looked around and decided to anchor off Linyard Cay where a couple other boats were anchored. We swam, ate, and went to bed. It was wonderfully calm and comfortable.

+

The cruising ground in the Abacos is mostly between the outer reef and the main island of Abaco, and the space available is generally two or three miles wide, though shallow areas here and there effectively make it less in places. There's one spot, around Whale Cay, where most vessels have to go out into the open ocean for a short distance to get around a shallow section, and people contemplating this can work themselves up into a real sweat, as you can hear on the local VHF net every morning. It is true that the passes through the reef, of which there are quite a few, can get nasty at times as the waves break in the shallowing water, and they can even become impassable at times. But in general there's little to worry about as long as you exercise common sense.

For the most part, inside the reef you can enjoy flat water sailing in water only a fathom or two deep with all the attendant colors—blues and greens and whites in infinite variety—that that implies. We had a taste of that the next morning as we threaded our way to Marsh Harbor, the main settlement, to check in, following a circuitous route around various obstacles and shallows.

I'd asked on the ham radio net about the procedure for checking in. A guy in Marsh Harbor said, "Just anchor and go to Customs by dinghy." We did. At Customs, the official said we had to bring the boat over to the main pier—so much for insider advice. I claimed I had engine trouble, but that didn't impress them, so reluctantly we dinghied back, got the anchor up, and brought the boat to the dock. I filled out the forms. The official was about to let me go when I reminded him that I'd brought the boat over so he could look at it. So, though he probably wouldn't have bothered if I hadn't said something, he came for a quick look around, then remembered he had to call Immigration to clear us. We waited an hour for the nice young girl from Immigration to show up, but once she arrived it was quickly done. Total charges were $3 (explained as a donation for a church organ!) and $10 for transportation for the Immigration girl. All a bit of a run around, but I'd long since stopped being surprised at *anything* that happens when entering a country.

The Abacos, we found, were more like an extension of Florida than anything, and in fact half the population of Florida, or at least half the condo owners, seemed to be over here in their boats. But we were still pleasantly surprised. There was more variety in a small area than in the rest of the Bahamas. Little settlements, each with their own characteristics, were scattered throughout, along with a slew of more isolated anchorages. Even better, there were actual trees of some size here and there, unlike most of the rest of the Bahamas where scrub vegetation rules, and even a few hills to break the landscape monotony.

After a few days recharging our energies in Marsh Harbor, we retraced our steps to Linyard Cay, stopping to snorkel at the delightful little reef off Sandy Cay. We intended to enter Little Harbor, the landlocked basin where sculptor Randolph Johnston had his foundry and gallery, but the entrance is shallow, only about four and half feet, if that, so we had to wait for high tide to get in. We made it in on the tide the next morning without touching and found a crowded scene with lots of boats on the rental moorings but still enough room to anchor.

Johnston had sailed into this harbor in 1952 and, after considerable difficulty getting established, had been casting his own sculptures in bronze for years in his island foundry. He was still alive at this point, though he would die the following year and leave his son, Pete, to continue the work. Ashore, there were two galleries and a restaurant, Pete's Pub. We strolled through the galleries. We liked some of the work; some was pretty conventional, birds, dolphins, and so forth. Pieces like The Ages of Man and Grieving Mother were more impressive. We were glad to have seen it, but it was all too rich for our blood.

Next morning we left about 45 minutes before high tide and got out without touching, though I could imagine our keel just grazing the bottom. We sailed back north to Hopetown, another landlocked little harbor clogged with moorings, though at that time there was still some room to anchor if you were careful. We were never ones to take a mooring if there was anchoring room, so we squeezed in. (Our rationale was twofold: we always felt safer on our own anchor gear than on somebody else's mooring—when was the last time they'd looked at it?—and we didn't like to encourage the proliferation of rental moorings, even if that's a battle we're not likely to win.)

The community at Hopetown was picturesque: New Englandy-looking houses up on a ridge overlooking the harbor with a lighthouse across the way and a nice beach on the ocean side, the sort of place tailor-made for tourist brochures. We stayed a couple days, then moved on to Man of War Cay, which wasn't as picturesque but had an air of prosperity about it anyway, even if everybody in town seemed to be named Albury. Then a stop at the settlement at Great Guana Cay, more laid back than the others.

Now we had to deal with the dreaded Whale Cay passage (so to speak). But the passage itself wasn't the biggest problem for us. As we sailed blithely along the coast of Great Guana, we noted a sizeable cruise ship moored at the north end of the island—unexpected to say the least—and then a maze of channel markers—substantial metal posts—came into view.

"What's going on here?" I said to Liz. I was thoroughly confused. We were using a 1986 edition of a cruising guide to the Bahamas (granted it was old, but not *that* old), and it made no mention of this either in the text or on the sketch chart.

Even more puzzling, a low sand island appeared ahead of us where no island should be.

"What's that island? Is it Whale Cay?" I said, hurriedly checking the sketch chart again.

"It's too close," Liz said. "And there's nothing growing on it."

True: it was just a humongous pile of sand, about a half a mile long. The guide made no mention of an island in that spot. Bear in mind, we had no GPS to clear up our confusion; all we had were our eyes and the bearings we could take on Great Guana. From all available evidence, it appeared that this sand island had spontaneously arisen out of the sea: disconcerting to say the least.

By ignoring the markers and following the directions in the guide for the passage around Whale Cay, we made it through to Green Turtle Cay without incident, though we were still confused. Later, we learned what had happened. A cruise ship company had decided that the beach at the north end of Great Guana at Baker's Bay would make a fine stop for tourists. The only problem was that to make it viable, they had to dredge a channel deep enough for their cruise ships to make it in. The markers delineated the cruise ship channel, and the sand island was composed of the material they'd dredged out and piled up— a hell of a lot material, I'd say. All that had occurred in 1987, after our guide had been written.

The sequel to the story is that when we returned to the Abacos in the mid 90s, the cruise ship operation had been abandoned, though all the markers, and the sand island of course, remained in place. They'd found there were just too many occasions in the winter when it was too rough to safely negotiate the channel; the company didn't like it when too many cruises had to be redirected, and presumably the passengers didn't either. So all the work accomplished nothing...except to confuse us.

The town of New Plymouth on Green Turtle Cay was another nice little community. There were two nearly enclosed basins where you could anchor, Black Sound and White Sound, but since the weather was settled and the wind in the east, the anchorage outside in the lee of the island was fine. I enjoyed walking around town in the afternoon, but Liz didn't. I suspected she was too focused on our imminent return to the States to enjoy much of anything now.

And it did feel like we were really headed home as we worked our way north. We stopped at Allan's-Pensacola Cay and walked over to the beach on the windward side to the APYC, not a yacht club at all, just a sign nailed to a tree and a collection of yacht names inscribed on this and that and various bits of memorabilia—or junk, if you prefer. Then on to Grand Cay, where it was difficult to see in the shallow twisty entrance channel and where we might've touched bottom briefly. We didn't find much of interest in the town. Far from picturesque, it looked relatively prosperous but totally disorganized: trash all over the place, everything half-finished, dogs yapping at us here and there. We weren't sorry to leave.

The forecast was messy though, and we dithered around trying to decide if it made sense to strike out on the passage to Beaufort in the uncertain conditions. We finally said the hell with it and left. The problem now was how to get off the bank and into the open ocean. The chart we had wasn't very detailed, but it looked like there was good water north of Walker's Cay where we could make it.

We could, but just barely. I think I stayed too close to the Cay because just before we reached the deep water we passed over a couple of shallow spots—shallower than they should've been—and had to maneuver to avoid a couple of coral heads that I'm sure were shallow enough for us to hit. A few tense moments that probably could've been avoided with a better chart...or a GPS. Failing that, I probably should've taken more care in establishing our position—we did have the radar going—before we got to the edge of the bank.

The trip to Beaufort proved to be a bit of a struggle. We had a good first day, making good time except that the boost we expected from the Gulf Stream never materialized: we had no northerly set at all. Then, in the morning, clouds and drizzle moved in, and the forecast was suddenly promising northeast winds. Where did that come from? Even though we hadn't picked up any current yet, that could happen at any moment, and the Gulf Stream was no place to be with the wind blowing against it. We decided to head for Charleston.

It wasn't a comfortable choice. In Charleston we'd still be more than 250 miles from Beaufort. We sailed through a hard rain squall and constant drizzle all morning. Luckily, it wasn't cold. As we approached the edge of the Gulf Stream, identified by the number of sport fishing boats there, all part of a marlin tournament as we learned when we talked to one of them on the VHF. No doubt we were being set north now. We were only about 50 miles from Charleston, but the sky cleared in the afternoon, and we decided to forget Charleston and try to work our way north *inside* the Gulf Stream. I was afraid to get back out into it even though it would've booted us along because of the messy weather picture.

The wind died, the sea went calm, and we ended up motoring all night: probably not the worst thing that could've happened under the conditions. The forecast was constantly changing. A cold front, previously unmentioned, had stalled to the north of us. What did that mean? I had no idea and apparently the forecasters didn't either. The one positive thing was that no strong winds were predicted. Of course that could change—everything else had..

We sailed the next day in northeast winds, increasing to 20 knots in the afternoon and raising a choppy sea. We went in to within 15 miles of the Cape Fear River, then tacked out again. We were basing our decision to keep going on a forecast of a wind shift to the south in the evening. I placed the odds on that happening at no more than 50-50. Decision-making with inadequate information was a big part of this passage. Perhaps it's a metaphor for Life as well.

We had to get around Frying Pan Shoals, and we had some trouble picking up the markers, at least partly because we had no clear idea what the current was doing to us. As we tacked in and then out again, the wind died just at dark, and we started motoring. We finally located the lighted buoy on the end of the shoal. I was still worried because of a comment on our 1974 chart: "6 feet reported 1956." But we found 25-30 feet as we finally passed over the end of the shoal, so the worry was for nothing.

We motored all night and into the next day, not getting any wind until we were a couple hours from the Beaufort Channel. But who cared at that point? We were in the channel at 1500, anchored by 1530. We had a total of 33 hours on the engine. It was hard for me to believe the passage had taken only four days: it seemed like we'd been out there forever.

15. The Voyage Ends

From our point of view, it really had been an ideal cruise. We'd been gone almost exactly six months, Beaufort to Beaufort, and we'd covered 4138 miles in that time. That's a lot of sailing, but we never felt rushed because we had a lot of in-port time mixed in, time to enjoy the places we'd gone to some trouble to get to rather than just rushing through, checking off the islands. In most respects, the cruise felt quite leisurely. Because we'd avoided the tedium of constant daysailing, we never got burned out or ground down. Our tactic of choosing a limited number of places we wanted to visit instead of trying to see everything worked well for us. The passages were easier to take too when we knew that we'd have plenty of time to recover from them when we got into port. And in fact, for the most part the passages were decent. There are always aggravations on a passage, usually weather-related, but we'd had no really *bad* weather; any strong winds we'd encountered had been short-lived.

We'd mostly enjoyed the places we'd visited, and we'd been lucky to be in the company of compatible people most of the time too. So what if it wasn't a super-adventurous cruise? Only Venezuela and Bonaire were new to us; the Abacos too, I suppose, though as part of the Bahamas they had much in common with the other islands in the group. But there's something to be said for revisiting familiar places, and we didn't regret it.

Now we had to face the fact that our voyage was over. According to my calculations, we'd covered 24,561 miles since we left in 1987, not quite equivalent to a circumnavigation but not that far off either. From a sailing perspective, it had certainly been a success. The boat had performed well in a wide variety of conditions, we hadn't had any serious gear failures, we hadn't got ourselves into any trouble we couldn't get out of, and whatever trouble we did have was relatively minor: hardly the stuff of high drama.

So why were we stopping? The answer is complex, though there were some very practical reasons. The most obvious was financial. We still had money, enough to keep sailing for a few more years, more if we could come up with a simple and agreeable way to earn a little along the way: that certainly was not out of the question. But sky-rocketing health care costs were worrying. Our bare-bones Major Medical policy's premiums had close to tripled in four years. It wouldn't take much more to price us out of it completely. That was a lot of uncertainty to bear.

I've alluded to another reason already: the ties to family. With Jeff still in an unsettled state, with our aging parents generally and my mother's problems in particular, sailing anywhere beyond the East Coast/Bahamas/Caribbean area, even if we wanted to, didn't seem practical when one or both of us might have to fly home at any moment. And we'd just done that kind of cruise. So what alternatives did we have now? What would we do? The same thing next year? Or confine ourselves to coastal cruising? I certainly had no interest in becoming one of those "cruisers" who plod up and down the Waterway each year. While some people find enjoyment and satisfaction in that activity, it never had much appeal for me.

More importantly, Liz was ready to stop. She clearly wanted a more settled life, a chance to develop continuing relationships and to explore new directions for herself; in short, to do her *own* thing. I couldn't fault her for that. She'd stuck with me through many years of voyaging and for all the years of preparation and boat-building and planning. She'd always been an ideal crew too, not only accepting a full range of responsibilities but also participating in the decision-making and helping to keep me together when I started coming apart. Without her, none of our adventures would've been possible.

But I also knew she hadn't been very happy in the last few years. That didn't mean she didn't enjoy many of the things we'd experienced: she did. And she never let whatever doubts or feelings she had interfere with the way she dealt with life on board, either at sea or in port. I always knew I could count on her in any circumstance for whatever needed doing. But it was also clear that she wanted and needed something more than life on a boat offered.

And what about me? After all, I was the one who made the decision to leave the Med before we'd planned to at a point when Liz was expecting to stay at least another year. Was I dissatisfied too?

It's not that simple. It's true that that Med had dampened some of my enthusiasm, that much as I enjoyed some of the places we'd been, I wasn't thrilled with the kind of sailing that prevailed there. Still, I might've considered another season worth it if it hadn't meant five or six months of holing up somewhere for the winter, waiting for reasonable weather. That was a big chunk out of my life to spend marking time. I was much happier in the Caribbean where you could almost always sail and where the weather was usually fine. But I recognized that even that palls after a while.

The fact is, just meandering from place to place was never very meaningful to me. I enjoyed sailing most when I had a clear goal, something to accomplish. I didn't need anything in the record-breaking, super-sailor category, but I liked to have something in front me that would give shape and purpose to the activity. The circumnavigation had certainly been that. So in a limited way had been our Atlantic crossings. And even the just-completed cruise had something of that about it, as we set about to accomplish a planned objective in a limited amount of time.

On our return to Beaufort, Liz was glad to be done with sailing and to have the chance to start forging a new direction for herself. I wasn't sure how I felt, but I knew I wouldn't have wanted to drag her along on another sailing adventure when she had little interest in it. Apart from that being unfair to her, I disliked being the one who has to constantly generate the enthusiasm, to try to ensure we're having a "good time." There'd been some of that in the Med, and I'd found myself resenting it.

With hindsight, I suspect that if things had been just a little different and especially if Liz had been more happily positive about sailing at that point, I could've found interest and excitement in some new venture. Maybe to the west coast or even Alaska. Maybe South America (though probably not to Patagonia!). But that wasn't to be, and for the most part I was okay with that.

One thing we'd learned with some force over the four years—and this was different from the way we'd experienced our previous voyage—is that shedding all the cares and concerns of land life (or "normal" life, if you prefer) was no longer possible for us. The pulls of family were stronger; worries about things like health and finances were more prominent; concerns about what lay ahead for us loomed larger. The idea of sailing off into the sunset and leaving all cares behind had become only an unrealistic fantasy now. Partly I suspect that was simply because we were older and starting to realize that our time on earth was much more limited than it had previously seemed. But it may also be that that kind of escape is no longer possible for anyone. Communication is much better; air travel is easier and cheaper; it's much more difficult to turn your back on what you've left behind, and that lends a different quality to the experience. And of course that's even more true today.

Still, thirty years later, most of the memories of that second voyage are positive. Maybe that just naturally happens, as we unconsciously censor the less pleasant aspects in our minds, as we tend to remember pain less vividly than pleasure. When I think about sailing in the Med, rather than dwelling on things we didn't like about it, I'm more likely to think about ways we could've made the experience more agreeable. Using what we learned, it should've been possible to adapt better to Med conditions. We'd done a ton of research before went to the Med, and we had a pretty realistic idea of what to expect, in a theoretical sense. But it's been said that in war no battle plan survives contact with the enemy, and that often applies to sailing as well. Being there is different than reading about it. With a bigger engine, better timing and route-planning, better options for the winter, the Med might've been quite enjoyable. I even considered going back there for awhile, though that never happened.

So, in Beaufort in 1991, both of us unsure of what the future held, we made preparations to return to land life. These transitions are never easy. We ended up storing the boat in a boatyard for three years while we concentrated on regaining a foothold on land. There were the usual crazy contrasts between life afloat and life on land: the intensity of the experience of life on a voyaging yacht is seldom appreciated by those who've never been there. Eventually, with more security and a house to come back to, we would return to sailing with renewed energy (and with scaled back ambitions), but that was still a way in the future.

Appendix: Passages of more than 24 hours

Date	From	To	Distance	Time
5 Nov 1987	Beaufort, NC	Provo, Turks & Caicos	855	7d 0h
25 Nov	Provo	Grand Cayman	584	5d 19h
14 Dec	Grand Cayman	Coxen Hole, Roatán	353	2d 22h
3 Feb 1988	Coxen Hole	Livingston, Guatemala	152	1d 1h
22 Mar	San Pedro, Belize	Cozumel, Mexico	170	1d 3h
25 Mar	Isla Mujeres, Mexico	Key West, FL	351	4d 20h
30 Apr	Miami, FL	St. George, Bermuda	977	8d 21h
21 May	Bermuda	Horta, Faial, Azores	1801	14d 11h
22 Jun	Horta	Cádiz, Spain	1078	9d 4h
21 Mar 1989	Vilanova	Pollensa, Majorca	115	1d 3h
1 Apr	Mahon, Menorca	Portovesme, Sardinia	190	1d 18h
5 Apr	Carloforte, Sardinia	Favignana. Sicily	203	1d 16h
14 Apr	Favignana	Malta	170	1d 8h
27 Apr	Malta	Zante, Greece	331	2d 17h
9 Aug	Alinia, Greece	Spinalonga, Crete	115	1d 3h
25Aug	Souda Bay, Crete	Sapientza I., Greece	150	2d 20h
31 Aug	Sapientza I.	Capo del'Armi, Italy	313	2d 23h

Date	From	To	Distance	Time
5 Sep	Capo del'Armi	Carloforte, Sardinia	374	3d 10h
10 Sep	Carloforte	Porto Colom, Majorca	282	2d 8h
12 Oct	Gibraltar	Las Palmas, Canary Is.	737	8d 3h
5 Nov	Las Palmas	Bequia, St.Vincent	2858	20d 23h
27 Feb **1990**	Grenada	Ponce, PR	461	3d 6h
25 Apr	Culebra	St. George, Bermuda	898	8d 5h
16 May	Bermuda	Block I, RI	664	7d 12h
8 Sep	Block I.	Cape May, NJ	200	1d 12h
7 Nov	Beaufort, NC	St. Thomas, USVI	1255	10d 13h
13 Dec	Trellis Bay, BVI	Bequia	413	3d 5h
29 Mar **1991**	Bonaire	Boqueron, PR	376	3d 6h
16 Apr	Boqueron	Linyard Cay, Abacos	807	6d 11h
8 May	Grand Cay, Abacos	Beaufort, NC	532	4d 6h

248

More about the MacDonalds

After a stint in the corporate world, the MacDonalds settled in Oriental, NC. They've since made a series of two-to-five month cruises on the east coast from Maine to the Bahamas. In 2018 they sold *Horizon*, having owned her for more than 37 years.

Additional photos of the voyage can be found at:
https://www.flickr.com/photos/111157836@N07/albums

Comments or questions? You can reach me at: **brmacd@gmail.com**

If you enjoyed this book, please consider leaving a review on Amazon, even if it's only a sentence or two. It would be a great help in getting the book to others who might enjoy it.

Sailing in the Caribbean 1989—Liz, Bruce, and Jeff